PRACTICAL GUIDES
ENGLISH

TEACHING WITHIN THE
NATIONAL CURRICULUM

Bill Laar, Liz Laycock and Lyn Watkins

Published by Scholastic Publications Ltd,
Marlborough House,
Holly Walk,
Leamington Spa, Warwickshire CV32 4LS

© 1990 Scholastic Publications Ltd

Written by Bill Laar, Lyn Watkins and Liz Laycock
Edited by Christine Lee
Sub-edited by Frances Hubbard
Designed by Sue Limb
Illustrated by Lynne Willey and Chris Saunderson
Photographs by:
Richard Butchins pages 5, 15, 53, 119 and 149
Mike Turner page 27
John Twinning page 75
Chris Kelly page 81
J Merrett page 105
Keith Hawkins pages 113 and 169
Bob Bray page 119
Ed Barber page 177

Every effort has been made to trace the sources of
the photographs used in this book, and the
publishers apologise for any inadvertent omissions.

Artwork by Liz Preece, Castle Graphics, Kenilworth
Printed in Great Britain by Ebenezer Baylis,
Worcester.

Front cover designed by Joy White
Front cover illustrated by Michael Helme

The publishers wish to thank Kelly Hayes, Jenna
Smith, Kathryn Smith and Danny Nuttall for their
help in preparing the artwork for this book.
    Examples of children's work were provided by the
following schools: Bannockburn Primary School,
Greenwich; Bental Junior School, Hackney; Bury
Church of England Primary School, West Sussex;
English Martyrs Roman Catholic Primary School,
Tower Hamlets; Gloucester Primary School,
Southwark; Mandeville Primary School, Hackney;
Robert Browning Primary School, Southwark; The
Rosary Roman Catholic Primary School, Camden;
Whitmore Primary School, Hackney; Wingfield
Primary School, Greenwich; Wix's Lane Primary
School, Wandsworth.

British Library Cataloguing in Publication Data
Laar, Bill
    A practical guide to teaching English within the national
    curriculum.
    1. Great Britain. Primary schools. Curriculum subjects:
    English language. Teaching
    I. Title   II. Laycock, Liz   III. Watkins, Lyn
    372.60440941

    ISBN 0-590-76235-4

Contents

Chapter four
Knowledge about
language   177

Appendix:
Bookmaking   183

References and
resources   189

Introduction

In compiling this book, the authors have drawn on the reports which preceded the formulation of the English Curriculum (Kingman, 1987, and the two Cox Reports 1988 and 1989) as well as the National Curriculum document itself and the Non-Statutory Guidance. These documents clearly state that schools need to develop coherent policies for their English teaching, based on a shared rationale and aims. In developing such a policy, schools will need to begin with the Programmes of Study for English, so we have used these as the framework for our consideration of the primary English curriculum.

The Programmes of Study set out the 'elements which must be experienced by pupils' to enable them to achieve the Attainment Targets and must, therefore, be the starting point for schools; they indicate the scope of the experiences and activities that must be provided. The Statements of Attainment outline the product of these experiences; they are the outcomes of children's learning and activity in school. Teachers will need to be aware of what these expected outcomes are, and may informally gather evidence of achievements over the years leading to assessments at Key Stage 1 (Reception to Year Two) and Key Stage 2 (Years Three to Six). However, these achievements need not be recorded formally until the end of each Key Stage. The Statements of Attainment are an indication of the range and levels of children's achievement, but teachers will need to be aware of much more than these. Nowhere, in all the reports and National Curriculum documents, is it suggested that the

Statements of Attainment should be used as a starting point. Concentration on these at the outset would produce a narrowly focused rather than a broad view of the English Curriculum.

The Non-Statutory Guidance for English begins with consideration of the context for learning. The learning context includes the classroom environment, namely the working locations, the range of resources and materials, and the opportunities for varied groupings. Also to be considered is the classroom ethos which comprises opportunities to participate and initiate on equal terms, attention to individual needs, access to resources and materials, and involvement in a range of activities.

It continues with consideration of the role of the teacher and the experiences which will need to be provided to enable children to develop as language users, and then suggests ways of 'gathering evidence of achievements' to demonstrate progress and as 'a means of informing the next stage of learning for the child and the teacher'. We have used a similar framework in the organisation of this book.

We have also followed the National Curriculum documents in dealing separately with the Profile Components (Speaking and Listening, Reading and Writing), although we believe it is impossible to separate completely each of these language modes from one another or from other elements of the curriculum. Whenever children are reading, an element of talk will arise; when they write, they will frequently talk about what they are doing, and the resulting text will be read. When children are investigating a topic from other curriculum areas (for example, plants, local history or different religions), they will certainly use all four modes of language.

There will, therefore, inevitably be some overlap between the Attainment Targets and teachers will be able to see possibilities for development across all of them in the examples we give. Potential writing and reading developments will arise from a talk activity and talk will

almost always accompany reading and writing. In following this organisation, it is not our intention to suggest that Speaking and Listening, Reading and Writing can be taught as discrete aspects of English and we hope that the text will be read with a recognition of their interrelatedness.

In this book the separation of the Programmes of Study for Key Stage 1 from those for Key Stage 2 is also somewhat arbitrary. In making suggestions and giving examples for elements of the Programmes of Study for Key Stage 1 (five to seven years), we often refer to work from children who would be in Key Stage 2 (seven to eleven years). This is because many of the activities are appropriate for children at both infant and junior stages. The differences will lie in the way they are tackled, what the children's previous experiences have been and the aims and expectations of both teacher and children. Similarly, resources that are important for younger children remain so as they get older (for example, a comfortable, inviting, well-stocked book area; materials with which to write and make books for other audiences; opportunities to use spoken language to solve a mathematical problem or to present their work to the class and to hear stories read aloud). We have dealt with some aspects of the Programmes of Study for Key Stage 2 by referring back to activities already mentioned for Key Stage 1. In the National Curriculum document, the Programmes of Study emphasise continuity by referring to activities and opportunities that the children should 'continue to have' or pay 'increased attention to . . .' or have an 'increasingly wide range of . . .', as well as referring teachers back to 'relevant material in the programme of study for Key Stage 1'. There is remarkably little detailed provision specifically presented for Key Stage 2, a fact which is reflected in the Key Stage sections in this book. It is important that language learning is seen as a continuum, beginning long before children start school and continuing after they have completed their formal education.

Rationale and aims

Any consideration of the way in which the requirements of the National Curriculum in English might be implemented must begin with an examination of the rationale on which the Programmes of Study and the Attainment Targets are based. The proposals for the National Curriculum – *English for ages 5 to 11* (November 1988) and *English for ages 5 to 16* (June 1989), known as the Cox Reports – provide a full statement and warrant detailed examination.

English in the primary school

In the Cox Reports, the role of the primary school in providing 'the vital transition from home to the outside world' is stressed, as is the cross-curricular nature of English. In *English for ages 5–11*, the Cox Committee asserts that:

'The best primary schools provide a stimulating environment where children are motivated to think about their experiences and to express themselves as fully as possible in speech and writing.' (2:4)

In such an environment all modes of language will be used for genuine purposes and teachers will provide opportunities for children to develop their competence in speaking, listening, reading and writing. This does not require the narrowing down of the English curriculum to a limited programme of isolated exercises and skills practice. Quite the reverse; what it does demand is an environment where children can be actively involved in their own learning, rather than becoming passive recipients of packages of knowledge, and where they are constantly challenged to extend their use of language.

David Allen's definition, in *English, Whose English?* (National Association of Advisers in English, 1988) of the needs of both the learner and the teacher, is quoted at length by the Cox Committee (*English*

for ages 5–11, 2:5; *English for ages 5–16*, 3:1):

'. . . the learner needs
expectation of success,
the confidence to take risks and make mistakes,
a willingness to share and to engage,
the confidence to ask for help,
an acceptance of the need to re-adjust,
and the teacher needs
respect for and interest in the learner's language, culture, thought and intentions,
the ability to recognise growth points, strengths and potential,
the appreciation that mistakes are necessary to learning,
the confidence to maintain breadth, richness and variety, and to match these to the learner's interest and direction (ie to stimulate and challenge),
a sensitive awareness of when to intervene and when to leave alone.'

To meet these needs teachers will need to develop practices which:

Aims of practices

● 'develop the successful language learning which children have already accomplished in the context of their own homes and communities' (Allen, op.cit);

7

- provide children with 'the best possible learning opportunities matched to their individual needs' (*English for ages 5-11*, 2:1);
- provide 'an "apprenticeship" approach to acquiring written and oral language, in which the adult represents the "success" the child seeks, yet offers endless help' (*English for ages 5-16*, 3:1);
- maintain 'a constant respect for the child's language' (*English for ages 5-16*, 3:1);
- enable 'children to reflect upon and organise their thinking about the activities which are provided for them' (*English for ages 5-11*, 2:6);
- provide opportunities for children 'to interact with each other and with the teacher' in oral language work and through this 'to gain confidence in their own ability as speakers' (*English for ages 5-11*, 2:8);
- help children to feel at home in the world of books and literature 'as attentive listeners and reflective readers' who find pleasure in books (*English for ages 5-16*, 3:9);
- 'allow children to behave like real writers' and to develop 'confidence in themselves as writers' (*English for ages 5-16*, 3:13).

The main features of current best practice in English can be observed in 'classrooms where, individually and collaboratively, pupils are seen:
- using language to make, receive and communicate meaning, in purposeful contexts;
- employing a variety of forms with a clear awareness of audience;
- working on tasks which they have chosen and which they direct for themselves;
- working with teachers who are themselves involved in the processes – albeit with special expertise – as talkers, listeners, readers and writers;
- reading literature for enjoyment, responding to it critically and using that reading for learning' (*English for ages 5-16*, 3:4).

For this to happen requires clear aims,

thought and planning on the part of the teachers working together. The teaching must be 'structured and sensitive' (*English for ages 5-16*, 3:10-3:13) if children are to thrive as users of spoken language and as readers and writers.

English in the National Curriculum

The Cox Committee examined the nature and purposes of English as a school subject, preferring to make their thinking explicit rather than leave it to be inferred from the rest of the reports. Their willingness to do this allows us to build a clear picture of what is involved in the teaching of English, whether at primary level or beyond, and makes a limited interpretation of the Programmes of Study and Attainment Targets less likely.

The English curriculum is enormously broad, encompassing 'language use; language study; literature; drama; and media education' and ranging from 'the teaching of a skill like handwriting, through the development of the imagination and competence in reading, writing, speaking and listening, to the academic study of the greatest of literature in English' (*English for ages 5-16*, 2:2).

In primary schools English is taught as part of an integrated curriculum, so it is important that teachers and schools identify and agree upon clear aims in order to ensure continuity and progression in this area of children's learning. It has not been the intention of the National Curriculum English documents (nor is it the aim of this book) to 'specify fully all aspects of the programmes of study for English'. The Cox Committee stresses 'it is important that our specification of the assumptions, principles and aims that underlie our approach to the English Curriculum should be seen as enabling rather than restricting. They should serve as a starting point for teachers, not a straitjacket' (*English for ages 5-16*, 2:5).

Teachers will need to be sensitive to the

needs of the children in their own school, recognising the knowledge about language that children bring into school with them, both of English and, frequently, of other languages. From this foundation schools will help children to develop competence in spoken and written Standard English within the context of 'informed discussion of the multi-cultural nature of British society' (*English for ages 5-16*, 2:8) and without denigrating or destroying what they already know. 'The presence of large numbers of bilingual and biliterate children in the community should be seen as an enormous resource' (*English for ages 5-16*, 2:11), not least because this resource makes discussion and investigation of knowledge about language – an important part of the English curriculum – that much more relevant and easier to undertake.

Aims

'The overriding aim of the English curriculum is to enable pupils to develop to the full their ability to use and understand English' (*English for ages 5-16*, 2:13). English is both spoken and written, so this aim must relate to all modes of language – speaking, listening, reading and writing – as well as to the 'personal development' and the 'adult needs' of each child (*English for ages 5-16*, 2:14-2:23). These two complementary aspects of English learning and teaching permeate all the Programmes of Study and the Attainment Targets. The personal and social development of the child are, therefore, inextricably linked (Figure 1). 'In England, English is different from other school subjects, in that it is both a subject

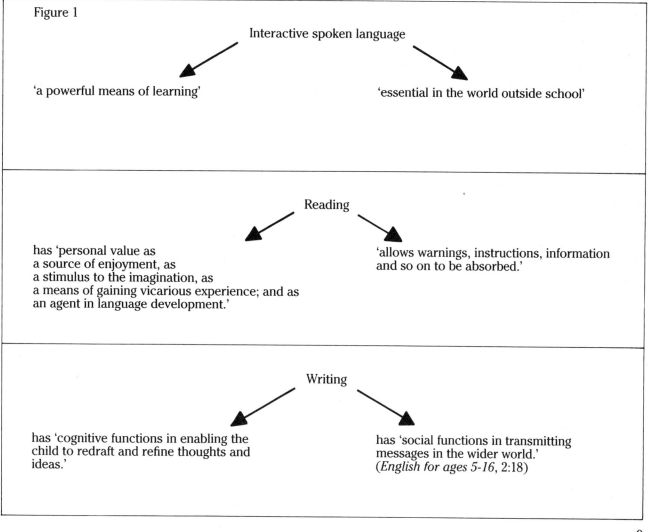

Figure 1

Interactive spoken language

'a powerful means of learning'

'essential in the world outside school'

Reading

has 'personal value as
a source of enjoyment, as
a stimulus to the imagination, as
a means of gaining vicarious experience; and as
an agent in language development.'

'allows warnings, instructions, information
and so on to be absorbed.'

Writing

has 'cognitive functions in enabling the
child to redraft and refine thoughts and
ideas.'

has 'social functions in transmitting
messages in the wider world.'
(*English for ages 5-16*, 2:18)

and a medium of instruction for other subjects' (*English for ages 5-16*, 2:22). Children learn both through and about language.

The cross-curricular nature of English is most apparent in primary schools. Whether children are talking and listening to each other whilst engaged in a practical activity (such as planting seeds or feeding the rabbit) or in solving a mathematical or scientific problem, reading a book about spiders or what life was like 100 years ago, writing an account of a pond-dipping outing or recording each other's preferences for food, they are using English in the service of other curriculum areas. English, whether spoken or written, is better developed through genuine activities and purposes than through discrete exercises and activities unrelated to one another.

'Knowledge about language' is best acquired and made explicit through real language activity: a close reading of Chapter 5 of *English for ages 5-16* will show clearly just how much knowledge very young children have and how a sensitive teacher can lead them to discover and understand new knowledge. Children are naturally curious about language and they love to play with sounds and words; teachers should be able to capitalise on those interests, extending what children already know. Grammatical variations, the structure of written language, spelling conventions and punctuation can all be discussed and taught within the context of children's own reading and writing, when the terms needed to talk about these matters will be introduced naturally. Identifying nouns, verbs or adjectives as an exercise is much less relevant than talking to children about the language you have used, refining that language and experimenting with new forms and vocabulary in your own writing.

Teachers will need to provide and create contexts for this to happen and to be constantly on the alert for opportunities and situations that can be extended and developed.

The language classroom

Through the social and curriculum contexts created by teachers in their classrooms, pupils are enabled to use and build on the language experience they bring to school. The setting for learning should provide opportunities to develop the language competence that virtually all children possess when they arrive at school. This language competence is not always in English, but whether it be Urdu, Arabic, Italian or Bengali, by the time children are five years old they already possess a highly developed ability to use and understand language and it is arguably the most important medium for promoting their learning. They already understand the conventions of taking their turn in conversation, asking and answering questions; they are aware of print in their environment and know rhymes and stories. They have heard the anecdotes of others and have told their own.

Classrooms which facilitate learning through language as well as learning about language itself do not develop haphazardly. They have to be carefully thought through, planned, prepared and managed so that they provide real opportunities for children to be talkers, listeners, readers and writers. The activities on offer have to be intrinsically worthwhile and provide something meaningful to talk, read or write about or to listen to. Resources have to be carefully selected, presented and arranged so that they support the learning and time has to be well managed so that the work can be developed.

The physical space

The classroom organisation should permit children to work alone when necessary. This will demand some screening off from the rest of the activities. They should also be able to work together in mixed or single-sex groups as appropriate. Bilingual children should be able to work with fluent English speakers as well as with members of their own community language group.

At times the whole class will need to meet together for the wider sharing of ideas so you will need a clear, permanent space where the class can gather.

Your organisation of the physical space will be crucial in determining possible groupings of children. If you arrange all the tables in groups of six or eight, then children will have to work in groups of that size and there will be little opportunity for an individual child, for example, to write alone or with a partner and without constant disturbance from others. With the best will in the world, children will ask for rubbers to be passed or help in spelling if there are others within asking distance.

The writing area

There needs to be an area for writing set aside in just this way. It will probably not be the only area in the room where children will write but it should be the central point where writing materials and aids such as dictionaries are stored and displayed. In addition it should be sited so that the materials will not come into contact with, and be contaminated by paints, adhesives, water etc.

If you take care to provide high quality materials in excellent condition you will be transmitting very important messages about the value you place on writing as an activity. In the same way if your own script is always hasty and dashed off without any care you will send messages about your expectations of the children's writing. A box of blunt pencils and a pile of scrappy paper torn from old exercise books will convey your views to the children very effectively.

The writing area should contain one or two surfaces where a few children can write without interruption, keeping their work clean if it is a final draft.

The book area

As already mentioned, the whole class meeting area is essential. In many classrooms this is also the book area. Some teachers are fortunate to have enough space to set aside an additional

reading area for one or two children to be able to read in privacy. The main book area is probably ideal for such a meeting place. It is likely to be carpeted so children can sit comfortably on the floor. The atmosphere you create in the book area will be conducive, particularly if it is lined with a marvellous selection of books displayed face-forward at child's eye-level. It should be a welcoming and exciting part of the room.

For some teachers the book area is the focal point of the classroom, situated in a cul-de-sac and not in a place where children have to pass through to get to other areas. It should be just secluded enough to ensure that it is a private place inviting reflection and reading in a sustained way, so that children develop both the habit of reading and the stamina to persist.

The listening area

Part of the book area might be a listening area, equipped with tape recorder and headphones. A stock of tapes of recorded stories accompanied by the books themselves can provide additional opportunities for children to hear stories read aloud. Published materials are available and these can be of very high quality but they can be supplemented by your own recordings. It is an ideal way of increasing your class's familiarity with voices other than your own, for example voices from different cultures.

Cross-curricular opportunities

Of course opportunities to use language and to learn about language do not only arise in areas designed for reading, writing, talking or listening. Every learning experience is a language experience and it is largely through talking with others that children, like adults, come to understand new ideas and internalise them. The Statements of Attainment in mathematics and science demand a growing facility to use spoken and written language. AT1 for science, for example, says that 'pupils should describe and communicate their observations, ask questions and suggest ideas, list and collate observations, interpret findings, record findings and describe activities, raise questions and follow written instructions.' In mathematics, 'pupils should compare and order objects without measuring, and use appropriate language' (AT8), 'give and understand instructions for turning through right-angles' (AT11), 'enter and access information in a simple database' (AT12) and 'list all the possible outcomes of an event' (AT14).

Each curriculum area has its own specialised language. Investigations of a scientific or mathematical kind give opportunities for discussion, for planning, for making suggestions, asking questions and reporting on results.

Play, role-play and drama

It is a vital part of human behaviour to play or to act. For young children it is one of the most important means of learning about themselves and others and about the way the world functions. Experience can be explored, rehearsed and re-enacted through language and action. Young children's self-directed role-play allows the world to be dealt with in a manageable way, through the exploration of events and relationships, in safe, controlled 'pretend' situations which 'for real' might be too dangerous, difficult or complex to handle.

The 'home corner' is a centre for role-play. At times this area can become a more intentionally stimulating space in the classroom. After hearing the story of the 'Sorcerer's Apprentice', a class responded enthusiastically to their teacher's suggestion that they make the home corner into the Sorcerer's Kitchen. This gave rise to a great deal of reading and writing activity as spell books had to be made, jars and containers had to be filled with appropriately spooky ingredients and labelled (toads' toes, slugs' blood, spiders' webs and so on).

In another classroom the area was for a while transformed into a building site, offering different possibilities for role play, for discussion of stereotyped gender roles and a new way of using the construction materials.

With older children, drama allows the more formal exploration of ideas and feelings. By participating in drama activity they can share their experiences and develop great self-confidence and self-esteem. Drama can be about anything relevant to the class – an event in the playground or street, a situation in a story or poem or an historical event. At times the children's own voices and language will be used for expressing ideas and feelings because the drama situation will be rooted in and sustained by their own personal experience. At other times it will be necessary to adopt the language and voices of others. Acting out familiar stories will have a place, as will the learning of lines for an occasional performance, but as a means of generating talk and extending the use of spoken language, improvisation and role-play have enormously greater potential.

Working in larger groups

Part of the daily routine of the classroom should be the whole class discussion or sharing time, so that there is a wider forum for the exchange of ideas. Often children engage in writing, for instance, for the teacher only; the general rule is that she is the only one who will read the piece and she may respond by marking it and possibly writing a comment at the end. When children know that they are expected to bring their writing to a whole-class sharing session they will begin to have a clearer notion of 'audience' and of writing for others. They will acquire a

sense of purpose to their writing and will come to expect their peers to give encouragement and constructive advice as well as appreciation for a piece of work well done. Also they will know that you, the teacher, are not the only person in the room who has ideas or the final say about quality. As a result, they will take an increased amount of control over the writing process and therefore increased responsibility for their own work. They will be able to make increasingly sophisticated decisions about content and will be much less reliant on you to make the decision for them.

As a teacher you are not abdicating your role but developing it. You can be a good model of audience for children to learn from, demonstrating easily and efficiently that positive, helpful comment is required; you can draw in the quieter members of the class and see that the more vocal do not dominate. You can ask genuine questions about the work as you also respond to the content rather than just to the transcriptional features.

14

Chapter one
Speaking and listening

The importance of spoken English

It is probably true to say that most people take for granted the ability to speak their own language. This is not particularly surprising, since there can be few activities that seem so natural, or more inseparable from the business of living, than the daily use of speech. However, most people, upon reflection, would not hesitate to acknowledge the importance of language in their lives, accepting it as the means by which much of their essential business is transacted, communication is achieved and knowledge gained and generated. Indeed, the more we reflect upon it, the more complex spoken language appears to be. We realise, for example, that our reactions to people and theirs to us, and the extent

to which they attract or influence us is significantly determined by the language they use and the way in which they utter it.

So our whole experience leads us to an understanding and acceptance of the importance of language. There is ample evidence, however, that once we begin to think about language in an academic or educational context, it is the 'literary' dimension or component that assumes overriding importance, rather than the spoken element. Parents seem to measure their children's progress in learning by the yardstick of their progress in reading and writing. Similarly, teachers often place particular emphasis upon writing and especially reading, and see success in these modes as being of greater importance than success with spoken language. The injunctions, 'Stop talking and get on with your work' and 'You waste far too much time talking' have become synonymous for many pupils with the life of the classroom.

In recent times, however, research and educational practice have increasingly helped us to appreciate that the ability to speak effectively is not merely important in the mastery of the whole language, but is central to the learning process generally. This viewpoint is expressed in *Better Schools* (HMSO, 1985) where we are told that: 'Talk is now widely recognised as promoting and embodying a range of skills and competence – both transactional and social – that are central to children's overall language development.' *English for ages 5-16* says, 'Our inclusion of speaking and listening as a separate profile component . . . is a reflection of our conviction that they are of central importance to children's development. The value of talk in all subjects as a means of promoting pupils' understanding . . . is now widely accepted.'

The Programmes of Study for English set out in *English in the National Curriculum* suggest that through spoken language children can, among other things, do the following:
• Describe experiences, express opinions, articulate personal feelings and formulate and make appropriate responses to increasingly complex instructions and questions (Programme of Study for Key Stage 1, 3);
• Ask questions, work in groups, explain and present ideas, give and understand instructions (Programme of Study for Key Stage 1, 4);
• Present factual information in a clear and logically structured manner in a widening range of situations; discriminate between fact and opinion and between relevance and irrelevance and recognise bias (Programme of Study for Key Stages 2-4, 6).

Language development and intellectual growth

The points above serve as a reminder of part of the formidable range of functions, some of them quite complex, that children need to command in order to be able to make sense of and to operate in the world. The important fact about these particular functions or skills, of course, is that they are dependent upon language. We have further reminders in the work of researchers such as Tough (1976) and Halliday (1975) (see Bibliography, page 189) of the diversity and complexity of functions that children need to command if they are to succeed in the world, and how dependent they are upon language to achieve them. Halliday identified functions or purposes for which children use language, including the heuristic function in which language is used to investigate, inquire and find things out, while Tough listed the following activities achieved by young children through the use of speech.

Collaborating towards agreed ends

A group of infants had been looking at snails found in the school garden. One child suggested that snails were blind, or had no eyes, could only feel things, and used their antennae mainly for that purpose. Other children argued that snails did have eyes, but that they were located at the tip of the antennae. The teacher encouraged three children, who were obviously very interested, to devise ways of solving the problem. They began by shining a torch into the snail's 'face' and declared themselves satisfied that it could see because it had veered away from the light. But shortly afterwards and following intervention from an adult, one of the children raised doubts about the conclusion, suggesting it may have been that the snail 'felt' the light, rather than seeing it. They appealed to the teacher who encouraged them to think about experiments that might provide a satisfactory answer. The children went away to reflect on this, and in the process sought the advice of other children. They finally described a number of increasingly refined experiments to the teacher and were helped to set up three of them. As a result of this they amassed enough evidence to 'prove' to their satisfaction that snails were blind.

Projecting, anticipating and predicting

Infant children were planting trees in the school field as part of a conservation scheme. Groups of children were allocated a tree for which they were to be responsible. The teacher wanted them to think about what might happen to the trees in the future, partly to avert disappointment on the part of those whose trees might not survive. The children suggested the following possible fates for the trees:

• 'Squirrels will come and eat them and break them.'
• 'The big boys in the village will knock them down.'
• 'Our tree will grow to a thousand feet.'

• 'They might be knocked down by another great gale and fall on the school.'
• 'People will have picnics under them.'

In further discussions the children were able to elaborate on the reasons for their predictions and what they anticipated as critical influences and factors.

Comparing possible alternatives

A teacher introduced children to the book *Would You Rather . . .?* by John Burningham which describes a series of difficult, embarrassing or positively dangerous situations in which the reader is offered a number of alternatives. So, for example, one scenario offers choices of being covered in jam, soaked with water or pulled through mud by a dog. Another offers £5 to jump in nettles, £20 to swallow a dead frog or £50 to stay all night in a creepy house.

The teacher found that these often bizarre situations engrossed the children to a remarkable extent. What proved to be particularly fruitful in terms of promoting language development were those situations where children did have an opportunity to choose from among a range of subtly graded difficulties, and where they had to justify their choice. The teacher found that they were responding in many cases in logical and quite sophisticated ways. For example, one child suggested that it would be preferable to clash cymbals or bang a drum at home rather than blow a trumpet through the open window because in the latter case you would 'annoy more people'.

Causal and dependent relationships

Some children had been growing tomatoes in a growbag. This maintained their interest simply because the rate of growth, especially at the beginning, was quite rapid. The children awaited the growth of the tomatoes with considerable excitement. However, not only was there a limited production of tomatoes (and these of extremely poor quality), but the plants began to die. The children were at a loss to explain why, since they felt they had cared for the plants. Then a visiting teacher, who was herself very interested in growing and keeping plants, explained to the children that they simply had not used enough water for these very thirsty plants. The teacher demonstrated this by having children grow some cress, and then deny one plant water for a period. It was very obvious to the children that failure to maintain proper care would lead to the plants dying.

Reflecting upon feelings
A teacher had been reading *I Will Always Love You* by Hans Wilhelm, a story of a boy growing up with his dog, to a group of top infants. After some years the dog dies of old age. The book is concerned about explaining how the boy comes to terms with this, and why, when he is offered a new puppy, he decides not to accept, but instead gives away the special basket of his beloved pet.

The teacher invited the children to explain why they thought the boy had refused the offer of another pet and why he had given away the basket. The children responded in a variety of ways, suggesting that he did not wish to be disloyal to his dog, he was afraid that he would not love a new pet so much, that he could not bear to lose another pet, that his parents would not allow him to bring a new dog home.

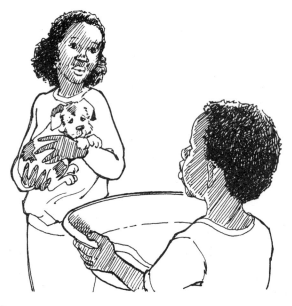

Even more interesting, perhaps, was the manner in which children seized upon the opportunity to recount a series of personal experiences that mirrored the disappointment and anxiety of the boy in the book.

Exploration through language

In fact, what such research, together with the Programmes of Study quoted above, are suggesting to us is that language enables young children to begin charting the world like an explorer putting down markers in a new terrain. They begin to get a purchase on that world by:
● Naming and describing things;
● Establishing the relationships and connections between things;
● Interpreting what they see and hear;
● Communicating needs, intentions, feelings;
● Interacting with the people with whom they come in contact.

We can see, therefore, that spoken language not only enables children to function effectively, but that it is a kind of instrument that enables them to enquire and learn further. Indeed, some developmental psychologists have claimed that our intellectual growth is significantly dependent upon our mastery of spoken language. The work of people like Chomsky, which identified shared structural features and shared rules in languages linked to common styles of reasoning, identified a close link between language and thinking. In other words, language rules gradually internalised become basic structures of thinking. As the Bullock Report points out, the 'higher processes of thinking are normally achieved by the interaction of a child's language behaviour with his other mental and perceptual powers and . . . that language behaviour represents the aspect of his thought processes most accessible to outside influences, including that of the teacher.'

Promoting fluency in spoken language

The growing awareness of the importance of language in children's lives, of the part it plays in their learning and of the critical connection between language and cognitive growth has increased teachers' concern to promote the development of children's fluency in spoken language. They accept that being 'fluent' implies not merely being able to speak coherently or possessing a wide vocabulary or being able to formulate sentences, but also having the ability to use language to pursue enquiry and to extend learning and insight. For example, it means that towards the end of Key Stage 2 some children will have developed the following skills in speaking and listening.

Statements of Attainment: Level 4
- 'give a detailed oral account of an event, or something that has been learned in the classroom, or explain with reasons why a particular course of action has been taken.'
- 'ask and respond to questions in a range of situations with increased confidence.'
- 'take part as speakers and listeners in a group discussion or activity, expressing a personal view and commenting constructively on what is being discussed or experienced.'
- 'participate in a presentation.'

Statements of Attainment: Level 5
- 'give a well organised and sustained account of an event, a personal experience or an activity.'
- 'contribute to and respond constructively in discussion, including the development of ideas; advocate and justify a point of view.'
- 'use language to convey information and ideas effectively in a straightforward situation.'
- 'contribute to the planning of, and participate in, a group presentation.'
- 'recognise variations in vocabulary between different regional or social groups,

and relate this knowledge where appropriate to personal experience.'

The role of the teacher

What kind of learning provision, what forms of classroom organisation, what resources and learning opportunities do teachers need to provide to ensure that children achieve that kind of language development? Firstly, we should consider the following issues:
- The language competence that children have already acquired before they begin formal schooling;
- The ways in which it is thought that children acquire language and the implications of this for their learning experiences in school.

Teachers not only have to remember that by the time children come to school they are remarkably competent users of language, but they have also to identify and be aware of what these competences and skills are. It is essential that they value children's previous experiences, identify their interests, enthusiasms and competences and relate the learning experiences they provide to these. Children's understanding is most likely to be developed by teachers who listen to what they have to say and respond creatively.

How can teachers be certain that children are competent language users before they arrive at school? How can they know what these competences are and how can they use that knowledge to further extend the children's understanding and skill?

In the first place, teachers need only reflect upon their own work, even with very young children, upon the myriad experiences, enterprises, exchanges and adventures that characterise their classrooms, to be reminded of the remarkable range of spoken language that accompanies the activities and actions. Children will be asking for, giving and utilising information. They will be answering questions, finding solutions to problems, issuing instructions, co-ordinating the work and activities of others, cajoling and persuading. They will be making and appreciating jokes, expressing surprise and excitement, trepidation, indignation and wonder and responding confidently to the language of adults.

By bearing these facts in mind, teachers can avoid wasting time in the futile business of trying to teach children what they already have mastered.

There are other important reasons why teachers need to take careful account of children's acquired language skills. Such awareness may help to reduce the concern that many teachers feel at the prospect of teaching the National Curriculum and fulfilling the apparently formidable range of Attainment Targets. For example, let us compare the Statements of Attainment, Level 2 to Level 4 in Attainment Target 1, Speaking and Listening, with a range of language skills that children are well on the way to mastering by the time they begin school (Figure 1).

LANGUAGE SKILLS	LEVEL	STATEMENTS OF ATTAINMENT
They can describe their experiences and tell in some detail and in logical sequence many of the things that have happened to them.	3	'Relate real or imaginary events in a connected narrative which conveys meaning to a group of pupils, the teacher and another known adult.'
They can, in many instances, make deductions about those experiences and why it is that certain things happened and others did not.	3	'Listen with an increased span of concentration to other children and adults, asking and responding to questions and commenting on what has been said.'
They can inform us of their needs, of things they would like to do, and can request assistance in doing them.	2	'Talk with the teacher, listen, and ask and answer questions.'
They can take part in discussions, can argue, negotiate, persuade and plan.	4	'Take part as speakers and listeners in a group discussion or activity, commenting constructively on what is being discussed.'
They will be able to reflect on and reformulate things they have already said.	3	'Relate real or imaginary events.'

Figure 1

We can see from this that the Attainment Target is, in fact, identifying critically important speaking and listening skills not as something totally unfamiliar to children which they have to learn from the outset, but as competences already acquired or mastered, at least to some extent. The teacher's task is not, therefore, to provide for the child a completely new map or diagram, but to help her develop and extend very useful and practical ones she has already begun to construct for herself.

What other reasons are there for identifying what children already know and how will such knowledge help us to develop further children's competence in speaking and listening?

If we accept that by the time they come to school children are so competent in speaking, then it seems important to discover how they acquired that competence. As Katharine Perera reminds us in *Understanding Language*, 'they can speak far more of their language at five than a foreigner who has studied it for several years'. So what experiences have they been exposed to, what instructions have they received, what techniques have they been taught?

Once we have determined what it is that has already made them such accomplished linguists, we can apply or at least adapt these factors to further extend their learning in school. Indeed, researchers such as Wells and Tizard (see Bibliography, page 189) suggest that, because schools do not always take sufficient account of the ways in which pre-school children acquire language and do not always maintain and extend these processes, children fail to make adequate progress, and in some cases even regress.

How do children acquire language?

Perhaps the first and most important thing to note is that it is most certainly not through the formal teaching of language rules. All available evidence suggests very strongly that it is not formal, decontextualised approaches, divorced from children's everyday lives that work, but rather approaches that are relevant and closely related to the natural activities and interests of young children. The following points are important for teachers to bear in mind as they plan children's language experience in the early stages of their schooling.

● In common with all human beings, children have a powerful need to make sense of the world. They need to understand it so that they can exercise power and control over it and over their own affairs.

● From the earliest stage, children are trying to establish an understanding of their immediate environment and are striving to make connections with the people in it. Quite plainly, to do this they have to and must be able to communicate with others.

● The most important drive urging children to speak is their desire to communicate, so that they can get people to do what they want.

● Children acquire language because they are powerfully motivated to communicate, and they acquire and reshape much of that language through the process of communication with others.

● Children acquire language through normal everyday interaction with the world in which they live, and the people with whom they are in contact. To do this they have to make sense of the language and communication about them. They therefore construct a set of rules by observing the ways in which language is used by others around them. This process enables them not only to make sense of the statements and sentences that others use but to construct their own sentences and statements in turn. Such rules, of course, are tentative and flexible and in particular cases cause children to decide upon technically incorrect – though usually functionally adequate – usage. Obvious cases are incorrect plural nouns such as 'sheeps' and 'mouses' or, more commonly, incorrect verb tenses such as 'I hearded you' instead of 'I heard you'.

- In the early stages of language development children will construct elemental phrases to serve their particular needs, often relying on three, two, or even one word sentences, frequently without verbs, participles, conjunctions or prepositions, but almost invariably with word order and selection that are correct and meaningful.
- Children take time to formulate their rules. Such rules are sometimes technically misleading and they are correctly reformulated only gradually through the child's own observation of the communication of others and the realisation that the rules need amending. Children move from simple to complex language, adjusting, adding to and changing the rules as they see the need. What they are doing is feeling out how language works and using it for their own purposes. In the early stages of language acquisition their understanding will not be changed by virtue of direct 'correction' or the direct teaching of the correct rules.
- Children use language for a number of purposes or functions. Halliday defined these functions as: the instrumental; the regulatory; the interactional; the personal; the heuristic; the imaginative and the representative.

It is essential for children to master the language necessary to accomplish these functions in order to manage and achieve things, to relate effectively to people, to analyse their personal feelings, to investigate the environment around them and to share their perceptions of the world. Teachers have to bear in mind that children have to acquire and develop these functions and to do so they need to be put in appropriate situations.

What factors influence language development?
We can identify other important factors from analysis of children's early experiences when they acquire the framework and ground rules of their community tongue.
- One very important factor is the influence of parents, and other adults, in the child's immediate environment. Not only do they expose the child to the majority of contexts, environments and opportunities to which the learner can respond and react, but they adjust and modify their own speech in a way that often encourages the speech of the child to be extended and elaborated. Very importantly they frequently allow and encourage children to take the initiative in learning to talk.
- Stories read to children are increasingly seen to be a powerful influence in the development of their oral language, and a helpful preparation for the acquisition of literacy.

Through listening to stories read or told children have their experience massively extended in a vicarious way beyond their immediate environment. As a result, they develop wider perceptions of the world and acquire related vocabulary. They gradually come to appreciate the power of language to create alternative and imaginary worlds. Stories provide children with the raw material to talk with others. They help them to construct narrative sequences themselves, to predict and anticipate what may happen in particular circumstances, to appreciate cause and effect. Story develops and extends understanding, enables the exploration of meaning, creates fresh perceptions and reveals new horizons. It nurtures the creative impulse and the critical faculty, the ability to be introspective and analytical.

The learning environment
It is important, especially in the early stages of school, to retain and enhance the features, characteristics and circumstances that have been instrumental so far in children's language development. One of the most critical of these is the environment. We have described children as seekers after meaning, who have a need to understand and control their world. The richer, the more challenging and stimulating that world is, the more children will be engaged and involved.

The outcomes of such engagement are obvious: their understanding of the world will be extended, their cognitive perceptions will be broadened and the language that both underpins and takes forward such developments will grow correspondingly.

The teacher starts with the advantage that the classroom affords opportunity for group working. It provides audiences with whom the individual can share and make meanings clear. What the teacher has to do is to extend and subtly and gradually complicate the child's experience so that she is constantly encouraged by the success she has already achieved and the stimulus of what is provided for her, to seek further answers and solutions. One of the first things that the teacher must do, therefore, is to consider the nature of the classroom environment and the elements of provision that will make it productive in terms of language development.

The classroom environment needs to be one where children can:
● Try things out, explore, experiment, find out by trial and error, ask questions, demonstrate, explain and generally talk about what they are doing;
● Work individually and in small groups;
● Have their curiosity and interests aroused;
● Find adult help at hand when needed, and have adult intervention available to pose questions, supply possible alternatives and generally help to take matters forward;
● Have opportunity for a wide range of play;
● Be encouraged to make, build and construct things;
● Grow things and care for pets;
● Encounter a wide range of stories, nursery rhymes and poems and a diverse range of books;
● Compose stories and make books.

The enriching classroom will encourage people of any age to linger there. Ideally, it will stimulate curiosity and intrigue, wonder and excitement. It will do so because of a carefully selected and organised provision. There will be:
● Objects that encourage children to hypothesise and solve problems by suggesting mysteries and puzzles;
● Objects that children have to take apart, construct or re-assemble in order to make sense of them;
● A wide range of junk materials that enables children to construct, represent, reproduce and in the process, reflect and comment upon what they have observed;
● Magnifying glasses, hand lenses and binoculars to facilitate close observation;

- Materials that can be used to make, substitute or be used for a variety of other things: levers, wheels, pulleys, cogs and electric motors;
- Small living things and growing things and the opportunity for children to work with them;
- Tools to develop drawing skills and materials that promote exploration of colour, pattern, texture and form;
- Opportunity for children to experience scientific and technological development and observe how elements of the natural world, weather, landscape, inanimate things, plants and animals behave;
- A wide variety of materials and fabrics that can be improvised for play purposes;
- A wide range of illustrated books, both with and without text. There will be more than one copy so that children can work together. Many of the books available will relate in some way to the general experiences of the children. There will be books that deal with human dilemmas and help children to project into other people's feelings, books that represent the ethnic diversity of society and reference material appropriate to children of varying experience, ability and age;
- Natural materials to work with including sand, water, clay, soil, stones and timber.

Managing the classroom environment

This creation of the environment is, however, only the beginning and perhaps the easiest part of the task. It is how these resources are used that is critically important. How the teacher interacts with the children, to ensure the most successful use of that wide, varied and changing environment will be critical to the children's development. The range of experiences such an environment represents has to be carefully mediated and interpreted for children. Human beings learn a great deal by experimentation, exploration and trial and error. To expect them to come to terms with the whole of their world through this process, without the help of others, and without reference to

knowledge and experience that already exists, would be both futile and frustrating. We would be constantly asking people to 're-invent the wheel'.

The situation applies even more so with children. They cannot learn effectively, cannot extend their language without the active co-operation of other human beings, including other children, but especially without sympathetically collaborating adults. The teacher and other adults should be seeking to:
- Extend what has been the common experience of children in the home;
- Treat what the children say with respect and interest;
- Listen to help them to define and articulate what they are trying to say, and intending to do;
- Discuss what they are doing and act as a sounding board providing feedback about how they are developing, both in practical and linguistic terms;
- Extend the range of what they are doing by feeding in encouragement, suggestions, further queries and challenges;
- Support them through difficulties, by providing explanations, and by interpreting complexities;
- Provide them with language where it is required, thereby extending language exchanges.

But the teacher has to go even further. She has to develop a precise awareness of different stages of language development. The teacher needs to know precisely what the difference is between a child's competence in spoken language at five years of age and the same child's competence at seven. She needs to understand, for example, the differences between Statements of Attainment in speaking and listening at Levels 1, 2 and 3, and perhaps even more crucially, how she can help the child to develop through these stages.

There is no doubt that a rich environment and stimulating tasks will be important factors in helping the child to progress through these various levels. But even more important to the process, will

be the way in which the teacher manages that environment, and manipulates and orders the tasks so that the development can be secured. In short, it cannot be left to chance.

It is here that the real skill and insight of the teacher will be most evident. A particular example may serve to illustrate what is meant. A group of infant girls, wearing commercially-produced nurses' uniforms, were playing at hospitals. However, despite the fact that these were lively, confident children, apparently interested in the subject, their talk in relation to it was desultory and limited until the teacher intervened. She insisted on playing the role of patient and being examined for a range of ailments located in various parts of her body including stomach, kidneys, liver, eyes, brain and tonsils. Initially, the children were quite defeated (and tried to escape from the situation by insisting that they were nurses and not doctors!), largely because they had not yet thought about the nature of a hospital environment. There were no

implements, tools or equipment to make a diagnosis, complete the examination, record the outcome or prescribe treatment. There were no thermometers, stethoscopes, X-Ray machine, indeed, not even clip boards, temperature charts or prescription pads. They had not yet given thought to where the patient should lie down, or whether she could be provided with a cup of tea! The 'patient's' complaints led to the children constructing the equipment required and the creation of a proper medical environment in which patients could be both examined and treated.

Here we have a fine example of deliberate intervention by a teacher to create a challenging situation for children that massively enhanced the opportunity for imaginative play and language development. If we were to categorise the activities in which the children engaged, following the intervention of the teacher, then we could certainly include play, speaking and listening, reading and writing (making lists, writing diagnoses, producing a brochure of the hospital and a book about the operation, bulletins and prescriptions), mathematics (weighing, measuring, taking pulses, temperature, blood pressure, making up prescriptions), science (using thermometers, testing sight) and design and technology (planning and making the range of instruments required for the diagnosis and the operation). The children had been put in a situation where they were challenged and encouraged to use a range of language to:

● Co-operate and articulate plans to working partners;
● Use names for instruments and the materials they were using to construct them;
● Plan the various sequences of action;
● Discover what was needed for a real hospital and the various routines and procedures they should follow;
● Communicate with their 'difficult' patient;
● Discuss the examination, the diagnosis and the correct treatment.

What the provision did not include was ready-made equipment. To have done so would have greatly limited the opportunities for creative play and language development. The teacher made crucial contributions in other ways to what was eventually an experience very rich in opportunities for language development. She entered into debate with the children about the kind of equipment that a modern hospital would need, encouraged research in relation to this, provided the materials and, where necessary, advice and suggestions for the construction of the instruments, and asked helpful questions. She exploited the fact that the children were used to working in groups and when invention flagged or inspiration was missing, she did not hesitate to steer developments in certain directions.

Most powerfully of all, she encouraged the children to articulate their intentions and needs. When children struggled to find the name of particular implements, she helped them to describe the function the implement would fulfil and the material from which such implements were made, and to speculate about how they worked and what information they were likely to provide. What she was seeking to do was not merely to use the situation to get the children to talk, but to add to their innate competence by encouraging precision in what they said.

We shall now turn to the Programmes of Study for Speaking and Listening and consider the ways in which the issues raised and the suggestions made can assist teachers in providing for the fullest possible development of the language competence that children bring with them to school.

Key Stage 1

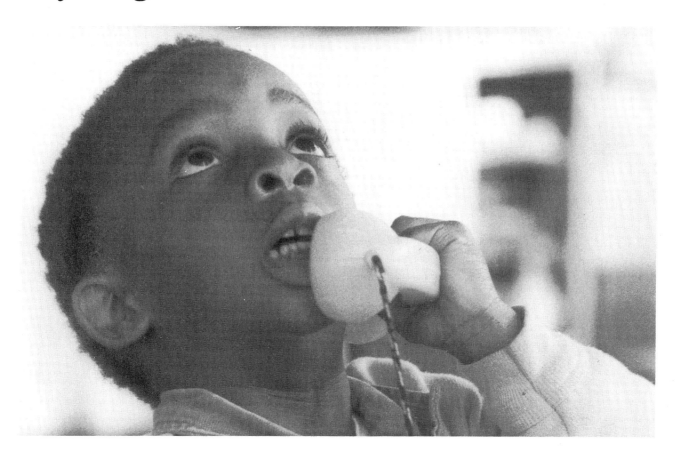

In the general introduction to the Programme of Study for Key Stage 1 it is suggested that:

'Through the programme of study, pupils should encounter a range of situations, audiences and activities which are designed to develop their competence, precision and confidence in speaking and listening, irrespective of their initial competence or home language' (2).

We have already referred to functions that are thought to be essential to children's development (see pages 22-23) and we know that by the end of Key Stage 1 many children will be – indeed should be – able to concentrate for substantial periods of time on what people are saying, and to query and debate what they have heard. It will be clear, not only from what has been suggested here, but from teachers' experience generally that such skills are developed by young children when they are placed in certain circumstances or when they take part in certain activities

that oblige them both to listen and to talk. That is what much of growing up is about, especially in the early years.

The task of the teacher is to provide a range of situations and activities that enable the child not merely to maintain, but to extend the competences she brings from home. Teachers need not only to structure environments and provide stimulating situations but also to have a language plan that will map children's development in a precise way. In many important aspects that plan is comprised of Attainment Levels and Statements of Attainment. These should show broadly where the child is going, and also serve as reference points that enable us to check on the progress made and provide indicators about where to go next.

We shall describe learning activities, situations and audiences that will enable children to engage in a wide range of language experiences and master the competences and skills set out in the Programme of Study.

These competences and skills are:
- **Grasp of sequence and cause and effect, reasoning, sense of consistency, clarity of argument, appreciation of relevance and irrelevance and powers of prediction and recall;**
- **Ability to adjust the language they use and its delivery to suit particular audiences, purposes and contexts and, when listening to others, to respond to different ways of talking in different contexts and for different purposes;**
- **Reflecting on and evaluating their use of spoken language and reformulating it to help the listener;**
- **Asking questions, working in groups, explaining and presenting ideas, giving and understanding instructions;**
- **Clear diction and audibility (4).**

Mastery of these skills is the key to development through the levels of attainment that comprise the Attainment Targets.

Planned situations and activities will be dealt with in the chronological order in which they are set out in the Programme of Study. It is important to remember that the activities described will often involve children in more than one objective or language experience. They will do so because both the activities and objectives represent aspects of linguistic behaviour and development that are inter-dependent, impinge upon, influence and nurture each other, and that do not occur in a regular and sequential way.

For example, children who are designing a treasure hunt for younger children might find themselves doing all of the following things:
- **Listening to, and giving weight to, the opinions of others (3a);**
- **Expressing opinions (3c);**
- **Voicing disagreement courteously with an opposing point of view (3d);**
- **Discussing their work with other pupils and the teacher (5c);**
- **Giving and receiving simple explanations, information and instructions; asking and answering questions (5i).**

It would probably also be safe to say that involvement in such an activity helps children to develop through the following attainment levels:
- 'participate as speakers and listeners in group activities, including imaginative play' (Level 1a);
- 'participate as speakers and listeners in a group engaged in a given task' (Level 2a);
- 'convey accurately a simple message' (Level 3b);
- 'give . . . precise instructions when pursuing a task . . . as a member of a group' (Level 3d).

In suggesting a range of activities and provision, we shall bear in mind the need to structure them so that in time children are given a chance to master all the skills set out in the Programme of Study. It is suggested that all activities should contribute, through a variety of means, to achieving the skills and competences. But different activities are more likely to provide effectively for particular language objectives than for others. Just as involvement with story and drama, for example, is likely to provide children with opportunity to 'express opinions and articulate personal feelings', so planning different kinds of games and making choices will help children to 'take turns and to voice disagreement'. The business of designing a rudder to steer a model boat may help to develop in children's speaking and listening 'a grasp of sequence and cause and effect', while reporting to others how they did it, or making and reading a book for younger children are likely to contribute more to 'adjusting the language they use and its delivery to suit particular audiences'.

What teachers have to ensure is that the total language environment and the general experiences provided in the classroom combine to ensure reference to all the objectives.

Organising for group learning

'These planned situations and activities should cover:
• working with other children and adults – involving discussion with others; listening to, and giving weight to, the opinions of others; perceiving the relevance of contributions; timing contributions; adjusting and adapting to views expressed' (3a).

This recommendation requires us to think carefully, first of all, about classroom practice and organisation and the ways in which learning and teaching can be managed to enable children to work together in a variety of ways and for a range of purposes. Every one of the recommendations in the Programme of Study is dependent on children being enabled to work in inter-active situations with other children and adults on common tasks and towards shared objectives.

Teachers, therefore, need to provide learning environments that will stimulate

and challenge curiosity, response and inventiveness. Forms of organisation should allow children to work in a variety of ways, sometimes privately and individually, sometimes as a whole class, and where speaking and listening are concerned, in a range of small groups.

The organisation of their classrooms has always been a priority for teachers because they have recognised it as probably the most important of the factors that under-pin effective teaching. One of the main difficulties they have to overcome is the need to provide adequately for each child in classes that may exceed thirty children. Consequently, primary phase teachers have relied to a considerable extent on forms of group organisation enabling children to work together on common interests, assignments and activities and to support each other in the process. This has also reduced the possibility of children being isolated or left to struggle on their own and has provided greater opportunity for teachers to spend longer periods with groups or individual children.

The grouping of children is often set up initially as an organisational strategy. In such cases some tasks are of the kind that children themselves can maintain for relatively protracted periods without the need for prolonged adult intervention (eg the construction of a model, making a puppet show or producing a playlet to be performed to the whole class). Grouping children together for shared activities in a carefully organised way can play a very important role in their learning and the development of their language.

It is now widely accepted that individual children bring valuable diversity of experience to a group, can challenge and extend each other's thinking, enlarge the range of skills available, encourage each other to persevere and are stimulated by each other's language, ideas and enthusiasms. In carefully organised group situations children learn to assume responsibility, to listen to others' views and opinions, to discriminate between conflicting arguments, to decide between options, to give and take instructions, to make judgements about personality and characters and on occasions to assume responsibility for leadership.

Let us consider examples of and opportunities for group learning and ways in which they promote the language objectives set out in the Programme of Study. The group activities are not confined to a particular subject or discipline. They may often begin in a definable area (eg science, environmental studies, play or drama) but frequently, in common with much primary practice, run across and involve a range of subject areas.

Group learning through play and drama

In the early years much group learning will be tied up with play and, to a lesser extent, with drama. Of course, a considerable proportion of children's play, and even some drama, will be effectively carried out on an individual basis.

The majority of activities, however, with their great potential for learning, are most profitably conducted in groups and are dependent upon the participation and support of others. The incident of the children setting up a 'proper' hospital will be recalled (see page 25). Similarly, some teachers who were seeking to involve children in collaborative problem solving with the major objective of fostering language, took the chance offered by a visit to a new shopping centre to encourage the construction of a range of classroom shops. These included a travel agency, garage and restaurant, each with the appropriate equipment, materials and stock, and all requiring the services of a group of people to make them function.

These shops, once established, led to both play and drama. For example, the travel agency came to be the scene of heated disputes with aggrieved customers making complaints or people vying with each other to describe their holidays.

In the restaurant, which was Greek, bookings had to be made by 'phone and

recorded in a book, the menu had to be translated into English for customers, bills had to be paid using cash, cheque or credit card transactions.

The garage provided breakdown and carwash services as well as petrol, leading to various 'emergency' situations. Such activities helped to develop the following language skills:
● Describing experiences;
● Expressing opinions;
● Making appropriate responses to increasingly complex questions;
● Developing speaking and listening skills when role playing.

Levels and Statements of Attainment developed included:
● Level 1 a) 'participate as speakers and listeners in group activities, including imaginative play';
● Level 2 a) 'participate as speakers and listeners in a group engaged in a given task';
● Level 2 b) 'describe an event, real or imagined, to . . . another pupil';
● Level 3 a) 'relate . . . imaginary events in a connected narrative which conveys meaning'.

Events related included the following:
● 'There's something the matter with my car. I had to stop because there's smoke shooting out of the back. I want to have it repaired. What do you think is the matter with it?'
● 'I don't know. I suppose I might have to examine it. You'll have to wait . . . I'll have to put my goggles on. I'll crawl in underneath then . . . oh! this is a mess. I know now – its your exhaust thing . . . that's what it is.'

Another opportunity for group learning was perceived by a teacher when a child in her top infant class brought in a copy of a Valentine message that her brother was sending to the local newspaper for his girlfriend. This so intrigued and amused the children that the teacher encouraged further conversation through questions, and feeding in additional information, until the subject of marriage was arrived at. There was considerable discussion about why people marry. This was an area where many of the children thought themselves to be quite expert. Many of them had been to a wedding; some had even participated as bridesmaids or pageboys. They had a surprising amount to contribute about the rituals and paraphernalia of weddings. Eventually the teacher suggested they should have a class wedding, an idea that, somewhat to her surprise, was enthusiastically taken up.

As a preliminary the children were helped to discover and put together as much information as they could about different kinds of weddings by obtaining information from their parents, brothers and sisters and accounts of weddings in story and song. The local vicar was invited to come and talk about the way in which weddings were conducted in his church.

Eventually the bride and bridegroom were voted for and they in turn chose their immediate supporters and the type of wedding. The teacher subtly arranged for sufficient roles so that everyone in the class had a part to play. There was a vicar, chauffeurs, photographers, a choir and band, ushers, confetti throwers, parents, an organist and a whole range of people associated with the kind of wedding chosen. The ceremony took place in the school hall with the whole school invited as guests.

This major project began as a casual conversation, focused on an interesting item a child had brought into school. Even at that stage the teacher found the occasion not only valuable for promoting group activity, but full of language opportunity. Children listened to and took account of what other children, some of whom had been involved first hand as bridesmaids and so on, had to say about weddings. They 'expressed opinions' about weddings and 'articulated their personal feelings'. The conversations gave them opportunity for 'turn taking' and encouraged them 'to gain and hold the attention of others'. However, the considerable task of actually arranging a wedding presented both a severe challenge to their imagination and ingenuity and an opportunity to deal with quite complex aspects of language. They were dealing with an exclusively adult issue and were having to seek information from and conduct some of their negotiations with adults. As a result the project demanded precise questioning and sharp and consistent attention on their part.

The various tasks they had to complete – the wording of invitations, the preparation of an order of service, the allocation of roles and the formulation of these roles, the speeches that would be made at the wedding – all required a mastery of particular forms and styles of language.

Working with other adults and children involved not only 'discussion with others; listening to, and giving weight, to the opinions of others; perceiving the relevance of contributions; . . . adjusting and adapting to views expressed', but in addition the process extended children's vocabulary and put them in situations where they had to deal with extended and complex sentences. It encouraged them to develop the language they used 'to suit particular audiences, purposes and contexts and, when listening to others, to respond to different ways of talking in different contexts and for different purposes'.

They were obliged to 'reflect on and evaluate their use of spoken language and to reformulate it to help the listeners'. Their grasp of 'sequence, cause and effect, reasoning, sense of consistency, clarity of argument, appreciation of relevance and irrelevance' were all naturally enhanced (Programme of Study, General introduction, 4).

Some group situations in the project were much less tightly structured, were worked out on a smaller scale and yet provided opportunity for the children to work constructively together and generate, in the process, language experiences of value. For example, one group of children who were not particularly interested in the wedding itself jumped at the opportunity to make a band which would provide music for the occasion. They made drums by stretching plastic and paper tightly over tins, constructed a wide variety of shakers by filling various containers with pebbles, peas and lentils, made stringed instruments by fixing rubber bands that could be plucked on different sized boxes, improvised musical combs and whistles from tubes and pieces of bamboo.

They talked with the teacher about the kind of music they should play for the wedding and decided on a fanfare for the entry of the bride, a rousing march for the procession afterwards and 'disco' music for the wedding party celebrations.

This group activity began as 'play' and developed into a mini-project combining science, technology, music, research and investigation. As it developed there was growing teacher involvement. It provides a further example of an activity which covers:
- **'working with other children and adults – involving discussion with others; listening to, and giving weight to, the opinions of others; perceiving the relevance of contributions' (3a);**
- **'development of speaking and listening skills, both when role-playing and otherwise' (3c);**
- **'making appropriate responses to increasingly complex instructions and questions' (3c);**
- **'asking questions, working in groups, explaining and presenting ideas, giving and understanding instructions' (4c).**

There are numerous other situations, arising naturally from the daily life of the classroom or from the children's own experiences, that will stimulate and encourage group work in play and drama, and in turn provide for language development.

Themes and situations might include:
- Domestic mishaps, crises and adventures;
- A visit to the dentist or the doctor, to the vet with a sick pet, to the hospital for an operation;
- Going on a sailing expedition, flying a kite, visiting an aunt, building a house, setting up a tent;
- Acting out fairy tales and stories.

32

Play arising from material provision

Other forms of play will arise from materials provided in the classroom. These will often involve only pairs or very small groups and will 'cross over' from play into exploration, investigation and experimentation, into science and technology. Children will use:
- Small bricks and blocks and off-cuts of wood to build towers, castles, blocks of flats, cars, lorries, boats, aeroplanes, houses, forts, rockets, space ships, farms and villages;
- Junk materials (string, buttons, containers, packages, cotton reels, magazines, corks) to construct all kinds of objects, many of them fantastic and fanciful;
- Water trays to discover what will sink or float; make boats of all kinds from a range of materials and discover how they can be made to go faster or sail in particular directions; colour the water, make it flow from one level to another, agitate it so that storms are blown up; speculate about the ways in which container shapes alter the volume; fill bottles to different levels in order to make a water organ.

With the materials to hand, children can be engaged in solving problems within their everyday experience – developing their investigative skills and understanding of science in the context of genuine exploration and investigation.

Whatever the context and however apparently simple the level at which creation is taking place, this kind of play provides children with the opportunity to be absorbed for extended periods, to work effectively together in groups, to produce acceptable and pleasing outcomes, and leads naturally to further activity, and obviously is rich in terms of language development.

Opportunities across the curriculum

'All activities should:
● **draw on examples from across the curriculum, and in particular those existing requirements for mathematics and science which refer to use of spoken language and vocabulary, asking questions, working in groups, explaining and presenting ideas, giving and understanding instructions' (4c).**

Opportunities for group work and the language development that it stimulates are not confined to play and drama, but are found across the whole curriculum.

Science, design and technology, mathematics

Science, design and technology and mathematics provide natural opportunities for group work. For example, in science the Programme of Study, Key Stage 1, for Attainment Targets 1-6 and 9-16 suggest that children should develop and use a variety of communication skills and techniques involved in obtaining, presenting and responding to information. They should have the opportunity to express their findings and ideas orally to other children and their teacher and also through drawings, simple charts, models and writing. They should be encouraged to respond to the reports and ideas of other children and to become involved in group activities.

Children should be encouraged to develop their investigative skills and understanding of science in the context of exploration and investigations, largely of the 'Do . . .', 'Describe which . . .' and 'Find a way to . . .' type.

As a result they should have opportunity to find answers to how and why things happen, and what the outcomes might be if certain things are done.

For example:
● Arising naturally from water play children might make boats from a variety of materials, discover how to make them move in certain directions, find ways of propelling them at a faster pace, experiment with different shaped sails and rudders, test them with different masses of cargo;
● Discovering what magnets do and how they affect particular materials; devising tests for establishing the ways in which they work and hypothesising about jobs that magnets could be used to do;
● Finding ways of moving heavy objects without the aid of transport;
● Investigating shadows, what causes them and how they behave; finding out what the purpose of a sun dial is and how one can be made;
● Observing and drawing conclusions about the behaviour of insects and small animals in a wild patch of garden;
● Devising ways of measuring time;
● Making a collection of simple tools and non-motorised machines and discovering how they work; examining mechanical toys and establishing how they operate;
● Finding out about themselves, how their bodies work and how they differ from other people; mapping their growth and development; establishing similarities etc with parents;
● Discovering all they can about their pets;
● Finding how certain instruments (such as thermometers, spirit levels, gear wheels) work; investigating a bicycle and building a working model;

- Discovering how light bulbs and batteries work and experimenting to use them for a practical purpose (eg to make a torch or to illuminate a doll's house);
- Making working models such as a periscope, a kaleidoscope, a pin hole camera, a windmill.

All such activities will involve children in collaborative work, problem-solving, communication and discussion. Sometimes the conversation may be desultory and will go unremarked by an adult. Sometimes the experiments will peter out because the challenge is beyond the children, or because they lose interest and want to move on to something else, or because materials are inadequate. However, even where there is no finished outcome or completed product there is likely to be some language development.

The following examples will give an indication of how much can be achieved through science-based activities that represent a natural extension of play and exploration.

- An infant class responded to a piece of research which suggested that hexagonal potato chips would represent both an economic and more wholesome means of production. The children completed a variety of experiments and proved that hexagonal cutting would yield a larger production. They then went on to design a series of machines that would produce a hexagonal cut. The children described – in this case on a radio programme – why they had become involved in the process n the first place and indicated clearly their understanding of what it was they were trying to establish. They also described their designs for the cutting machine and how their machines would operate. It was clear from their conversation with the interviewer and their responses to him that they had, for example, encountered a **'range of situations . . . and activities . . . designed to develop their competence, precision and confidence in speaking and listening . . .' (2).**
- A group of children who had uncovered large worms in the school garden were encouraged by the teacher to discover whether the worms had legs and eyes, whether they could see, had teeth, what they ate and drank, and how baby worms were conceived and born. The children themselves posed questions about a slime trail that one of the worms created, whether worms had brains, could manoeuvre round obstacles, could cross water, whether they preferred the light to the dark. The questions came naturally, but the real difficulties arose when the children had to devise strategies, tests and experiments for finding answers. With many of the problems, they were obliged to give up at the outset. However, they decided that worms did not have eyes because they looked exhaustively at them with a large magnifying glass; that they 'hundreds of tiny legs' because they made a rasping noise when moving across corrugated card; that they preferred the dark to the light because one moved violently when a torch was shone on it (although one child suggested that this was because it disliked the heat from the torch) and 'anyway it lives in the earth'; that worms could think for a variety of obvious reasons and that they could 'swim' because one hauled itself across a tin-foil tray filled with water.

One group of children found themselves bogged down in trying to satisfy one member's determination to discover the age of a worm. Speculation about this began with the suggestion that they count the rings on its back. When asked to explain the reason for this suggestion, the child responsible suggested that that 'is how you find out how old trees are'. After this promising beginning and various tamperings with the worm to hold it secure for the 'count', a child said, 'I don't think we should be doing it to him any more'. When asked what he meant by 'it' he said, 'teasing him, because it's cruel'. This viewpoint found sufficient agreement among the group to end the enquiries and to lead to the release of that particular worm.

In both these activities children had

been involved in **'working with other children and adults – involving discussion with others; listening to, and giving weight to, the opinions of others; perceiving the relevance of contributions; timing contributions; adjusting and adapting to views expressed'** (3a).

Many of the mathematical activities that have been seen to prove most fertile for children in terms of stimulating debate, questioning, planning strategies and communicating ideas are those connected with play, with outings, and with the incidents and enterprises that grow naturally out of the life of the classroom. The following cross-section of issues, drawn from a number of classrooms, leading to both mathematical activities and language development, are typical of those that children might encounter in any school day.

- Making 'zig-zag' books to tell a story;
- Making boxes to keep rubbers;
- Working out the cost of feeding the class guinea pig for a week: from this arose discussion about the cost for a year, about the life expectancy of a guinea pig and what it would cost to keep one for life, about how much any one of the children ate and how much it cost to feed them;
- How much could be bought in the school shop with certain sums of money;
- The total amount of pocket money individual children were given over a period of a month and then a year;
- Estimating the number of matchsticks in a box or the number of floor tiles in the school hall;
- Making a number line and posing each other 'add on' and 'taking away' problems;
- Working out how many school dinners were served in a full week;
- Estimating and measuring each other's heights and weights; putting the class in order of height and weight.

History and geography
The National Curriculum has given history and geography a specific place in the primary school curriculum as foundation subjects. These areas of experience are essentially concerned with the ways in which civilisation has evolved and people have developed, the nature of the world and its multiplicity of inhabitants and the ways in which they have impinged on, influenced and affected each other. Because they are disciplines that deal to a considerable extent with human concerns, they are inextricably bound up with language and communication.

The earliest stages of children's conceptual development in history and geography will be marked by prolific opportunity for a wide range of speaking and listening. For a start, much of history and geography, both in the initial stages of children's learning, and indeed later, is communicated and acquired through story or has the elements of story tied up in it. For example, one class considered the following points:

- How their forenames were decided on;
- What their parents did when they were children and where they lived;
- Where the family lived before they came to their present house;
- Whether their grandparents live nearby and what they did when they were young;
- What their garden is like, how it is shaped and what grows there;
- What the streets around their house are like;
- How they travel to school and how long it takes;
- Where they go on holiday and what their longest journey has been;
- The story of the person the school is named after;
- Why the road opposite the town square is called Windmill Lane;
- Why there is an old stone water trough outside the Town Hall and a torch quencher on the railings of the large red brick house in the High Street;
- Why people go to so much trouble to prop up the old oak tree in the park;
- Some events that took place in the year they were born;
- Why people in the class speak a number of different languages;

- Why men are digging a ditch outside the school;
- Why there is so much fuss over the new motorway being built near the school and what the motorway is for.

Teachers should help young children develop a sense of time and chronology, some understanding of cause and effect and a realisation that their lives are influenced by circumstances, things and people. They should encourage children to draw conclusions from the evidence that is around them, to classify things and make deductions. They will be anxious to extend children's knowledge of the world beyond their immediate environment and to provide them with the language of enquiry, data collection, description and classification.

The following types of experience could be used to enhance the knowledge and understandings that children bring with them when they first come to school.

- Organise class or school museums, amassing over a period of time collections that comprise old coins and medals, postcards, scrap books, photographs, cigarette cards, magazine and newspaper cuttings, old toys, items of clothing, cutlery and crockery, souvenirs and so on. Invite donors to talk about their treasures, experts to bring in their own collections and describe them. Invite children to speculate about the objects, to search for clues as to their use and date and to make up stories about them.

- Get the children to make their 'life-lines', that is to select from their own memories the five most important events in their lives, to draw them on a long strip of paper in chronological order and then to describe them.

- Provide small groups of children with a carefully selected group of objects and ask them to place the objects in what they think is the correct chronological order and give reasons for their decision.

- Ask children to play 'detective'. They might be presented with a jacket with pockets filled with various objects (a comb, lipstick, photograph, train ticket, theatre programme etc) and asked to decide the kind of person the owner is. A series of photographs can be given to them and they can be invited to make deductions about the environment, period, people and so on.

They can be shown photographs of the school and neighbourhood in the past and asked to identify the changes that have taken place. They can be shown some objects found in a waste paper basket and asked to decide what kind of building or office it came from.

• Children could be given wheeled toys to work with and, ideally, trails, tracks and terrains for Dinky toys. The school environment may have a chequer board garden, habitats for minibeasts and butterflies, places to sit, observe and think, to gain a sense of perspective. Creating indoor habitats for fish, hamsters, gerbils, guinea pigs will call for designing and making. Small world play with zoos, farms, dolls houses or Noah's Ark will help in representation and general geographical understanding.

• Experiments can be carried out with shadows in the sunshine, and attempts to record the weather. They can be asked to construct a simple weather vane, an anemometer and a rain gauge. Children can be asked to find the best place to plant the sunflowers, or to let the rabbit out to play.

• Children could be encouraged to sing the songs, speak the language, display the costume and tell the stories of the countries in which they or their parents were born.

• Children might make collections of holiday postcards received in the class and note that the captions are sometimes in another language. Encourage them to note the different languages that their class can lay claim to, make multilingual captions for displays of work, for paintings and models, compose messages of greetings for visitors in a variety of languages, identify words and phrases that have similar features in different tongues.

Environmental studies

Guarding the garden

A group of young children had been invited by the headteacher to care for a small patch of school garden where some planting had been freshly done by older children. The children were determined to keep the garden free of damage from any source. Their teacher suggested that they should make a list of possible sources of danger and provide ways of guarding against these. The children identified a range of possible dangers, including volcanoes, but decided in the end the most likely sources of trouble would be:

• Vandals;
• Cats;
• Dogs;
• Birds.

Means of guarding against these were identified as:

• Putting frightening masks on poles;
• Electric alarms;
• A searchlight;
• Traps dug in the ground;
• Nets for covering the seeds;
• A scarecrow;
• A watchdog.

Through discussion it was decided that many of the suggestions were impractical because they were beyond the possibility of invention by the children. Great enthusiasm was expressed for the scarecrow – lists were made of materials required, and plans and sketches drawn. Finally, a scarecrow was constructed from crossed bamboo canes covered with a shirt and with a flowerpot on top.

What language activities were involved in the task?

• '. . . discussion with others, listening to, and giving weight to, the opinions of others . . .' (3a). For example, the proposal to have an electric alarm was seriously discussed, with children citing instances of burglar alarms in various premises and how they worked, but it was reluctantly discarded. The idea of the searchlight intrigued them, but was quickly dismissed because 'it would keep everyone awake and it could damage the plants'.

• '. . . perceiving the relevance of contributions . . .' (3a). Children who came up with realistic propositions were seriously listened to. For example, the child who suggested a watchdog was given time to develop his idea, but he in turn accepted that the need to look after the dog would only add to the difficulties, while a couple of children who were eager to promote the idea of traps dug in the ground were quickly dismissed by some of the others who explained the impracticality of the proposal to them.

Away on camp

A group of infants was spending a weekend away from home at a camp not far from the school. The teacher in charge invited a group of junior children who had been to the camp the previous year to visit the class and describe their experiences. The junior children's teacher, in turn, helped her class to prepare an exhibition of photographs, slides and drawings to complement their description of the visit. Children were allocated various aspects of the trip to describe and all were required to provide one 'tip', one piece of useful advice gleaned from their experience. These tips ranged from helpful suggestions about warm pullovers and wellington boots 'in case you fall in the cow muck', the value of binoculars and the need for extreme quiet if the badgers were to be seen, to more ambiguous and alarming advice to take sticks to hit the snakes hiding under the huts, and the urgent necessity to prick sausages in order to prevent them from 'blowing up'.

The younger children gained much from this seminar, however. They seemed to listen to the older children with at least as much enthusiasm as they would have done to teachers, asked a range of questions and retained and utilised much of the information in their own planning.

The teacher divided them into groups for this purpose, with each group required to plan a particular aspect of the trip. One group charged with the responsibility of preparing the menus were obliged not merely to consult the whole class for preferences, but then had to arrive at a realistic consensus. They also spent a considerable amount of time conferring

with the school cook as to how food might be prepared in bulk and were somewhat disconcerted to discover that her expertise did not extend in every case to outdoor cooking. A child's suggestion that the Brown Owl of their Brownie Pack could provide useful advice in relation to this aspect of the camping was rejected in favour of the more practical suggestion that they should talk and obtain detailed advice from the group of junior children who had described things to them in more general terms.

Other groups were responsible for planning:
- Rotas for chores and assignments;
- The programme of activities – with considerable input from the teacher;
- Contingency plans for emergencies (the recommendations of this group ranged from the sensible and practical – what should be done in the case of fire, accidents, children being lost, ill or homesick – to the more fanciful and alarming, including children being kidnapped, or eaten by a bear in the bear hunt which was to comprise part of the programme of activities). This group was also responsible for the medicines and first aid provisions that should be taken.
- Sporting activities and entertainments. The main concern here was the planning of a successful sing song on the Friday evening and the reception and entertainment of a range of visitors who were due to assist at some stage during the course of the weekend. Two interesting and useful outcomes emerged from their discussion: the production of a programme sheet for the entertainment – with much debate as to whether it could be seen in the light of the campfire – and the provision of a mentor drawn from the children for each individual visitor.

In the main, the discussions were productive and of genuine value to the trip, especially where groups were required to come up with practical plans and decisions. When teachers and other adults in the school were able to contribute to the groups or provide a lead where necessary, then obviously discussion was more focused and less inclined to get off the track. One of the most interesting and productive features of the exercise in terms of language development arose from the need on the part of some groups to turn for information or clarification to other groups or individuals: to the cook and the previous visitors for information about catering and cooking; to the rest of the class for consultation about dietary likes, fads and dislikes; to teachers for confirmation about equipment and materials that would be required, and so on.

What was in no doubt was the range of language opportunities that the exercise provided. Children were obliged to listen, to give weight to and make sense of the contributions and advice of others. They perceived the relevance of some contributions and dismissed others as unhelpful or even frivolous. For example, they accepted advice about food and how it should be cooked, about the clothes they should take with them, about the equipment they would find useful, but they rejected as silly the notion of taking class pets along with them, or suggestions from one quarter that they would need umbrellas and hot water bottles.

Children adjusted and adapted their initial plans in the light of others' advice and opinions, especially those of the group who talked from previous experience. They expressed personal feelings and opinions, especially in relation to food and the activities that should comprise the programme. The group work and the presentation by the older children encouraged them to concentrate, to take turns and to gain and hold the attention of others. In time, they came to listen with more patience and increasing courtesy to the views of others, where, previously, especially in the whole class situation, they were not above treating certain opinions and suggestions with outright scorn and derision.

In the course of discussion there was, for many pupils, development of 'understanding for the spoken word and the capacity to express themselves effectively in a variety of speaking and listening activities, matching style and response to audience and purpose' (ATI). The children were enabled to:

- 'participate as speakers and listeners in a group engaged in a given task' (Level 2a);
- 'describe an event, real or imagined, to . . . another pupil' (Level 2b);
- 'talk with the teacher, listen, and ask and answer questions' (Level 2d);
- 'respond appropriately to a range of more complex instructions given by a teacher and give simple instructions' (Level 2d);
- 'relate real . . . events in a connected narrative which conveys meaning to a group of pupils, the teacher or another known adult' (Level 3a);
- 'convey accurately simple messsages' (Level 3b);
- 'listen with an increased span of concentration to other children and adults, asking and responding to questions and commenting on what has been said' (Level 3c);
- 'give, and receive and follow accurately, precise instructions when pursuing a task individually or as a member of a group' (Level 3d).

In all, a formidable range of learning developed from this enterprise. Children applied mathematics to practical situations; they produced a range of writing of different kinds, business letters, requests for information, invitations, logs, diaries and records; they did field work, studied natural history and set up scientific investigations; made maps and sketches, drawings and paintings; had experience of a diverse environment; worked in groups and engaged in a range of social activities. In the process they were presented with experiences, challenges and problems that required language to solve them and fostered its wider development in the process.

The life and routines of an infant school are full of events and occasions, many of them apparently commonplace, that can be used and developed to enhance children's language development.

Let us consider some of these situations and activities and how they might be used in the **'development of speaking and listening skills, both when role-playing and otherwise – when describing experiences, expressing opinions, articulating personal feelings and formulating and making appropriate responses to increasingly complex instructions and questions'** (3).

Local outings: a neighbourhood walk

Teachers often take children on local outings, which are potentially rich in language development opportunities, involving planning, speculating and seeking the advice of others.

Children can be asked to describe their own immediate neighbourhood, the streets in which they live, the route they take to school, the shops, houses and unusual buildings, the elements about which they have to be careful, the different people they encounter and so on. They can recount particular adventures and incidents they have experienced. In planning a walk around the neighbourhood of the school children can be asked to focus on specific aspects, so that eventually they can produce a guide book or brochure for other children in the school. Different groups can make observations about specific buildings, about their purpose, appearance and construction. Speculation and deduction can be encouraged. Are some houses divided into flats? How can you tell? Is it an area where many young people live? Are the houses expensive? Are the inhabitants concerned to protect their property? How can you tell? Do people keep many pets?

What do the shops tell us about the nature of the locality? Can we learn anything from the names of the roads and street? Can we make informed guesses about the neighbourhood in the past?

In preparatory work, groups can formulate the questions they need to ask in order to complete their particular assignments. They can decide on how they might secure information, whether it will be possible for them to conduct interviews en route, whether it would be helpful for them to make sketches and to take notes, to take photographs, to record sounds even to dictate impressions into a dictaphone.

The teacher may wish to develop the experience into a larger project, such as producing a guide book, or setting up an exhibition, incorporating written descriptions, photographs, drawings and models, with children acting as guides and providing oral commentaries.

Local outings: a visit to a police station

A visit to a police station will take children into a very different area of debate and pose different kinds of questions and challenges. Children will already have a range of perceptions about what policemen do, much of it gathered, perhaps, from the television or indeed from the local police who may have made visits to the school.

As with other outings, teachers will find it worthwhile to group children for planning purposes. Clearly defined tasks will help the children to focus their discussion and give them a framework for reporting back their decisions to other groups. This will oblige them to define clearly their intentions and to communicate them efficiently. It will also make it incumbent upon the listeners to take careful account of what is said and to frame questions designed to clarify matters without upsetting or intimidating those who are being questioned.

In a visit of this nature, where the children already possess a considerable body of knowledge, however fanciful some of it may be, then the issues likely to cause interest are not difficult to predict: why people are arrested and what happens to them when they are, whether there are cells in which they are confined, the use of dogs and police cars, the complex communications and record systems which are used, the use of fingerprinting and so on.

Preparation for a visit of this kind will provide ample opportunity for children to contribute from their own experiences, to share information, weigh up ideas and suggestions, seek factual information, **'formulating and making appropriate responses to increasingly complex instructions and questions' (3c).** However, it is the unpredictable aspects of the experience that may often provide the richest opportunity for development of speaking and listening skills. No matter how well children may be prepared, there will be encounters and experiences in the course of the visit – being handcuffed, having fingerprints taken, listening to messages on the radio, being able to 'call up' a police car – all things that will oblige them to adapt to situations they had not anticipated and to formulate fresh questions and suggestions. They may well have the opportunity in such situations to develop **'listening (and, as appropriate, reactive) skills in non-reciprocal situations' (3b),** for example, when listening to and replying to police car messages.

Further inputs to language development can be provided by follow-up activities. Not only may children wish to report back orally on their experiences to others at school, but teachers can provide for a range of play and drama situations. Children can establish their own police station with a radio station, dog training facilities, panda cars, finger printing or recording provision, a rogues gallery, 'wanted' notices, information about missing persons, a large wall map of the neighbourhood. Such provision will call for thought, ingenuity and planning on the part of the children and will only be successfully accomplished through a great deal of group interaction. It will not be enough for the children just to 'construct' the police station. They will also have to decide how they are going to use it. One teacher has suggested that a way of getting the best from such situations and ensuring that they do not degenerate in to meaningless exchanges is to encourage children to make a set of rules for the management and running of whatever they have established. This not only contributes to more controlled and productive situations, but generates a significant exchange of conversation in the process. The children have to evaluate a range of suggestions, decide how far they are relevant and useful, resolve ambiguities, remove overlap and duplication, and finally formulate suggestions into a coherent set of rules for publication.

Teachers will find it worthwhile to encourage children to make large books based around such outings, for example, 'Class Four at the Police Station'. They can be designed for sharing with other children, especially younger ones. Children working in pairs and small groups for such purposes have to decide on what they want to describe and the information they wish to give. They have to select a 'cast', make a plot, plan the illustrations and compose the text. A great deal of oral language will be involved in the planning stage, before work begins on the production of the book itself. But it is subsequently, when children come to present their work to other children, that they may be most frequently called upon not merely to:

- '. . . gain and hold the attention of their listeners . . .' (3d);
- provide 'clear diction and audibility . . .' (4e);
- '. . . talk and listen in groups of different sizes and to a range of audiences . . .' (4d),

but may be required to respond to unexpected questions or to listen to and incorporate the views of children who want to relate their own experiences.

To a considerable extent this whole activity of making a book for a particular audience will achieve one of the requirements of the Programme of Study for Key Stage 1. That is, that they should **'develop pupils' ability to adjust the language they use and its delivery to suit particular audiences, purposes and contexts and, when listening to others, to respond to different ways of talking in different contexts and for different purposes' (4b).** In many ways, this also encourages the children **'to reflect on and evaluate their use of spoken language to reformulate it to help the listener' (4b).**

Outings and visits are only one aspect of the range of experiences that the life of a school provides and that teachers can structure to promote learning in general and language development in particular. Other events might include festivals, celebrations and fêtes, sports days, parties and exchanges with other schools. There will also be the whole varied series of happenings and incidents that illuminate the days of a normal infant classroom.

Such experiences will naturally provide children with numerous opportunities for talk in a variety of forms. But teachers with the Programme of Study in mind will realise the value of shaping some of the experiences and intervening directly in others, of providing and involving audiences to develop children's **'competence, precision and confidence in speaking and listening, irrespective of their initial competence or home language' (2).**

Let us look at some of the ways in which this might be done.

Festivals and celebrations

These have always provided opportunities for children to hear stories, dress up, sing, paint, dance and have parties. There is even greater opportunity now to draw from the faiths and cultures that enrich our society and that are widely represented in schools.

Children can be encouraged to talk about the festivals and celebrations that are part of their lives and to describe their purpose and significance. Teachers can help them to set up exhibitions of their national costume, garments used in religious services and cherished artefacts that have particular meaning for them. Children can be given the opportunity to tell their stories, describe how they celebrate, sing their songs and perhaps bring in samples of their food. Parents, grandparents, community and religious leaders can be invited to contribute in a variety of ways. Opportunities can be seized to draw comparisons with stories from different cultures and even comparisons in languages.

Such experience will emphasise for children of different ethnic backgrounds the importance of their cultures, traditions, customs and religions and the respect and value that are accorded them. As well, it will provide a powerful impetus to their acquisition of English as a second language. The challenge of explaining their customs and traditions and, where relevant, of telling what they know of their country of origin, will provide genuine opportunity to develop competence and precision in terms of description and narration.

British festivals and celebrations will provide opportunities just as rich in fostering children's language development. At Christmas time children can be encouraged to design the celebrations for the occasion. Groups can be assigned particular tasks and, as far as possible, have an adult attached to each group so that discussion can be directed and decisions about what ought to be done can be recorded. Assignments might include:

● Planning and making decorations: one group would be responsible only for the planning and designing stage. The group might be supplied with brochures and illustrated books of decorations that will offer ideas for discussion. Having decided upon the decorations they wish to make, the children in this group would be obliged to negotiate with children in another group about how this would be done. This would require them to explain their plans, to demonstrate what they want and to negotiate with the other group about its contributions.

● Organising the party: this group might be concerned with planning the food for the party, deciding how it is going to be obtained, whether some of it (cakes, biscuits, jelly etc) can be made by them in school; how they should appeal to parents for help; deciding upon and issuing invitations and then announcing their plans to the rest of the class, involving

them in the process and negotiating what their specific roles will be.

● Planning the entertainment: another group could be responsible for arranging this provision, for deciding upon the games that will be played, for planning solo and group contributions in terms of singing and dancing and persuading other children to take part.

All the groups may be encouraged to publish their final plans in some form or other, either by writing them themselves or dictating them to an adult. They will need to ensure that the plans are being carried out.

Such assignments represent considerable challenges for children. The objectives are achievable; they are consistently managed in infant classrooms, but often with adults taking major directing roles. Such activities would represent enormous opportunity for language development. Children would be obliged to come to a group consensus about what they want to do, to plan, create roles and tasks for others, convey their intention to others, secure their agreement, involve them in the task, and then supervise it through to a successful conclusion.

Often the less spectacular or less well-known occasion will prove to be just as rewarding in terms of the learning and language opportunities it provides. Children in a school named after St Francis were read a version of the Saint's encounter with a wolf and were particularly struck by a portrayal of the animal as vulnerable and frightened. This led to discussion as to why the wolf was 'misunderstood', why he had gained such an unfortunate reputation and why people feared and disliked him. As reasons were advanced for this, taking children into areas of speculation and hypothesis, a child suggested that there were boys in the school who aroused similar feelings of fear and anxiety. This stimulated so marked a response that the teacher focused on it and gave the children an opportunity to reveal what were obviously deeply seated anxieties on the part of many of them about bullying. She steered children away from individual cases and helped them to concentrate on what they perceived to be the reasons for bullying and what could be done to deal with it. She read them poems from *The Roundabout by the Sea and Other Poems* (John Walsh) which tells of a girl who is terrorised by the school bully and subsequently attempts to help him because she realises he is a sad and pathetic figure. The children were, in many cases, able to relate this to the story of the wolf, but, the teacher realised, did not find their real fears of those who intimidated them in school in any way diminished. It was clear that this was something that they would come to terms with only in time and through experience. But there was no doubting their ability to have some understanding and sympathy with the plight of the wolf and to be able to respond to language, both in the story and the poems, that was suggesting in quite subtle ways deeper meanings underlying the basic plot. Here the children were responding to language to think themselves into other roles and situations in order to understand different ideas and to make valid responses to increasingly

complex situations and issues.

The opportunity for children to work in groups is essential to the language activities, experiences and opportunities that have been described here. They have included:

- 'discussion of their work with other pupils and the teacher';
- 'collaborative planning of activities in a way which requires pupils to speak and listen';
- 'talking about experiences in or out of school *eg a school trip, a family outing, a television programme*';
- 'collaborative and exploratory play';
- 'imaginative play and improvised drama';
- 'giving and receiving simple explanations, information and instructions; asking and answering questions' (5).

Children's own experiences

But children's response in learning and language terms will often be made in individual and personal terms. The planned situations and activities outlined in the General Introduction to the Programme of Study must cover: 'development of speaking and listening skills, both when role playing and otherwise – when describing experiences, expressing opinions, articulating personal feelings and formulating and making appropriate responses to increasingly complex instructions and questions' (3c).

Much of young children's talk naturally arises from describing their experiences for a number of reasons: to gain attention; to seek approval; to test the value of what they have done; to seek an explanation of aspects of experience that may have puzzled or alarmed them; to interpret things for themselves; to impress others; to raise self-esteem; to discover why things went wrong.

A quick analysis of such purposes shows that all of them are connected in one way or another with cognitive, emotional or maturational growth. As children seek to describe their experiences in a way that will achieve their intentions, they are obliged to fashion and shape the descriptions so that they present to the listener what they wish to convey. Whatever forms of development, emotional or cognitive, that maybe taking place in the process – and often it will be so gradual or minimal as to be almost imperceptible – there will be certain language development.

Very young children will:
• Make decisions about the words they need to use, discriminating, selecting and rejecting (these will include nouns, verbs, adverbs, prepositions and conjunctions);
• Decide the order in which the words should be put;
• Select some words as subjects and others as objects and 'talk in sentences';
• Use, in some cases, subordinate clauses;
• Decide upon particular emphases;
• Reformulate words and phrases and arguments;
• Take account of responses and adjust and adapt to cope with them.

Teachers can work with children individually and in pairs as well as in groups. They can call on the children's personal experiences, and encourage them to talk about their best friends, their pets, their most memorable holiday, their favourite foods, their three most treasured possessions, the story they like to tell most of all, the jokes that make them laugh, to name but a few ideas.

Children could then be paired with an older child or an adult to develop their personal experience into drama or story.

Story-making as a stimulus for language

Drama can provide a powerful impetus to children's language development, but a story is at least as potent a factor, involving constructing the story line, talking it through, deciding upon reasons for certain decisions and behaviour, investing characters with personality, formulating conclusions and outcomes.
• A class of infants had had the story *The Willow Pattern Plate* by Barbara Wilson read to them. Some of the children designed a series of plates based upon their own favourite stories; one group told the story in a series of captioned pictures which were shown to another class on a model television screen; while another group gave a 'lecture' about it using an overhead projector.
• Children who had seen a televised version of *The Little Match Girl* by Hans Christian Andersen produced a taped description of the comments of people coming from a great banquet who pass the child in the street. They made up stories about some of them – a rich selfish woman disgusted by the shabby and grimy appearance of the girl; her daughter much kinder, but diffident and unable to influence her mother; the tyrannical man who employs the match girl – and described their own 'visions' as the match girl describes her vision in the story.
• Top infants had been sharing the book *Joseph's Yard* by Charles Keeping with their teacher. She encouraged them to find words to describe Joseph's changing attitudes and state of mind as the story develops. They decided that Joseph's problem was that he was lonely and had

nothing to love or cherish. They went on from there to make a book of lonely people. They talked about what Joseph's plant meant to insects, birds and even cats. They considered how the destruction of a forest or a hedgerow impinges on wild life. They turned over a large stone on a piece of waste ground adjacent to the school and observed through magnifying glasses the results of the disturbance of the colony beneath.

They might have been encouraged to relate Joseph's story to that of *The Selfish Giant* who tried to keep his garden to himself; to make a book of beautiful gardens; to have a flower arranging competition; or to invite a gardener to talk about growing and caring for plants.

● Children who had been reading *Charley, Charlotte and the Golden Canary* by Charles Keeping made a book about their best friend, because they had identified that as the main theme of the story.

The story could also have stimulated children to describe their own street; to make a book of birds; to set up a bird table outside the classroom window and observe what happened; to locate their homes on a map of the area surrounding the school; or to talk about open air markets.

● A group of infants who had been sharing *On Friday Something Funny Happened* by John Prater made a large illustrated diary of their adventures over a week, accompanied by a tape recording.

● Another group made a picture book with further adventures of Clare, whose extraordinary exploits they had been party to in *On the Way Home* by Jill Murphy.

Most people will accept that experience of stories will expand children's vocabulary and their command of grammar and sentence structure. But as the examples cited here serve to illustrate, story is capable of taking children far beyond that in terms of language development.

Story is one of the most powerful starting points in children's learning and in their development as language users. Teachers know from their experience that story must be allowed to work its own

wonders in subtle ways over long periods of time. Growth and development will not come from squeezing a story dry in order to generate work, imposing demands for particular types of work on every encounter children have with story. Story will inspire children and take their language into a variety of realms where it is available in profusion, and used with finesse and enthusiasm. There seems good reason to believe that a rich experience of story and literature will help children to match the demands and expectations of the National Curriculum and to grow through the Levels of Attainment, not merely with confidence and success, but with pleasure as well.

Structured activities to develop listening skills

'These planned situations and activities should cover: . . .

● **development of listening (and, as appropriate, reactive) skills in non-reciprocal situations,** *eg radio programmes*' (3c).

The ability to listen, to determine what is being said and to respond appropriately are often thought of as skills that are naturally and easily acquired. However, the physical act of listening is only part of the process. Where children need help is in the cognitive part of the task, in assimilating, interpreting and making sense of what they have heard and in deciding what the appropriate responses might be. In order to provide support for children in relation to these often highly complex and demanding processes, teachers will often have to set up carefully structured activities.

These activities could include:
● Playing a variety of games which require children to listen to spoken instructions, for example simple board games or physical education activities and games;
● Listening to taped stories (commercially produced material is available with accompanying text, but in order to derive the fullest possible value

from these tapes, adults should share the stories with children afterwards);

● Making story tapes that feature teachers and other adults in the school, parents and children;

● Making sound effect tapes about which children can speculate, including animal noises, a police or ambulance siren, a whistling kettle, a motor car starting, a 'phone ringing, a fog horn, a door bell, water dripping, someone moving across the room, closing a door, opening a parcel;

● Recording someone reading from a book like *Peace at Last* by Jill Murphy, devising and making the sound effects and listening afterwards and commenting on how successful they had been;

● Recording people describing activities such as washing up, pitching a tent, learning how to use a skateboard or eating a juicy orange, then asking the children to guess what they are;

● Taping descriptions of, for example, a teapot, a spider, a bicycle, a tin opener, a recorder or a telephone, then asking the children to guess the objects.

A variation on this would require the children to prepare descriptions which a partner would then attempt to guess.

The power of story

In recent times there has been a growing understanding of the importance of story, both in relation to children's language development, and their learning generally. It seems likely that through listening to and reading stories children have their knowledge and understanding of the world extended, have new horizons and fresh perceptions revealed to them, rather like a traveller on a journey. Story possesses in a very powerful way the means to develop the creative impulse and the critical faculty, the ability to be reflective and analytical; it enables the listener or the reader to impose order and understanding upon diverse experiences. As story helps children to move beyond the here and now and acquire ever widening perceptions of the world, so their command of language structures and vocabulary grows. They are provided with the raw material to talk with others, and are enabled to construct narrative sequences, to predict and anticipate what may happen in particular circumstances, to appreciate cause and effect. Perhaps most important of all, children learn from story that language is the great resource out of which they can create their own world.

Teachers, influenced by the evidence of their own experience of the power of story, have increasingly begun to give much wider value and significance to it in the routine of the classroom and in the general experience that they provide for the children.

This has been done most effectively where:

• Stories are selected, told and read for their own intrinsic worth, and because they seem likely to give children pleasure, to cause excitement, to broaden and enrich their experience and understanding, to engage and challenge their imagination, to stimulate debate and speculation, to suggest possibilities and alternatives, to provide comfort and support;

• Stories are selected within a whole school policy for literature, which carefully provides for continuity, progression and development;

• Story reading and telling is provided regularly by various members of staff, by parents, children, visitors in assemblies and book-weeks and on festival and party occasions;

• Books clearly play an important part in the life of the school, through the provision of extensive and carefully planned libraries, where children have the opportunity to be members of a book club and buy books over a period through an 'instalment' plan, and can bring their own books from home and share them with others;

• The school collaborates with parents in providing the richest possible reading opportunities and experiences for children;

• Non-fiction is as carefully selected and valued as fiction, and is available to support children's learning, research and exploration across the whole curriculum.

It is almost inevitable that story, even casually presented, will extend children's language. It would be virtually impossible for children not to have their sense of sentence structure and their vocabulary enhanced by listening to *Alexander and the Terrible, Horrible, No-good, Very Bad Day* by Judith Viorst, or *I Unpacked My Grandmother's Trunk* by Susan Hoguet which can even be played as a game in pairs or larger groups ('I unpacked my Grandmother's trunk and out of it I took an acrobat, a bear, a cloud, a dinosaur, an eagle, and . . .') or *A Lion in the Night* by Pamela Allen ('They had what they usually had for breakfast; all except the lion, who tied a napkin around his neck, then gobbled up . . . one bowl of porridge, two eggs, a slice of hot buttered toast, some crumpets, bread and honey, fruit yoghurt, muesli, a bag of biscuits belonging to the little dog, and last of all, a big bowl of strawberries and red jelly').

Young children find *Rosie's Walk* by Pat Hutchins irresistible for many reasons. They are charmed by the way she glides unaware and ignorant (or is she really?) through a world of danger, leaving a trail of destruction behind her and outwitting the villainous fox at every turn. They are invited to participate from the outset, to anticipate what will happen on the next page, as in a cartoon film. The story provides obvious and natural opportunities for language development, but in some respects the most valuable of these goes almost unnoticed; the way in which the story helps children to come to terms with prepositions of location, words that are crucial for children to master in terms of being able to formulate critically important language functions, but are extremely difficult for young children to comprehend outside meaningful contexts.

Similarly, it might be tempting at first sight to see *A Walk in the Park* by Anthony Brown as merely a collection of clever visual jokes and miss the opportunity it provides for debate about reality and fantasy, about ambiguities and anachronisms.

However, the potential of story and literature to enhance and enrich children's learning and language development will only be fully or partially realised where story is used sensitively and creatively, and where children are encouraged to pursue lines of enquiry and development that

genuinely engage their interest and curiosity.

Children are unlikely to respond enthusiastically, and certainly not creatively, if they are frequently put in situations where they feel obliged to dredge from the stories they encounter a particular meaning or some visible piece of 'follow-up' work, like a trophy won in a race. But where children are constantly given the chance to enjoy and savour a story for its own sake, to reflect upon it, to let it mature in the mind, to make connections between it and other stories, between characters, places, episodes and incidents, then a rich source of reference and vicarious experience will be built up that will furnish the raw material for extensive learning.

Starting points

Let us consider briefly some examples of story and books that have provided fertile and natural starting points for language developments, and suggest others that could prove as valuable if used naturally in a rich context of story provisions.

● A group of infant children were listening to a reading of *The Bears on Hemlock Mountain* by Alice Dalgleish. At a crisis point in the story, when Jonathan is trapped by the bears under the cooking pot, the sequence was interrupted by a child who called out, 'He's like the boy with his hand in the hole in the dyke keeping out the water'. What this girl had remarkably succeeded in doing was to make the connection between Jonathon's dilemma and the predicament of the Dutch boy and to perceive the likelihood of their experiencing similar emotions and responses. She was expressing **'opinions and viewpoints with increasing sophistication' (Programmes of Study for Key Stages 2-4, 6a)** and 'taking part as speaker and listener in an activity, expressing a personal view and commenting constructively on what is being discussed or experienced' (Level 4c, Statements of Attainment).

This young child was able to make that connection and draw that conclusion only because she was used to an environment, both at home and in school, where books were always available, where stories were discussed and shared, where other opinions and viewpoints were sought and seriously considered. She was able to form judgements and perceptions, to make deductions and conclusions because she was already a familiar traveller in the world of books and was developing an understanding of its conventions, codes and rules.

● A small group of infant children were sharing the illustrated book *The Great Flood* by Peter Spier with a visitor. The book described the adventures of Noah and his family as they filled the great Ark with animals. While the children provided the 'text' for the uncaptioned pictures they speculated as to why 'Noah found grace in the eyes of the Lord' (one of two lines of text in the whole book); named the creatures who came into the Ark; discovered that some are now extinct; explained why the tigers had to be confined to a cage; guessed why the mule had to be dragged in resisting and why the snails came last.

When they came to the page where, the doors having been locked, there is still a great mass of animals shown outside the Ark, the visitor jumped to the conclusion that the pages had been mis-assembled, and expressed disappointment that the story had been disrupted. One of the children, however, pointed out that the animals they were looking at had been left behind because, 'Noah could only take two

of each . . .'. She had drawn together the evidence available to her from the pictures, from the storyline up to then, and from a previous knowledge of the story to make sense of a quite complex and ambiguous situation. But in an important respect she had gone even further. Her valid conclusion showed an understanding of subtle literary processes and a very sophisticated response to the visitor's comment, which represented both a recognition of the visitor's misunderstanding of the situation and an appreciation that her explanation would be comprehensible to him. This conclusion on the part of the child was based upon an ability to follow the sequence of action, to use the visual evidence available to construct an appropriate narrative, to predict and speculate and to hypothesise; if Noah could only take two of each animal, then by implication, some animals had to be left behind.

How could the response be assessed in terms of the requirements of the National Curriculum? For Attainment Target 1, Key Stage 1 it would match: 1(a), (b); 2(a), (c), (e); 3(c); and possibly 4(b).

In an illustrated book of this kind where there is no text, save for a couple of lines, then the children become the 'authors', constructing the storyline themselves, talking it through, deciding upon reasons for certain decisions and behaviour, investing characters with personality, formulating conclusions and outcomes.

The following suggestions for story-stimulated activities are straightforward and quite routine. It is likely, however, that the richest outcomes will be those that are unexpected and unpredictable.

Children could be invited to:
● Describe their own happiest birthday surprise, having shared Sam's adventures in *Happy Birthday, Sam* by Pat Hutchins;
● Talk about occasions when they have been rude or thoughtless like the naughty baby in Elfrida Vipont's *The Elephant and the Bad Baby*;
● Describe with drawings adaptations they would like to make to particular toys

to make them more effective as Mrs Armitage does in *Mrs Armitage on Wheels* by Quentin Blake;
● Describe the most unusual, most welcome or most difficult person who has visited their house, having heard of the embarrassment created by *The Tiger Who Came To Tea* by Judith Kerr;
● Provide a text for *Creepy Castle* by John Goodall;
● Make their own 'junk' models after looking at *Bored, Nothing To Do* by Peter Spier.

Summary

Teachers may find the following summary of major points useful.
● Children will generally use three forms of speaking and listening: to help them to share and talk with others in the normal everyday business of living; to help them learn; to communicate.
● Teachers are very good at providing context, opportunities and environments for developing all these modes of speaking.

What is harder to do is to make sure that all three are being provided for in proper proportions, so that, for example, children do not spend most of their time in social conversations, which is probably the easiest of all to provide for. It is more demanding and complex to ensure that children are using languages as a means of extending their knowledge and learning.
● Equally it is probably easier to provide for speaking than listening. It will help if teachers think of listening as the 'receiving' part of speaking and remember that good provisions for speaking can do much to ensure good reasons for listening. When planning speaking activities teachers will find it helpful to reflect upon the implications for the listeners. *sheet speaking/listening*
● Teachers at primary level have provided creatively for language development for many years, but have not always ensured that systematic progression is being achieved. The Programme of Study properly implemented will help provide for this and the Statements of Attainment and the Attainment Levels will provide a yardstick for evaluation.

- Much assessment can be accomplished in the course of the learning activity. It is well to remember that the everyday assessment done by teachers can be spread over a period of time. Opportunities for assessment of language occur not only across the entire curriculum but in the whole range of the social activities and life of the class. Responses, for example, to a story can provide teachers with opportunity for on-the-spot assessment of aspects of children's language development that can be recorded subsequently.

- Opportunity for speaking and listening and their development occur naturally across the whole curriculum. The other profile components in English are critically interlinked with the speaking and listening components.

- It will help teachers not only to make effective provision but also to assess if they can build up a kind of aide memoire in relation to all the children in their class; identifying which ones are confident and outgoing, which shy and diffident; which activities and experiences seem to be most productive in relation to speaking; which children can speak more than one language.

- Teachers will find it helpful to obtain some adult assistance, however briefly, at least once a week to enable them to observe and effect language activities in the classroom. Other helpers may make a note, for example, of the repertoire of ways of talking shown by a particular group of children.

- It is helpful for teachers to remember that most children come to school as pretty competent speakers, and that the more they use language the more adept they are likely to become. Furthermore they are most likely to be involved in language activity by working in a group.

- Literature is crucial to children's language learning, especially in speaking and listening. It will be productive for all staff to review and consider together their provisions in this area.

- Bilingual children will respond positively in the kind of learning context and environment and to the language opportunities we have discussed in this book. Teachers must be confident about the potential of the provisions they make to cater effectively for bilingual children. Equally they must not worry about bilingual children using their community tongue when it is easier and more appropriate to do so.

- Schools should involve parents as partners in their children's learning and share with parents the knowledge they both have of individual children's development and also of the experience they are encountering both at home and at school. It is particularly important that schools should strive to involve parents of bilingual children in this process.

- Finally it is probably not an exaggeration to claim that children are amused by, attracted to and intrigued by language. Some of the most valuable language learning occurs when children are encouraged to have fun with it.

Key Stage 2

The Programme of Study for Key Stage 2 says that

'Pupils should be given the opportunity to learn how to:

● express and justify feelings, opinions and viewpoints with increasing sophistication' (6a).

It is easier for children to express how they feel and to justify the opinions they hold when they are discussing matters that are of genuine concern to them. Such matters will be those that relate most immediately to them or affect them in a particular way: their parents, family and home; their friends and pets; aspects of school life that are enjoyable and exciting or, conversely, alarming or intimidating; teachers and other adults in their life; rivals and those they dislike; bullying and threatening behaviour; what they watch on television; play and hobbies; personal enthusiasms, ambitions and aspirations, worries, fears and concerns.

It may be neither realistic nor helpful to expect most children to respond to abstract issues at this stage. There may also be areas of intense personal concern and delicacy about which even very young children are too shy or inhibited to speak. On the other hand, children will often take advantage of certain circumstances or activities, of play or drama, or the chance to respond to a particular story or book to express deep personal and private feelings.

A teacher who was concerned about feuding and bad feeling between two ethnic groups of older junior boys read the class the book *Babylon* by Jill Paton-Walsh. She then divided the children into groups of four and appointed a chairperson and a scribe to record their final decision. This was a process the children were used to and were learning to refine. The teacher normally used it in connection with more practical matters: planning assemblies;

comic remarks or even embarrassed by the manifest unhappiness of some of the children.

allocating tasks in connection with outings; the organisation of the classroom; making preparations for guests and so on.

On this occasion she asked the groups to decide why it was that David's mother had said to the young girl Dulcie that she would 'surely have somethin' to weep for by and by.' In this way the teacher was hoping to explore as sensitively as possible the issue of racial hostility and to help the children appreciate how damaging to them all it could be – indeed was being.

To her surprise the children almost without exception ignored the question in so far as it related to Dulcie. Instead they turned it to deal with their own personal situations – mockery of their parents by other children; reflections upon their own appearances, intelligence, and family; fear of going to the secondary school and some of the older children they would encounter there. The children listened with deep attention to the views of other groups, in many cases acknowledging and agreeing with what was said, in others rejecting strongly what were seen as unjustified

allegations, and in a few instances being either amused by what they took to be

What this teacher discovered was that:
● Deep concerns sometimes require the kind of trigger that story or drama provides before they can be expressed.
● It is necessary to adopt certain strategies if children are to be assisted to respond in increasingly sophisticated ways. For this reason the children sometimes worked in pairs which made it easier to construct their arguments and points of view. It facilitated both collaboration and mutual feedback, initiated children into agenda-making and note-keeping and prepared them for the challenge of working in larger groups. The latter was often achieved by simply merging pairs together and encouraging them to share the ideas they had already formulated in the small grouping. Clearly formulated rules governed the group work; many of these had been generated out of the children's own experience of less ordered and ultimately frustrating occasions. People took turns to fill the roles of chair and secretary.

The main task had to be clearly defined, a time limit was established and children were encouraged to review periodically the progress they had made and to analyse what decisions they had reached.
● Story and drama are among the most powerful agents for evoking feelings and responses in children, for helping them to formulate perceptions and to develop opinions and viewpoints.
● Children will achieve sophistication in what they are trying to express when they are helped to reflect systematically on the nature and quality of what they are saying. Teachers have to work consistently at this, sometimes taking individual children back over the main points of their argument, sometimes working with a group or even the whole class. Children can be encouraged to rehearse with partners, to provide feedback for each other, to make drafts of what they wish to say, to record what has been said and to analyse it critically.

Discussions and reflections

Many children, before they are ready to discuss personal issues, will need to have experience of working, ideally in pairs, discussing and reflecting on matters that are interesting for them but not likely to be painful or threatening.

So, for example, they will talk for two or three minute periods with children and adults they know well about a variety of things:

- Descriptions of themselves;
- Descriptions of their parents, grandparents, homes, pets, favourite toys, clothes;
- Accounts of their favourite hobbies;
- Description of a vivid dream;
- An account of an unpleasant chore;
- Their favourite food or entertainment.

The partner can be required to feed back what they have learned or have discovered from the talk. Sometimes a third person can be allocated as an observer to the pair to ask questions at the end of the conversation, to seek clarification and to comment on what she has gained from the exchange.

A variation on this requires the children to share photographs or postcards; incidents or people likely to evoke a reaction or response such as actors, singers or dancers in histrionic contexts, or animals in danger; or situations that cause amusement or surprise. The pairs should share their viewpoints or feelings for not more than two minutes each. They then go on to join another pair and assume the responsibility of interpreting their partner's opinions.

In time and with practice children will go on to discuss increasingly complex issues. They can be encouraged to talk for longer periods, to work more frequently in groups of four and to consider broader issues. Because it remains likely that many children will continue to express what they think and feel and deal confidently with increasingly complex issues where they relate it in some way to themselves, then the following areas for discussion are likely to foster development:

- Who would I be if I were not myself? Why?
- What two things would I change in this class/school if I could do so immediately? Why?
- What one thing would I give myself, my best friend, my father, mother or teacher for the purpose of improvement?
- What kind of person would I like to marry? Why have I chosen these particular qualities?
- What kind of person would I want to take with me on holiday and why?

Wider issues

As children mature and move through Key Stage 2, they will be capable of focusing on and discussing issues of wider and more general concern and can be expected to make thoughtful responses to matters, for example, that feature in local and national news:

- Should all people who keep dogs have to pay for doing so? If there are to be exceptions to this rule, who should they be and why?
- Should everyone be prevented from travelling abroad in support of the national football team, in order to prevent hooliganism?

Children can be helped to reflect on complex issues arising out of the work they do in school. For example, one class had made a survey of a large beach with prolific sea life. They made a collection of some of these, including crabs and a sea mouse, intending to preserve them in formaldehyde for their class museum. As they headed back in some excitement, one of the children asked whether a feebly moving crab in one of the jars was dying. When this was confirmed it dawned on the children generally that all the specimens would have to perish. They then debated whether they wished to proceed and eventually, and with an element of reluctance on the part of some, returned all their hard-won specimens to the sea. On their return to school, the teacher helped them to reflect on the matter at more length obliging them to identify the real reasons for their decision and asking them to relate this to the fact that some of them, for example, went angling. Some of the children were able to justify their decision at a sophisticated level ('. . . we put them back because we did not really need them' or '. . . they would have died slowly and that would be cruel . . . when animals are killed for food they don't know it has happened to them . . .'). The teacher pushed the matter further and began a debate about whether they should be keeping their pets in the classroom. The children were more confident and at ease with this issue: '. . . pets are good for you because they help to calm you down . . .', '. . . if they were let out in the wild they would die or be killed . . .', '. . . at least they are sure of food and shelter here . . .' and '. . . we know they are happy because they run up our hands and they like playing with us.' And perhaps what clinched the debate: 'They'll calm you down, Miss, when you get upset!'. As a result of this debate, however, it was agreed that only a limited number of children in rotation, could play with the animals, and then only at particular times in the week.

Everyday matters

A whole range of matters connected with everyday life in the classroom and school can give rise to discussions of varying levels of complexity:
- How to ensure that classroom jobs and responsibilities are equally shared;
- How to guarantee privacy and quiet in certain areas of the classroom;
- How to ensure equal access to classroom facilities eg the computer;
- What can the children do to improve their classroom/school environment and why should they be concerned to do so.

Literature

We have said that story and drama are among the most powerful agents for evoking feelings and responses in children and for helping them to develop opinions. Because of its power to select and shape events and to represent experience in meaningful patterns, literature can raise complex matters in a concentrated and explicit way for both adults and children alike. So, for example, children who encounter books of the kind mentioned below might find themselves wrestling with any of the complex issues referred to in connection with them:
- *Dogger* by Shirley Hughes – The qualities that imbue objects with value for people; what other criteria, apart from material ones, determine worth; the notion of sacrifice, what inspires it, whether it is laudable and desirable, where else it is found both in literature and life, whether ordinary people, including children are capable of it.
- *Storm* by Kevin Crossley-Holland – The dilemma here hinges on the identity of the mysterious rider. If it is a ghost, what clues or evidence are there in the book to indicate that it is so? How does the writer create a sense of the eerie and supernatural without recourse to 'ghostly' paraphernalia? What things create a genuine sense of unease as distinct from the wild excesses of horror films and comics?

- *How Tom Beat Captain Najork and his Hired Sportsmen*, Russell Hoban – This poses complex technical issues. The task of writing the rules for the three complicated games that are vaguely described represents a considerable intellectual, linguistic and technological task. When the rules are completed those responsible must surely be invited to discover by experimentation whether they really work out in practice.
- *Three Pigs*, Tony Ross – This has the capacity to be read and talked about at a number of levels. It may be just a blatant lie, a piece of 'make-up' and deceit. On the other hand, there may be just a possibility that the wolf has been maligned and misunderstood. In some respects it offers an early way in for children to consider alternative points of view and the ways in which facts and issues can be distorted and misrepresented. Children can be encouraged to examine other stories and consider alternative story lines.
- An able group of fourth year children had been sharing the novel *Smith* by Leon Garfield with their teacher. They explored the novel in a range of ways, including following the route of Smith's adventures across London. The teacher provided them with a particularly complex challenge. She suggested to them that every major character in the novel was evil, that the book was about human corruption and invited them to prove or disprove this thesis 'by reference to the text'.

Four of the children, working in pairs, supported the proposition and 'proved' it satisfactorily by quoting from the book. A fifth child suggested an exception, the philanthropist Mansfield, and again was able to justify her view by 'reference to the text'. The final member of the group refuted this, claiming that Mansfield was not just 'blind outside' (in the novel the character is blind) but was 'blind inside' and provided evidence of moral frailty from the book.

In this striking example we see exemplified two of the skills that the Programme of Study seeks to develop across Key Stage 2: the ability to **'discuss increasingly complex issues' (6b)** and the ability to **'assess and interpret arguments and opinions with increasing precision and discrimination' (6d).**

The other books we have referred to similarly facilitate children's discussion of complex issues and challenge them in varying degrees to weigh conflicting arguments and opinions. Where the children are additionally obliged to furnish evidence and reasons for their own decisions and viewpoints, then they are being helped to seek for **'increasing precision and discrimination'.**

Drama

Drama can powerfully support children's developing abilities to discuss complex issues and to analyse, interpret and represent argument and opinion. Drama situations will vary widely. Very often they may lead to little more than an exchange of dialogue; involve only pairs or small groups of people; seek to do no more than retell a story or to express an alternative to it; be finished and discarded as soon as the particular issue is resolved and have little or nothing recorded on paper.

In other cases children will work in a variety of groups, may have to confront other groups with arguments that are meant to secure an advantage or even outright victory, may require the action and the outcomes to be recorded and presented as part of a coherent argument to an audience.

Sometimes groups will seek to involve other groups in their enterprise by inviting them to participate in aspects of the action or plot. Children who have seen Theatre in Education groups will be quite accustomed to this approach.

Typically, therefore, drama that is likely to raise complex issues and to call for the weighing of argument and opinion may focus on issues of the following nature:
● How to decide upon a leader for a range of purposes and different contexts;

● What to reply to the king who demands your most valued possession;
● Providing arguments for the opening of a letter that contains either disastrous or highly beneficial news, but does not need to be opened, rather like Pandora's box;
● Selling winter clothes from a stall in high summer;
● Explaining to the police why the other driver was at fault in an accident;
● Trying to mollify someone whose window you have broken with a rashly thrown cricket ball;
● Persuading people going into a circus that they should turn back because they will be contributing to the degradation of the animals.

Historical drama
Later through Key Stage 2 some children will be competent to create drama based around historical situations:
● The priest who persuades the villagers of Eyam to stay within the village when the plague strikes, rather than run the risk of spreading it across the neighbouring countryside;
● The first person to ascend in a hot air balloon explaining what he intends to do and inviting on-lookers to join him;

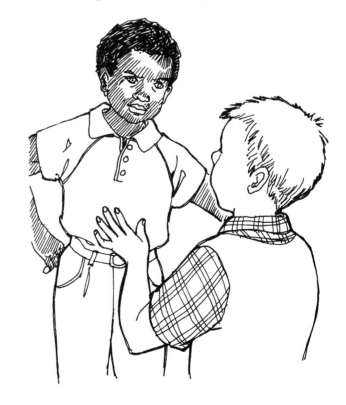

• An episode in which the person who tests the Davy Safety Lamp first goes down a mine to do so;

• The first people to cross a river by raft, to light a fire, to experiment and operate with chloroform, to build a bridge across a gorge or to invent a wheel explain the value of what they are trying to do to a sceptical audience and attempt to involve them in the process.

Children may also select particular characters from story and literature and either adapt their adventures into drama, which they script for formal presentation, or create new adventures for them to be presented as live drama or through puppets.

Many of these situations will require children:

• To research the characters and periods they are presenting, especially in the case of historical contexts;

• To consider the scientific, historical or geographical ideas or concepts with which the characters, incidents or places are associated.

Children who present a play about the Davy Safety Lamp, the heroic work of Florence Nightingale, the life of Joseph Damien or Scott's last journey will find themselves considering and analysing scientific and medical matters. Why could the experiment with the lamp have proved fatal? Why was Damien doomed from the moment he set foot on Molokai? How did Scott actually know how to find his way to the South Pole and what exactly is it? What was the great work Florence Nightingale achieved after the Crimea? They will also have to consider the nature, qualities and characters of the people they are playing and construct satisfactory roles for them.

These experiences in drama will give them the opportunity to **'use, and understand the use of, role-play in teaching and learning, *eg to explore an aspect of history, a scientific concept or a piece of literature'* (6m)**. It will enable them to **'work with or devise an increasing range of drama scripts, taking on a variety of dramatic roles'(6l)**.

Audiences

These situations will also call, of course, for audiences; children will not only create and present, but will observe, take note and criticise as well. They have to be educated into this difficult and challenging role, to match their judgement and perceptions against the intentions and objectives of those playwrights and actors who are creating and performing for them. So before plays are presented it will be a valuable exercise for those responsible to give an introduction to their audience, to deliver a synopsis of their production, and even to explain what it is they hope to achieve. The critics in turn, must learn to take account of this, to make their judgements within realistic parameters and to justify by reference to the play or the acting, the criticisms they are offering. These children will be not only 'reporting on and summarising' in certain contexts, but will be helping the performers to **'reflect on their own effectiveness in the use of the spoken word' (6q)**.

In the process many of the children will be listening and responding to **'an increasing range of fiction, non-fiction poetry and plays, including those which have been seen' (6j)**. They will also be required to **'recite and read aloud in a variety of contexts, with increasing fluency and awareness of audience' (6k)**.

Reading aloud

Children will not be dependent on drama alone for opportunity to read aloud to audiences, with increasing fluency.

• They may do so quite often in assembly, when they not only read, but create and compose the material for the reading.

• They might read stories they have composed for younger children, including those at the nursery stage.

• There might be occasions when they, in the capacity of secretary, read back notes for the whole class or for groups, of discussions that have taken place or decisions that have been taken.

- They could read drafts of their writing to other children in a writing 'conference'.
- They might present readings on the occasion of presentations to retiring members of staff, to groups of parents or to guests who are visiting the school.
- They could read descriptions of scientific experiments they have undertaken or of models they have made and exhibitions they have set up.

Children will learn through experience, through listening to the feedback from audiences, through being encouraged to reflect as frequently as possible on the effectiveness of their presentations, that different work and varied audiences call for particular forms of presentation and for appropriate language. A tragic drama about the death of Icarus will demand, for example, language of a certain intensity and gravity, at least at crucial moments. It will be strikingly different from the language and conversation of a play based on the attempts of Jack, a comic and accident-prone bumpkin, to win the hand in marriage of the beautiful princess.

They will also learn to appreciate that neither of those forms would be appropriate to describe an enterprise to electrify a doll's house, or a maths experiment to find out how long it would take to travel to Pluto at 100 miles an hour, or to write a letter of thanks to the teacher from the nearby school who has helped them to keep locusts in the classroom. The stories they offer to senior citizens will be different in context from those read to children in the reception class. Such experiences all help children to reflect on the complex nature of language, on its immense capacity for endless variation, its power to gain attention, to startle or alarm, to amuse, to enthral, to inform or to teach.

Dialects and accents

This leads naturally to a consideration of Standard and Non-Standard English, of the fact that people not only speak in different accents, but also use very different forms of English (see also the section on Knowledge about language, page 177).
- It will be valuable for children to collect examples of dialect, to see written forms of dialect and to contrast this with, or 'translate' it into, standard forms. Both accents and examples of dialect can often be identified in a school, both in children and adults. Children can be encouraged to listen to both 'live' accents and to taped versions and then to differentiate between them. Collections of dialects, in taped form, can be made.
- Children may examine some of the easier medieval verse, compare it with a modern translation and identify the ways in which words have changed and developed.
- They can make slang collections and invent words of their own for particular purposes. They can be helped to understand that language grows and changes through popular usage, by being led to reflect on those words that their own generation have brought into use eg 'brill'.

Effective communication

'Pupils should be given the opportunity to learn how to:
- **recount events and narrate stories'** **(3c).**
One of the most prevalent of all human instincts is that which impels us to tell others of the experiences we have had, the events in which we have participated and the things we have managed to do. Equally we will give personal accounts to win sympathy, to excuse ourselves, to secure the views or opinions of other people, to clarify matters by talking them through.

But we learn very quickly that the business of conveying what we want to say is a complex one. Many people struggle all their lives to 'find the right words'.

Ability to communicate effectively derives from a complexity of sources, including personality and experience. Children need to develop confidence at an early stage about describing what they are doing or thinking, or what their plans and intentions are. They must be helped to understand that language is an instrument that helps them to sort out their thinking, that enables them to take things apart and analyse them just as their hands shuffle and re-arrange the pieces of a puzzle or a jig-saw.

They will find it easier to accept and comprehend this in a natural way where, from an early stage, they are encouraged to talk with a wide range of people – children and adults – and, above all, where they have a large spectrum of events to discuss and describe. This brings us back to the critical importance of the learning environment and the nature of the experiences they encounter both at home and in the school.

Throughout Key Stage 2, it is essential that children have problems to solve, are accustomed to working collaboratively in groups and expect to communicate to others what they have been doing and what they are achieving. Quite often this will amount to no more than two children sharing ideas about the right way to tackle a mathematical problem, to find the appropriate tone of colour for an evening sky in a mural, or to reading and criticising

each others' first writing drafts.

But if children are consistently to have things they are anxious to talk about and recount, if they are to have stories of all kinds to tell, then they are most likely to do so where:
● There is consistent opportunity for science activity which requires children to pursue solutions and report back to others;
● They are encouraged to investigate the immediate environment of the school and the surrounding neighbourhood, to focus on particular aspects and to present their findings about these;
● Drama is a regular feature of the classroom experience, both in problem solving contexts and in terms of writing and presenting a range of drama to others;
● A variety of people visit the classroom for particular purposes over a period of time to talk about their hobbies or interests, to display and talk about items of interest and to involve the children in what they are doing;
● Children are encouraged to write for particular purposes, where they expect their writing to be 'published' and where they have a clear conception of who the audience is likely to be;

- Story-telling and bookmaking are central to the life of the classroom, where there is a wide range of books available, including all kinds of illustrated books, fiction and non-fiction;
- Personal reading is consistently encouraged and where children have frequent opportunity to share what they are reading, both with adults and other children;
- There is a class or school museum, to which the children can themselves contribute;
- Work in history involves children in problem solving, and the analysis of evidence.

The kinds of experiences that such contexts offer both demand and inspire the recounting of events and the narration of stories. These contexts will also enable children to **'present their ideas, experiences and understanding in a widening range of contexts across the curriculum and with an increasing awareness of audience and purpose'** (6e).

Effective listening
'Pupils should be given the opportunity to learn how to:
- **assess and interpret arguments and opinions with increasing precision and discrimination'** (6d).

A major part of the Programme of Study for Speaking and Listening is concerned with enabling children to communicate effectively and to express their opinions, feelings, needs and intentions. But it is equally important for children to be confident in the role of listener, receiver, interpreter. Effective listening is a crucial part of learning, the means whereby information, important arguments, viewpoints, perceptions and conceptual cues are picked up and intellectually scrutinised.

This is as important, complex and demanding in cognitive terms, as the matter of active communication. Listening and speaking are the two elements of an interactive process. Teachers may well

seem to provide more fully for the more active side, the speaking element, than they do for the receptive and 'passive' one. Of course, in creating the language environment and context in which all the aspects of speaking can flourish, they are creating the circumstances in which people will want to listen. People in general will want to listen to what is being said when it is likely to impinge upon and effect what they themselves may do, or what may happen to them. But effective listening calls for intellectual action. This is especially so where the listening is intended to help the listener assess and interpret argument and opinion. Most children will not easily develop this ability without active support.

Teachers will need to help children understand that their ability to act correctively or effectively, or to realise their intentions, may often be dependent on getting the right information and data, sorting out what is useful to them and making the right choice. Children will develop the ability to assess and interpet particular opinions with precision not merely by cultivating the ability and patience to listen, but by acquiring the skill to present cases and arguments effectively themselves.

Assessing what has been said
The ability to assess the worth and value of what others are saying will develop as pupils are encouraged to reflect back on how effectively they have said things themselves in certain circumstances:
- In presenting on behalf of a group the report of a science experiment they have concluded;
- In explaining how the group reached a decision or completed a certain piece of work;
- In telling a story to some younger children;
- In asking for a privilege on behalf of a group of children;
- In telling a joke;
- In responding to opportunity to speak in a range of contexts and for a variety of

purposes, whether drawing conclusions from a scientific or mathematical problem, giving their opinion of a book, or working out how to present a story through a play.

This will not only allow children to **'report and summarise in a range of contexts'** (Programmes of Study for Key Stages 2-4) but will enable them to **'reflect on their own effectiveness in the use of the spoken word'**. They can be encouraged to consider how their explanations might be made clearer and more explicit, how arguments could be more powerfully or subtly conveyed and how evidence can be presented most effectively and quickly.

The following experiences and activities will contribute to children's language development in a variety of ways but are also likely to help them to develop the skills of assessment and interpretation:

- A consideration of jokes and 'tall stories' and identifying and suggesting what it is that makes them funny or unlikely;
- Analysing the humour of books like *On The Way Home* by Jill Murphy and *The Enormous Crocodile* by Roald Dahl;
- Making judgements about appropriate ways to behave and talk in particular circumstances, for example, at a christening, a party for a shy friend or delivering a harvest festival parcel to an old lady;
- Considering and commenting on a series of opinions such as: all small people are poor at games; a person who runs away from a dog is a coward; boys should not cry; a camera always conveys the truth; or all people who beg are lazy.

Debating issues

Children should be given the opportunity to make judgements and provide reasons for their opinions and decisions about debatable issues, through a series of hypothetical situations.

- A boy finds a kitten which is lost and starving, looks after it devotedly over a year and then has it reclaimed by the true owners. Should he have to give the kitten up?
- A girl plays in the school team for several months, training in the evenings and turning up faithfully every weekend to play. A newcomer to the school who proves to be a brilliant player replaces the girl on the team immediately. Is this fair treatment?

Children might be invited to present cases of treatment of themselves and others which they consider unjust. They might also talk about cases from story or history in which people have been treated unfairly. They can be encouraged to present a devil's advocate view of relatively straightforward cases devised by the teacher.

Alternatively, pupils could be invited to devise, in pairs, brief but persuasive advertisements for a particular group of objects selected by the teacher; compose 'headlines' to describe romantic stories such as 'The Owl and the Pussycat', 'Cinderella', 'Sleeping Beauty' or 'Snow White and the Seven Dwarfs', or be asked to present news headlines in order of priority, eg 'Erupting volcano engulfs South American city', 'Airliner with 200 passengers hijacked in the Middle East', 'International pop idol to wed', 'Serious traffic hold-up blocks Central London for two hours', 'Cow gets trapped in stream in Oxfordshire'.

Working as a group

The Programmes of Study for Speaking and listening for all the Key Stages are in many respects dependent for their implementation on children working together in groups of various sizes. Since talking and listening occur in the main in social contexts it is clearly vital that children are given as much opportunity as possible to operate together.

The Programmes of Study for Key Stages 2 to 4, for example, refer to group activities on a number of occasions.

'Pupils should be given the opportunity to learn how to:
- **communicate with other group members in a wide range of situations**

eg an assignment in science or mathematics where a specific outcome is required;
• **discuss issues in small and large groups, taking account of the views of others, and negotiating a consensus;**
• **engage in prediction, speculation and hypothesis in the course of group activity'** (6 n, o, r).

'The range of opportunities provided should:
• **allow pupils to work in groups of various size, both single sex and mixed, where possible, with and without direct teacher supervision'** (7b).

'The range of activities should include:
• **taking part in shared writing activities'** (8e).

The ability to work effectively with other people at a common task is comprised not merely of technical skills, but of subtleties of insight and maturity of behaviour that have to be acquired and developed over periods of time. Children will need sensitive and carefully organised support if they are to work successfully in groups.

That is not to imply, of course, that teachers have to regard children, when they first come to school, as wholly inexperienced in collaborative work. Just as they come to school already capable in the use of language, so they may already have considerable experience of relating to other children and adults in group situations. They will have played and explored, participated in outings and parties, all with groups of people. They will have learned that certain things can only be done with the involvement and support of others.

But just as teachers have to help children build on the language expertise they bring with them, so they have to support them in developing specific skills if they are to get the most out of working in group situations.

Any group will comprise a range of qualities and characteristics, tendencies, conflicting aspirations and intentions.

Participants need to learn to recognise these facts and take account of and utilise them in the best interests of the group as a whole as well as the individuals within it. Some children will be shy and diffident about making contributions, others will find it difficult to concentrate for long on a task. There will be those who have no confidence in the contributions they might make, while others will want to dominate matters. Some will be reluctant to take turns, others will find it hard to listen.

Children have to learn how to conduct group business efficiently, how to decide on and realise objectives. They have to learn to listen to what others say, to identify what is most valuable or useful in it, and determine how to put it to best use. They have to learn how to discard the irrelevant, decide on what is feasible, allocate tasks and responsibilities, set timetables for action, and find ways of reviewing progress and evaluating what has been successful.

Children will learn to work in and contribute to groups through experiences of the following kind.
• During a class discussion, teachers can encourage children to respond and offer suggestions, inviting others to comment constructively on what has been said. Opportunity can be provided, even in whole class situations, for children to reflect on what has been done, 'to predict and speculate' about events in which they are going to be involved, about places they are going to visit, about what is likely to happen next in books and stories they are sharing etc.

This will accustom them to contributing individually in class discussion, help them to understand that others have contributions to make from which they can learn, to take turns, to ask increasingly precise or detailed questions.
• Discussion in pairs will be particularly helpful for shy and diffident children, especially if they are working with a friend thus giving them opportunity to express ideas without feeling under scrutiny or pressure. A natural and useful development

Group work will support children's language development for two very important reasons. Firstly, it is a social process that generates language because it is dependent on language for its very existence. Secondly, because group work is prolific in the forms it takes and the objectives it pursues, it will nurture a variety of language.

Children working in groups are likely to be required to:
- Express and justify opinions and present arguments and information logically;
- Make suggestions;
- Give precise instructions to others;
- Mediate in arguments, identify a range of opinions and decide upon a consensus;
- Listen to, take account of and make sense of the opinions of others;
- Reflect on effectiveness in the use of the spoken word.

Of course, group work will not be confined to oral discussion, especially where primary children are concerned. There will be group work in which practical work is conspicuously predominant, but where the language input, although quantitatively slight, will be of crucial importance to the operation. This will be true of many situations where children have to secure the support or ensure the involvement of others. The Programme of Study for Key Stage 2 suggests, for example, that children should be given opportunity to learn how to **'communicate with other group members in a wide range of situations, *eg. an assignment in science or mathematics where a specific outcome is required'* (6n).**

Such situations might include activities as diverse as making a cake, devising a maze, inventing a code, making a scale model of the planetary system, working out the speed of model cars on a sloping ramp, inventing home made clocks, making a book of personal statistics, etc.

Assignments such as these will involve children as much in practical activity as in discussion and communication. However,

of pairing is for pairs to share their views on a common theme with another pair, and to seek to come to a consensus of opinion. Children can also be asked to represent a partner's viewpoint to another pair.
- Groups can be encouraged to select chairpersons and secretaries, and to define clearly the rules for discussion and group management. Care should be taken to ensure that every child in the group has some task to discharge; children who are initially unwilling or reluctant to take part in discussion might record how many times each person spoke or might act as timekeepers.
- Children can be helped to establish group rules, to define the task and set objectives, to review periodically the stage the discussion has reached, to record decisions and make an action plan to ensure that every member of the group makes at least one contribution to discussion.
- The teacher or another adult can act occasionally as the leader of a group, encouraging shy children to comment on others' ideas, obliging the garrulous to be precise and helping the group to reflect on the effectiveness of their planning. The adult should lead them to reflect on what makes a successful and effective meeting and what tends to confuse or delay progress.

not only will the initial planning involve significant use of language, but as assignments are carried through there will be constant need for re-evaluation, for progress reports, for adaptation and new approaches as difficulties arise. Such work will provide an even greater impetus to language development when, as so often happens, it leads to areas of investigation and activity that had not been originally planned, as the following examples show.

● A group of children making a record of personal statistics found themselves involved in comparisons that led to interviews not only with other children in the school, but with members of their families as well.

● A class who had read *Carrie's War* by Nina Bawden set up an exhibition, comprised of artefacts they had collected and interviews they had conducted with people who were able to provide personal recollections of the war.

● Children who were depositing a 'time capsule' in the school garden ran a competition to find the parent or 'friend of the school' who could suggest the most appropriate representative collection.

● The setting up of a school museum led to an 'antiques road show'.

● Children who were given the responsibility of organising guest speakers to the classroom involved the local library and over a period succeeded in arranging visits from an archer, a water diviner, and a racing pigeon expert.

As these activities developed, the children had varied linguistic demands made upon them. They were involved in:

● Shared writing;

● Drawing up lists of speakers and experts, discovering how they could be contacted, making formal invitations – sometimes by 'phone – organising the presentations, conducting the events and subsequently thanking their guests;

● Rehearsing and carrying out interviews using tape recorders, cameras and dictaphones;

● Providing precise instructions and information.

Presenting information

'Pupils should be given the opportunity to learn how to:

● **present factual information in a clear and logically structured manner in a widening range of situations – discriminate between fact and opinion and between relevance and irrelevance and recognise bias' (6i).**

Children who have had experience of the processes outlined in the Programme of Study for Key Stage 1 will have had ample opportunity to present factual information in a clear and understandable manner and will certainly be capable of making distinctions between at least some fact and opinion, between truth and fiction. Indeed children are often extremely concerned to get the truth of the matter established, especially when it touches them directly (one has only to deal with playground disputes to have clear evidence of that!) and to determine whether a story is real or made-up.

So a good basis exists on which the initially important skills in this section of the Programme of Study can be built. They are crucial skills because without them people are at a loss in the complex, information-saturated contemporary world. It is crucial for children to acquire the expertise that will enable them to present their perceptions of the world as accurately and efficiently as possible, and to analyse and use the varied information with which they will be inundated.

Many of the activities and experiences that comprise the Programme of Study will naturally require children to utilise the skills of clear and logical presentation and of discrimination. The following are typical of examples encountered in classrooms.

● A group of children who had constructed a model of the planetary system identified the apparent conflict between the claim in the reference book they had consulted that the world was millions of years old and the statement in the Old Testament that it had been created by God in six days. This led to a long discussion with the teacher which went some way to resolving the contradiction. However, one child brought to school a few days later another reference book, containing an account of a celebrated case in the Southern United States involving the trial of a teacher who had taught the Theory of Evolution, and made the remark, 'Maybe they wouldn't believe what you said about the planets in America!'.

● Children who had been building boats posed the question, 'all the things made of iron and steel that we tried to float in the water tank sank to the bottom. Why is it then that a ship made of iron can float on the sea? Something doesn't make sense!'

● A group of children read that a pound today would have been worth four times as much in the year they were born. They set up an exhibition of objects in the classroom ranging from a bar of soap and a Mars bar through to a bicycle and a 'diamond ring', complete with current price tags and asked the class to work out what the prices would have been in the year they were born. They then held a 'speed competition' to establish what prices were likely to be in ten years time at the same rate of inflation.

● A class had been set a task to fill the final hour of a day at the end of term. They were divided into groups of four, provided with a limited number of offcuts of card and invited to construct a bridge of any style and in any way they liked. The children were so interested in the challenge that the teacher later took the topic further, providing them with more elaborate materials and resources that would allow them to research and plan in advance. The task became a competition to find the most durable bridge, with each group required to describe how they had arrived at and constructed that design.

One bridge collapsed almost immediately, sending its convoy of model cars and lorries crashing into the 'gorge' beneath. Subsequently some children who had read about the Tay Bridge disaster in the course of their research, proposed that the group responsible for the failed bridge

should be 'tried for negligence'. The teacher agreed, but with the proviso that trial procedures should be thoroughly researched.

As a result of the 'trial' the group was instructed to construct a satisfactory model. They asked permission for help from parents who had themselves become interested in the 'court proceedings' and the collaboration produced a spectacular model which the group was happy to display and lecture about in some complex detail.

● A group of junior children produced 'guidelines' for infant children to help them recognise a witch and an alien. This arose from particular books that both classes were reading at the time.

The following range of activities exemplify other kinds of experience that will help children become competent in the logical presentation of factual information and to discriminate between what is relevant and irrelevant and what is fact and fiction.

Children might be invited to reflect on how they would present news, publicity, information in relation to particular circumstances or how they would convey appropriate messages in connection with specific events. More specific activities might include:

● Playing games in which children have to re-arrange picture sequences to create patently ridiculous or impossible situations;

● Compressing accounts of things they have done into minute long reports;

● Reading selections of 'real' news and fiction to other groups, then asking them to distinguish between the two and give reasons why;

● Converting stories, fairy tales and historical events into news headlines and brief reports;

● Describing certain images, such as postcards, pictures of fashion models, scenery, furniture and so on, in two diametrically opposed ways;

● Looking for words and phrases in a story that indicate possibility and speculation, finding perjorative and critical phrases in a book or story, then finding the clues in a story or book that indicate the villain;

● Making a collection of tragic/happy pictures. What differentiates them? How would descriptions of them differ?

Such activities should be helpful in developing children's ability to be logical and structured in the way they present information and to be perceptive and discriminating about the information with which they are presented. They will also be likely to develop other skills and to provide other essential experiences:

● To give increasingly precise instructions;
● To ask increasingly precise or detailed questions;
● To respond to increasingly complex instructions and questions;
● To engage in speculation and hypothesis.

They will provide natural opportunity for children to reflect on 'the range of purposes which spoken language serves' and to identify in the activities they have undertaken examples of ways in which they have arranged, shaped and ordered language to achieve particular ends:

● To elicit sympathy;
● To win admiration;
● To persuade;
● To deceive;
● To inform and guide;
● To answer questions;
● To amuse;
● To startle and alarm;
● To warn;
● To advise;
● To flatter or encourage;
● To publicise.

Responding to literature

'Pupils should be given the opportunity to learn how to:
● **listen and respond to an increasing range of fiction, non-fiction, poetry and plays, including those which have been seen' (6j).**

We have already emphasised the central importance of story, whether it be fiction or the story of the development of the human race in the context of the world, in children's learning and in the development of their language. As children advance through the primary stage, however, there is a tendency for teachers to commit less of the time available to them to story in whatever form it might be presented. This tendency may well be largely attributed to the demands that an expanding curriculum makes upon the timetable. But there is also a feeling common to many teachers that older primary children have a diminishing need to have stories read or told to them. It is suggested that competent readers can be justifiably encouraged to 'get on on their own', thus releasing precious time for teachers to devote to children with particular learning needs.

It is easy to sympathise with teachers who feel the pressure of coping with an expanding curriculum, where science and design and technology have had to be accommodated only relatively recently and where history and geography now have to

be provided with a securely established place. In such circumstances teachers may well feel that 'an increasing range of fiction, poetry and plays' represents something of a luxury to be fitted in where possible.

It is important to stress, however, that language is the vital instrument that gives children control over the curriculum, and that story, literature, drama and poetry are among the most powerful contributors to a developing competence in language, both in speaking and listening.

The following examples provide evidence of the complexity of cognitive challenge that literature can provide for children and the intellectual level at which it can motivate and enable them to operate.

• A headteacher had been working with a group of older primary children on an intensive reading of *Watership Down* by Richard Adams, and was focusing on both literal and inferential comprehension in the opening chapter. The chapter, which had been largely concerned with a lyrical description of the rabbits' territory, concludes with a brief account of the erection of a noticeboard announcing large scale industrial development in that area. A girl in the group pointed out without any prompting that this was the 'vision of horror' quoted in the lines of poetry that comprise the chapter heading.

This is a striking example of a developing ability to read between the lines and, at a deeper level, to pick up subtle signals from the author thus participating creatively in the reading process. In this particular case, the headteacher drew the attention of the group to the other chapter headings as they progressed through the novel, so that they became involved in the business of prediction and detection.

• A group of children had been reading *The Way to Sattin Shore* by Philippa Pearce in a literature club held after school. Their teacher felt they were at a stage of competence and interest where this particular novel could be used to develop an awareness of metaphor. She explained

that this was a device, a kind of clue or hidden signal, used by writers to convey an important message to the reader, and that this was particularly appropriate in a mystery story. Inevitably, perhaps, the children initially found metaphors everywhere, whether intended or not. The teacher therefore allowed the issue to drop and continued with the shared reading.

However, by the conclusion of the novel the group was clearly developing a perceptive awareness of the writer's intentions and proposed the following examples. 'Syrup' the cat was like a barometer; when the story was sad or tense, then Syrup was alarmed. When the mystery is solved, he is free to enjoy himself. The way in which the heroine, Kate, treats Syrup shows that she is growing up. When she solves the mystery, she feels able to give Syrup to her grandmother. One child commented, 'The book should not be called *The Way to Sattin Shore*, but The Way to Certain Sure.' When asked to elaborate on this the child explained that since Kate was seeking to discover who she really was, the book was really about trying to make 'certain sure'.

Teachers may well be convinced by such examples of the capacity of literature to promote not only children's competence in language but their broader intellectual development as well. Equally, many teachers may feel that the provision, organisation, and financial overlay in terms of books, that such practice calls for are beyond their resources.

In approaching this vital element of the Programme of Study, teachers may find it helpful to consider the following suggestions:
• Teachers should continue to read and tell stories and poetry to the children through their whole primary experience. Stories can, for example, comprise a natural part of the school assemblies.
• Build up teams of people who can help with story-telling and reading through work with smaller groups of children or even with individuals.
• Organise story telling competitions in

which children can tell stories they have heard, read or composed themselves.

• Set up lunch time or after school literature or story clubs to which parents and invited guests can contribute.

• Ensure that displays throughout the school are accompanied not merely by relevant fiction, but have collections of carefully chosen reference and non-fiction material available to amplify, elaborate and clarify what is displayed.

• Arrange family reading circles in which a few families come together to share a book they have been reading over the last few days.

• Try to provide up to four copies of good texts, whether fiction, non-fiction, poetry or plays, so that groups of children can share the reading experience. Have an adult presiding to provide direction, to amplify what is in the text, to focus readers' attention on particular aspects, and to help children read between the lines.

Through a primary school where such opportunities are provided, and where there is a clearly defined policy designed to ensure progression, children will accumulate experiences that will enrich their language development in a multiplicity of ways; extending vocabulary, providing insight into the ways in which sentences are put together, stories are constructed and characterisation is built. They will come to recognise and understand the devices that story-makers use to create tension, excitement and crisis, the ways in which they win sympathy, achieve a sense of grief or tragedy, evoke horror, alienation, humour or laughter.

High quality literature puts children in touch with their heritage and the world at large, conveys the values of their civilisation, provides a commentary on human affairs, gives a sense of extraordinary possibilities.

Words and pictures

Let us consider some examples of how story and poetry can lead naturally to deeper engagement with language, without need for the material to be manipulated in a way that would rob it of the freshness and intrigue it can hold for the children.

Anno's Journey by Mitsumasa Anno is a picture book without text describing the author's journey through Europe. What we are faced with is an infinitely stimulating and highly complex detective story, like a gigantic jigsaw that can only be assembled if we find the right words. We are told that as we travel with Anno we shall encounter the paintings of the French Impressionists, find a phrase from Beethoven's Ninth Symphony, tilt at windmills with Don Quixote and help to pull up the Big Enormous Turnip. We are reminded also that we can create our own versions of the stories.

Such a book will inspire numerous accounts, theories and explanations. Understanding can only be reached and meaning fully revealed where children are prepared to hazard guesses, opinions, propositions and speculations.

Stories of one kind will lead to others: of the deaf Beethoven who had to be turned round on the concert platform to see the audience applauding; of Mozart and his wife obliged to dance to keep warm; of Purcell locked out of his home because he came home late and dying of fever caught in the night air.

Anno's Counting House by the same author is a different kind of detective story. A non-fiction book, it uses similar exploratory devices to take children into areas of mathematical concepts such as matching, comparisons, conservation and ordering, and the language that defines them.

By contrast, an illustrated book such as *Jacko* by J S Goodall seems at first glance merely an invitation to write or re-tell the story inherent in the picture sequences. In fact, what is represented by this apparently straightforward little book is a combination of historical, social, technical and inferential contexts that demand precise and formally ordered language for realisation. The powerful storyline takes children into situations where they become marooned unless they find the necessary language to 'float themselves free'.

The power of story, whether in pictures or in written form, can set the imagination free and soaring, and in the process release and generate language. Nowhere is this more evident than in the opening pages of *Come Away from the Water, Shirley* by John Burningham, where the heroine, with the cautions of her parents ringing in her ears, proceeds to transform the deserted beach into a world of dazzling creation.

Poetry

Poetry invites children to make their own pictures, while offering examples of the language and style in which it can be done. So 'How to Catch Newts' by John Walsh invites stories of other feats and adventures, whether in a cornfield or in the city centre; 'Today Was Not' by Michael Rosen calls forth accounts of similar heart-stopping moments that transform the hum-drum day; 'You'd Better Believe Him' by Brian Patten maintains hope in the miraculous, the fantasy come true. Themes such as power, compassion, the freedom of choice, complex ideas and abstractions are all brought within the children's reach by the immediacy and urgency of the language of poetry.

Eleanor Farjeon's 'It was Long Ago', leads irrevocably to the recalling and describing of the first memories of childhood; 'Daddy fell into the Pond' by Alfred Noyes, to recollections of the hilarious and comic; 'Where go the Boats' by R L Stevenson, to speculation about the world and the people beyond our immediate vision; Auden's 'Night Mail' to wondering about that array of letters (what was so timid about the lover's and what was the heart outpouring? What were the faces scrawled in the margins?). We grieve and wonder why Causley's 'Cowboy will never see twenty one', and reflect on Chesterton's Donkey's, 'fierce hour and sweet'.

Story

It is probably story that brings children most immediately and powerfully to confront a world they know only too well in some respects and, in others, find painful and bewildering. They recognise too, very soon, that it is a world they have to come to terms with in various ways if there is to be harmony and security in their lives.

It may well be that they are the more able to understand their own struggles and to appreciate their own inherent capacities because they have opportunity to observe in some detachment the struggles of Steve in *The Short Voyage of the Albert Ross* (Jan Mark), and Benjie in *The Eighteenth Emergency* (Betsy Byars), against fears that seem likely to overwhelm them. Through reading what happens to Jess and Lesley in *A Bridge to Terabithia* by Katharine Patterson, they may be the more readily helped to gain insight into true friendship, the importance of personal relationships and the real nature of heroism.

Story has the rare power, on the one hand, to create for children a world of imagination where things of the spirit flourish and, on the other, to help them understand and manage the material world in which they live.

The benefits of literature

How can we summarise the contribution of literature to the language needs of children as outlined in Speaking and Listening, Key Stage 2?

Through a deep experience of literature, story, poetry, drama and non-fiction, children will be enabled to learn how to respond to most of the expectations set out in Section 6, Programme of Study for Key Stages 2 to 4. Such experience encountered in language-rich classrooms, where children have opportunity to work in 'groups of various size, both single sex and mixed where possible, with and without direct teacher supervision' will enable them to:
- **'reflect on their own effectiveness in the use of the spoken word' (6q);**
- **'engage in prediction, speculation and hypothesis' (6r);**
- **'enable pupils to talk with wider**

audiences, *eg. in repesenting the views of a group or taking part in group or class presentations'* (7d).

Few areas of learning experience will offer more naturally to children the opportunity that story, literature and poetry do, to come in contact with and focus on 'regional and rural variations in accents and dialects of the English language', and to consider and explore with less danger of personal slight or embarrassment 'attitudes to such variations'. Equally they provide probably the most practical and least bewildering way for children to be helped in their initial explorations of the forms and functions of spoken Standard English.

Teaching about language

By the time pupils are working toward Level 5, speaking and listening should focus on:

• Regional and social variations in accents and dialect of the English language and attitudes to such variations;

• The forms and the functions of spoken Standard English.

Children are keenly conscious of styles of speaking and are invariably interested in the way in which people sound when they speak. Indeed it has been said that children have at least three languages available to them: one for the playground, one for home and one for the classroom. They generally take notice of accents and attempt to imitate them. In the same way they will frequently imitate phrases used by adults. They will of course, be used to hearing a wide range of accents, both national and international through television and films.

In any classroom there is a strong possibility that a number of accents may be represented, especially in urban areas where mobility of population is common. Equally most children's language will reflect, at least to some extent, regional and social variations and in some areas there will be uniform usage of dialect by a large proportion of the children.

The danger is of course, that we may easily form negative and unhelpful expectations about people that are likely to be inaccurate and misleading. It is dangerously easy to assume that because a child speaks in a dialect or uses language that can be categorised as deriving from a particular social class that he will be deficient in specific respects and experiences. Such expectations can be translated into perceptible attitudes and behaviour that convey negative viewpoints to children.

What can teachers do to help children focus positively on regional and social variations? The following suggestions may help.

• Exploit children's curiosity about accents. Make a survey of accents in the classroom, including the teacher, and record them. Listen to, analyse and discuss the different examples. Extend the survey to the whole school. Invite adults and children to visit the class and 'demonstrate' their accents. Tape accents of people in the school and ask children to guess who is speaking. Make a listening corner with taped accents and photos of speakers. Ask children to 'connect' them up. Make a listening gallery of famous people with marked accents.

• Ask children to speculate about why and how accents have developed. What advantages or disadvantages accompany them?

• Find examples from literature and television of people speaking with particular accents.

• Adopt similar strategies with dialect. Tape examples of dialect from across the country. Produce examples of written dialect with Standard English equivalent to allow for understanding.

• Collect any of the numerous examples from story and literature of characters speaking in dialect. A wide range of poetry in dialect form exists, including some lovely examples of accounts of the Nativity and Genesis in Black Country dialect.

° Dialect   Standard °
           English

It ain't there!   It isn't there!

I didn't get nothing   I didn't get anything

It ain't 'alf good   It is very good

She's after her dinner.   She has had her dinner

Where you be going?   Where are you going?

- Help children to speculate in broad terms as to how dialect has evolved. Stress the similarity between dialects and Standard English rather than the differences.
- Discuss the fact that international languages differ. Collect common phrases in a group of languages, put them on display, compare their 'appearance', record examples of them spoken by native speakers and identify similarities.
- Stress the fact that it is an accomplishment to know another language and that being able to 'call upon' a dialect is, in a sense, to add to one's linguistic repertoire.

Forms and functions of spoken Standard English

Children will have an awareness at Key Stage 2 of what Standard English is. As we have said earlier children are confident in assuming language styles appropriate to occasions and places; they know the styles that will be acceptable to and understood by their friends in the playground. They know what constitutes rude or 'bad' language. They are adept at speaking slang and indeed are major modifiers of language themselves. They can certainly be helped to an understanding, and even more important, to an appreciation of the value of Standard English. They will have a range of perceptions of what Standard English is, including 'lah-di-da' 'stuck-up' and 'posh'. They need to be helped to appreciate that Standard English is a form that is acceptable to and conveys consistent messages to the majority of people. They can be invited to advance their own reasons for the necessity of this. On which occasions, for example, would it be essential for Standard English to be used? Why is the national news in Standard English? Why when a doctor is conducting a diagnosis is it likely that Standard English will be used?

What is Standard English?

Provide the class with examples of Standard English in books, newspapers and from the national news and invite children to translate items into slangy or colloquial speech and then to reflect on the differences. Make a collection of appropriate words and phrases from different occupations and activities. Make a collection of the correct names or descriptions for a range of artefacts used in different occupations. Get children to reflect on why it would not be economical or efficient to be unable to label or describe these objects correctly. Decide on an appropriate form of address and conversation for a range of people including:

- An old man or woman;
- A nervous person;
- A patient in hospital;
- Passengers in an aeroplane;
- An archbishop visiting the school;
- Someone you are meeting for the first time;
- Someone whom you wish to congratulate.

What is perhaps most important of all is for children to grow into an understanding that language is formed mainly out of usage. It is not something to be feared or be timid about or regard as sacrosanct, but to treat as an infinitely varied and sensitive instrument that children can utilise appropriately as occasion demands. They should be helped to see that developing confidence in the use of language is as important and desirable as competence in swimming, dancing or playing games.

Assessment

It is not so long ago that teachers were sceptical about the possibility of assessing spoken language. They would have been confident about their ability to recognise a 'good' speaker, but not so much thought was given to the criteria that defined that competence.

There is now a general acceptance that we are less likely to be able to offer children proper support in the development of oracy unless we are using assessment in a formative and diagnostic way. Furthermore we now have stages of development and progression available to us in relation to speaking and listening, maps that enable us to identify where children have 'come from' in terms of experience and growth, to 'locate' where they are at present and to plan forward routes for them. Teachers are now seeing assessment as a positive tool, essential to providing for speaking and listening, rather than merely something devised to test children. They are encouraged by the realisation that levels do not have to be assigned to children until the end of a Key Stage, that the emphasis is being placed upon the assembling of a broad profile of speaking and listening abilities and competences over an extended period of time. The areas that comprise such profiles can be derived from teachers' shared perceptions of the important elements in speaking and listening and from reference to the statements of attainment. They will incorporate the abilities to listen and respond creatively to stories, poems, anecdotes; to describe a range of personal experiences; to be able to give and follow instructions; to communicate feelings and intentions; in short, the repertoire of competences that we have discussed through these pages.

A teacher was recently observed reading *The Jolly Postman* by Janet and Allan Ahlberg to a group of young children, a choice that some people might quibble with for that age group in view of the sophisticated concept that underpins the book. A visitor to the classroom expressed ignorance about what had led to Goldilocks' letter of apology to the three bears. The children explained that Goldilocks had 'caused trouble in the bears' house'; that 'she hadn't meant to do it really'; that 'she had broken some of the beds because she did not fit them' and had 'eaten all the porridge'. This latter point was immediately contested, with one child advancing the viewpoint that she 'just could not have eaten all that porridge'. It was quite clear that these children were perfectly capable of fulfilling the following criteria of the Programmes of Study.

- **'listening to and responding to stories, rhymes, poems and songs' (5a);**
- **'giving and receiving simple explanations, information and instructions' (5i).**

They could moreover:

- **'express and justify . . . opinions and viewpoints' (6a);**

as well as having the ability to take turns, to gain and hold the attention of their listeners and to voice disagreement – quite courteously if a little impatiently! – with an opposing point of view.

So far as Statements of Attainment were concerned, it was clear that many of the children were able to:

- 'participate as speakers and listeners in group activities' (1a);
- 'listen attentively, and respond, to stories and poems' (1b);
- 'participate as speakers and listeners in a group engaged in a given task' (2a);
- 'describe an event, real or imagined, to the teacher or another pupil' (2b);
- 'listen attentively to stories and poems, and talk about them' (2c);
- 'talk with the teacher, listen, and ask and answer questions' (2d);
- 'convey accurately a simple message' (3b);
- 'listen with an increased span of concentration to other children and adults, asking and responding to questions and commenting on what had been said' (3c).

Had she wished to, the teacher could have recorded some firm evidence about the levels of attainment these children were reaching, information that had been acquired almost incidentally in the natural process of satisfying curiosity about a story. However, to record 'levels' at that stage would be inapproriate and unnecessary. Much more relevant and valuable was that she had acquired more evidence to add to the bank of information that was being amassed about these children's language development. Even more important, this information enabled the teacher to make plans about provision for future developments in the children's learning.

The National Curriculum and our understanding of the true purposes of assessment are combining to move us away from any notion that language development occurs naturally and inevitably, provided that one arranges stimulating and challenging learning and language environments. It is increasingly clear that progression and development will only take place, even in carefully organised environments, where there is sensitive and planned teacher intervention backed up by maps of where individual children are, and by awareness of how their present and future needs can be catered for.

For many children, language skills are only likely to develop where specific provision has been made to achieve them. It is leaving too much to chance if we rely only on the provision of a broadly stimulating learning environment to help children to achieve the necessary Statements of Attainment.

Such skills are not acquired at random and by chance. One might as easily hope that children will begin to think and operate as historians because we release them into museums or as geographers because we take them for walks by the river! The art of teaching lies in careful selection, organisation and provision of such experiences and opportunities, matching them with stages of development, need and aspiration, taking account of individual progress, having clear perceptions of where the investigation and learning can most appropriately proceed next and having systems for assessing and recording what is happening.

Such planning with its implications of precision, even of rigour, does not in any sense preclude 'inspirational' teaching, those illuminating and memorable learning experiences that teachers generate out of the unexpected happening or occasion. Indeed there are those who would claim that such teaching and the valuable learning opportunities that it creates is much more likely to flourish in the planned and organised contexts to which we have been referring. Careful assessment is certainly more likely to ensure that the needs of the individual children, wherever they may be on the learning continuum, will be met.

For example, on the occasion of *The Jolly Postman* story to which we referred earlier, a child, not yet five, said urgently to the other children when they reached an episode concerning a witch, 'I certainly would be careful about anything I ate in her house; you wouldn't know what she might do to you!'. The last thing the process of assessment should do is to encourage us to jump to hasty conclusions about stages of development, based on limited evidence. Nevertheless, that kind of response repeated in other contexts and documented on a language profile would influence a teacher in relation to the kind of learning experience she provided for the child involved. Just as the teacher of a six year old, engaged in a group construction of a model windmill, who remarked casually that 'in the war the Resistance arranged the sails to pass hidden messages to each other', would bear that apparent level of sophistication in mind when planning at least some element of that child's work. In the long run, of course, both children would find themselves involved in collaborative activities with less outgoing, more diffident and perhaps less informed children, to the general learning benefit of all.

Nevertheless, however relieved teachers may be to be reminded of the natural and gradual nature of much assessment, they will be the first to point out the practical problems of assessment, especially when working with classes of over thirty children, often with little or no other adult help. They are also very conscious of the fact that while valuable assessment can be done 'on the run' there is much that calls for time set aside with small groups of children for significant periods, in relation to quite complex concepts. No matter how conscientiously they have managed these sessions, teachers may still not be sure how far they can rely on the evidence they have laboriously gathered.

Practical suggestions

- Find a simple and informative format for recording. Remember it has to make sense to others, including colleagues and parents. Study examples used by other teachers; take account of the advice and suggestions provided by the ILEA Primary Language Record.
- Make sure that the format is capable of recording information over a period of time so that a map of the child's progress is evident.
- Design the record so that it conveys information of the broadest nature about speaking and listening.
- Remember that a record is intended to provide information based on your continuous assessment of the child's language development. Therefore you should choose headings that reflect the main body of opportunities, experiences and functions of speaking and listening. There is little doubt that they will be compatible in many ways with the Statements of Attainment.
- Rich language experiences and environments will enable children to respond linguistically in a variety of ways. The record should seek to reflect this so that as full a description as possible of their language usage is available.
- To obtain broad descriptions, teachers should ensure they are observing children in as wide a range of circumstances as possible. It is particularly important to bear in mind the multiplicity of children's backgrounds, language experiences and personality traits and to ensure they are given every opportunity to flourish in relation to their strength.
- Teachers observing children's language need to resist entertaining expectations of ordered and chronological responses. Language development does not occur in this way; children who have much to learn and acquire in some elementary areas may already be operating with confidence in other apparently more complex areas.

Recording information

Remember the more recording you do and the longer your acquaintanceship with particular children, the easier it is to collect and record information about their language development.

If anything, teachers will tend to find themselves surfeited with information about children's language, rather than the reverse. It can be collected from parents and from other adults in the school who encounter children in a variety of situations.

Teachers will find their own favourite ways of writing down material, but these are obvious points to consider:
- Target particular children in particular areas of activity for fixed periods of about 15 minutes.
- Keep a small notebook on your person for noting random examples.
- Decide upon two to four children for protracted periods of observation and recording each week.
- If you decide upon individual conferences with children make sure that everyone knows that these are private and not for disturbing.
- Have individual or small group conferences with children simply to talk about 'talk'.
- Explore the use of taped interviews with children. Use tapes made by the children themselves in connection with various learning experiences that take place in the classroom and outside to analyse their language.

Teachers will inevitably decide upon approaches and methodologies that best suit their circumstances and are most in accord with what their colleagues do. What matters most about assessment is that primary teachers, with their long traditions of basing children's learning upon careful and sensitive observation, should come to see it increasingly as a powerful support and a means of enriching the teaching and learning process in which they and their children are engaged.

Chapter two
Reading

Making a start on the Programme of Study

The Statutory Orders describe the Attainment Target as being concerned with 'the development of the ability to read, understand and respond to all types of writing, as well as the development of information-retrieval strategies for the purposes of study.'

Schools are expected to prepare written schemes of work which reflect their agreed general approaches to the teaching and learning of literacy, based on the Programmes of Study. Through following such a planned scheme of work, pupils will acquire the skills and concepts they need to meet the attainment targets.

A fundamental principle of good primary school practice with which most teachers would agree is that we start from where the child is. Teachers in the early years need to develop strategies to find out what their children know, understand and can do; in other words what stage they have reached when they come to school. Children's primary educators are their parents and teachers depend upon them to provide information about their children's achievements prior to schooling. Parents know about their children's interests, about their contacts with print and the drawing and writing they do at home.

Holding a 'conference' with parents early in the school year is one way of acquiring relevant information. 'Conferencing' is a term used by Don Holdaway in his book *Independence In Reading*, to describe a session in the school day when a teacher engages in sustained conversation with an individual pupil about her reading. Donald Graves describes a similar process in *Writing: Teachers and Children at Work*. Teachers in this country have developed these ideas to include individual discussions or conferences with parents so that parents can talk about their children's progress.

At such a conference parents are offered a time to talk privately with the teacher and it is made clear that this time is for the parents to inform the teacher about their child's language development. Open-ended questions about the child's interest in print, both in the environment and in books, will release useful background information upon which the teacher can build. Teachers who arrange conferences with parents often find that quite young children read newspapers, leaflets, letters and other printed material at home.

The other most powerful way of finding out what a child knows and can do is through observation. Spending a minute or two watching a child in the book corner or as she shares a book with another child or adult will reveal much about her knowledge of print, her attitudes to and her interest in reading.

Key Stage 1

Pre-school experiences

'Reading activities should build on the oral language and experience which pupils bring from home' (2).

The oral language competence children bring from home to school has been discussed in the Speaking and Listening section of this book. We know that all children come to school with a stock in trade of oral and written language experiences. It is important to recognise that children who may not have had a rich and varied book experience before school have had other valid language experiences and thus are not starting from scratch.

Some ways of building on children's existing knowledge are described below.

• Provide opportunities for children to tell their own stories and scribe these for them. If you write them in enlarged print and let the storyteller illustrate them they will become an important resource in the book collection.

• Bring (and get the children to bring) examples of environmental print into the classroom to make the link between the familiar and the unfamiliar, eg product labels, catalogues and so on.

• Make collages of known brand labels and use them to decorate and brighten dull areas in the room. Covered with plastic film, the collages can be used as table mats and coverings and provide talking points in some of the classroom activity areas, eg as desk blotters in the graphics area (see the section on Writing for a fuller explanation of graphics areas on page 121.)

• Make class books about favourite foods illustrated with product labels.

• Take (or let the children take) photographs of print in the immediate environment of the school. There are lots of examples, from street names and local bus destinations to road signs and shop signs, all of which will have real and immediate meaning for children. Use the photographs decoratively or to illustrate books.

• Create a display area where children can put drawing or writing done at home. This will not only place a high value on children's self-directed writing, but will also strengthen the link between home and school and provide motivation for the child who might not otherwise choose to write at home.

• Encourage the making and sending of greetings cards and the writing of notes and letters as a reflection of the kinds of literacy experiences to which children are accustomed.

• Provide magazines, TV guides, holiday brochures, cookery and other books, newspapers, calendars, telephone directories in the role-play or 'home corner' area.

Range of texts

'Teaching should cover a range of rich and stimulating texts, both fiction and non-fiction, and should ensure that pupils regularly hear stories, told or read aloud, and hear and share poetry read by the teacher and each other' (2).

'Rich and stimulating texts'

In *Read With Me*, Liz Waterland says that books are the reason for reading, not merely the objects by which people are enabled to read, and children should be shown that 'within the covers of a loved book is an adventure of the spirit – something that can speak to the child alone and lead her or him into a wider world'. Texts themselves play a vital role in the learning process, in that they provide the intrinsic motivation we all need to possess before we learn anything at all.

Some of the characteristics of rich and stimulating fiction texts are as follows.

• They contain expressive language. Among the most satisfying and enduring are the familiar favourite stories which have their roots in the oral tradition and which appear and reappear in the narrative traditions of many cultures. Common to them all is rich and potent language; rarely simple, it is always lively, rhythmic and frequently repetitive. There are hundreds of examples. 'The Little Red Hen' is one such, a story I remember as a child at school in the 1940s. There are many versions of this old tale but in Margot Zemach's there is a hilarious illustration on the last page of the hen and her chicks enjoying the fruits of their labours as they eat their own golden loaf of bread, while their lazy friends are excluded from the feast because they refused at every turn help with the work.

• They present moral issues in an interesting way. 'The Little Red Hen' appeals to the straightforward morality of young children, wherein laziness is punished and hard work rewarded.

A similar story about good and evil is the tale of Little Dog Turpie as retold by Simon

Sterne in *The Hobyahs*. I was initially nervous of reading this very old story to my class of six year olds, despite the fact that I loved it as a child. It seemed inordinately violent for present day tastes, yet they also loved this story, I believe, for its powerful message of wrongs put right, and for the dog who saves his family despite having been tied up to stop him barking.

• They often contain meaningful repetition. Beginning readers need and enjoy repetitive sequences in their texts. Stories with strong narrative, natural language and meaningful repetition are very different from the reduced and over-simplified language we find in books specially written to teach children to read. The language of these books is so different from anything children will have encountered, either spoken or written, that it is bound to create confusion. Generally this kind of repetition is based on high frequency use of a core of chosen vocabulary and it often sounds something like 'Here is the dog. We like the dog. We can play with the dog'. Because the vocabulary has been reduced and simplified we can easily be convinced that children will find it simple to read. Yet generations of teachers have been perplexed that, despite the fact that some of their children have seen the same word many many times, they still do not recognise it.

Repetition of words is less powerful for learners than repetition of meaningful sequences. For example, in David Mckee's *Not Now, Bernard*, the title sequence is repeated six times in twenty-four short lines of text. It is instantly memorable and always recognised because it belongs to a connected chain of events and does not rely only on memory of the shapes of the printed words.

Repetition may occur in a different way as new sequences are added one by one. Some really good examples which I have always found successful with classes of young children are, *The Elephant and the Bad Baby* by Elfrida Vipont, *Hairy Maclary from Donaldson's Dairy* by Lynley Dodd and *My Cat Likes to Hide in Boxes* by Eve Sutton.

The Elephant and the Bad Baby is a long text, with extensive vocabulary and complex sentences, but few children fail to sustain attention till the last minute and frequently they will ask to hear it again immediately. The other two books are written in verse form, which makes the shape of the language memorable. Such texts seem to work particularly well with beginning readers. For example, Nadine, a child in Year Two of an inner city infants school, had a sight vocabulary of a dozen or so words yet her teacher was worried about her. Nadine would choose her reading material from a small set of caption books with limited text in which she could be sure of 'knowing' the words. She decoded with great care, anxious not to make any errors and asked for help when she met a word she did not recognise on sight. She became upset if she was asked to try to 'work it out'. Her teacher read the story of *The Elephant and the Bad Baby* to her several times in a one-to-one situation and then suggested Nadine had a go herself. Her first retelling of the story was quite close to the text, full of self-correcting behaviour and not once did she ask for help. Her reading demonstrated a real search for meaning and not merely an intention to get the words right.

• They will present positive cultural images. Including books which present positive cultural images is, of course, vital in that they very directly affect children's self-esteem. For example, one of a series of books without text entitled *Phototalk* shows a Moroccan mother cooking some sweetmeats. Latifa, a six year old from a Moroccan family, was so surprised at seeing something familiar from her own culture in a school book that she asked to take it home to show her mother. The next day she brought a tray of the pastries for her teacher and classmates to taste. The teacher fortunately recognised the significance of this incident for her children's need to 'see themselves' in their books. She therefore seized on the opportunity to invite Latifa's mother to come in to school to demonstrate the cooking and a class book was made to record the experience.

• They will present positive gender images. It is essential that the books we offer children do not always present females as the providers of food or the primary carers for others. There are books available which portray males in these roles and it is important to present a balanced view. You should include titles such as *The Julian Stories* by Ann Cameron in which Julian's father is looking after Julian and his little brother while their mother is out and they make a wonderful pudding for her as a surprise. This is a humorous story which also happens to feature a black family, so the book satisfies several criteria of quality.

• They will contain good illustrations which support the text.

• They will be written in language which enables the reader to predict, using her innate sense of syntactic and semantic structure.

Simone, a child in reception, shows a bringing together of the prediction skills of the real reader in her retelling of *Red is Best* by Kathy Stinson, although she does not yet decode accurately. Her retelling is reproduced in the box below.

Text: My mum doesn't understand about red.
Simone: My mum doesn't understand about red.
T: I like my red stockings the best.
S: I like my red socks best.

Commentary
Does it matter that Simone substitutes socks for stockings or omits 'the'? Neither miscue affects the sense.
T: My mum says, 'Wear these. Your white stockings . . .
S: My mum says, 'Wear . . . your white socks they . . .
T: . . . look good with that dress.'
S: . . . look good with that dress.'
T: 'But I can jump higher in my red stockings.'
S: 'But I can jump high in my red socks.'
S: My mum says, '. . . to wear your blue jacket . . .

Commentary
Having omitted to read 'these', Simone inserts 'they' to make sense of this sentence.
T: 'I like my red jacket the best.'
S: 'I like my red jacket the best.'
T: My mum says, 'You need to wear your blue jacket.

T: It's too cold out for your red jacket.'
S: It's not colourful out for your red jacket.'

Commentary
The substitution of colourful for cold may indicate initial letter awareness.

T: 'But how can I be Red Riding Hood in my blue jacket?'
S: 'But how can I be Lit . . . Red Riding Hood in my blue jacket?'

Commentary
Self-correction – Simone predicts that 'little' is appropriate before Red Riding Hood then realises 'little' is not in the text.
T: I like my red boots the best.
S: I like my red boots the best.
T: My mum says, 'You can't
S: My mum says, 'Your . . .
T: wear your red boots in
S: wear . . . your red boots . . .
T: the snow. They're just
S: . . . are . . . only . . .
T: for rainy weather.'
S: for rain winter.'

Commentary
Again the substitution of winter for weather could indicate a combination of context, picture cue, and initial letter knowledge.

Bilingual pupils

In common with all children, bilingual pupils need to see themselves in their books, to have experiences of their own and others' lives. Stories with rich expressive language are all the more vital for bilingual pupils so that they have access to a richer language than the everyday currency useful for 'getting by' and simply understanding the daily give and take of the classroom. Simplified texts only reinforce minimal language patterns. Texts for bilingual pupils should possess all the qualities referred to above but good texts will also provide:

● Strong contextual support;
● Good illustrations which relate to and enhance the text;
● Settings which are familiar to the pupils;
● Settings which introduce the children to aspects of the new culture.

A good guiding principle is probably this: any book which satisfies the criteria of a good book for bilingual children or children from a minority ethnic group will probably be a good book for all children.

Telling stories

Stories introduce children to new ideas, experiences and cultures, of the present day as well as from times past. They introduce characters who invite us to reflect on their motivation and attitudes and sometimes to compare them with our own. They also introduce language of a kind pupils are unlikely to meet in everyday situations.

There are so many wonderfully illustrated books and well-written stories available to teachers that we can easily overlook the need to tell stories as well as read them. Freed from the constraint of holding the book and following the printed text closely (young children, as we know, quickly spot any deviation!), the storyteller is freer than the reader of a story to add descriptions or important explanations without spoiling the flow. It isn't easy to tell a story well the first time you do it and you will probably be quite worried about forgetting the words or the plot. Whilst it is quite important to know the plot of the story well it is not necessary to learn the whole thing off by heart. That way you can retain some flexibility and feel free to embellish it with as much detail as you like.

Support the telling of the chosen story with puppets or cut-outs of the characters. The children will use these props later as they try to retell your story.

Invite storytellers into schools to tell stories to the children. Some will bring traditional tales from other cultures and relate them in a way appropriate to the culture. Some of these very gifted storytellers support the telling with dance, mime, music or drama. Some run follow-up workshops where the children can express their response to the story in drama, dance or other creative activity.

Reading to children

Reading aloud to children is something most teachers of young children take for granted. It is generally a pleasurable experience and one that many adults continue to enjoy through listening to radio programmes. For teachers, 'storytime' has become the traditional way to end the school day.

However, now that we know it is also the most potent means of motivating children to want to read for themselves, it really cannot be consigned merely to that slot following afternoon playtime. Many teachers start each day with a story, or include reading aloud to the class as a way of setting the scene for a period of sustained or quiet reading. There is also a place for the children to read aloud at the end of the reading time, to encourage wider sharing of what may have been an individual or personal experience. There are two critical reasons for reading aloud to children:

● Reading aloud supports language development. Good authors communicate their ideas through the words they choose and they are able to convey deep and subtle meanings or images of places, people or times which take the reader beyond first-hand experience. Through having frequent experience of hearing 'book language', children will be more able to manage it in their own reading and incidentally they will be more likely to use such evocative imagery in their own writing if they have regular exposure to hearing it. For example, Robert Roennfeldt writes in *Tiddalick, the Frog Who Caused a Flood*, 'Very slowly and gracefully, Noyang stood upright on his tail. Weaving and swaying he danced faster and faster'. And later on, 'a mighty gush of water swept the animals far and wide, bumbling and tumbling them along creeks and water holes'. Such imagery and language will develop a particular sensitivity and the knowledge that such well-chosen words convey a unique atmosphere.

● Reading aloud to children enables them to become readers themselves. Through listening to stories read aloud and hearing favourites read and re-read, children will build up a repertoire of familiar texts. This

repertoire can become the basis of the child's own reading material. In *Young Fluent Readers*, Margaret Clarke appeals for reading and re-reading of stories to children before they start school, thus: 'Repetition of the same story read to a child has many values, not least the sensitising of the child to the features of book language which is probably a far more valuable preparation for school than any attempts at teaching the child phonics or even a basic sight vocabulary.'

For both those reasons it is vital to continue to read aloud to children right through their whole primary school experience and into the secondary school. The following are some suggestions for extending the experiences of listening to stories:

• Set up a permanent listening area equipped with a cassette recorder and four sets of headphones as a good means of providing more stories than you can tell in a day. Up to four children at a time can listen to a taped story. Published tapes are available in packs which include a copy of the book itself. If you provide multiple copies you will avoid the difficulties associated with sharing, when not everyone can see the text well.

• Record on tape a few stories which are clear class favourites and again provide at least two copies of each text. It really is worthwhile to invest scarce resources in the most popular texts. You can reduce the cost by buying paperback versions.

• Make story visuals or cut-outs of characters to support tapes or retellings of stories. Rolls of magnetic tape can be bought and patches can be stuck on the backs of the cut-outs. They can then be used with a magnet board as an alternative to the printed text.

• Try to provide some stories recorded in languages other than English for bilingual pupils, not only to show that you value their languages but to encourage their use. Research has shown that competence in the first language increases competence in the second. Parent participation in translating and recording will be essential and is a good way of encouraging parents in to school to work on a project which will directly affect their child's education.

Non-fiction

Reading for information is a different process from reading narrative and in general requires additional skills. The reader may simply need to search for a specific item of information which may be contained in a caption under a picture. Rarely will it be necessary to read a whole book word by word.

The main difficulty with information books for beginning readers is that if the information is readable it is rarely informational, in that it does not provide answers to questions in the way adult information books can. Good information books for beginning readers will most likely be those which present the information visually through high quality illustrations, such as David Macaulay's, *Castle* or *Cathedral* or in photographs such as *Small Worlds Close Up* by Lisa Grillone and Joseph Gennaro, and not those which present it in simple language. 'We went to the zoo. We saw the elephants. Elephants are big', is an example of text which purports to be informational but actually tells a child nothing she did not already know.

It is important that the information in the 'non-fiction' collection is not misleading or out of date. Do your books present people from Africa as shoeless or as living only in villages or do they show the more balanced picture of urban societies with blocks of flats, cars, buses, traffic lights and so on?

Making your own information books

Apart from those well-illustrated information books you can buy which do not rely solely on the text to convey the meaning, the class can make its own books. They will be more relevant and the language more accessible.

- As a class or group activity, make a guide book for visitors to the school. There will be a genuine need for the collection and publishing of information, supported by appropriate photographs or illustrations. There may be a need to draw maps or diagrams which will support early work on geographical skills.

- Invite parents and other adults from the community to come into school to talk about their work or their personal histories, for example, 'Growing up during the War'. Scribe their stories or get them to write them out themselves if they feel confident.

A teacher in a London school asked the mother of a British-Caribbean child in her class to come and tell the children about her schooldays in Jamaica. They were enthralled by her account of schooldays in a rural area and her stories of the long walk to school (most London children live within yards of their school not miles!) and the very different curriculum – Melodie described taking care of the goats and chickens as part of the normal school work! She wrote the story down working closely with the teacher, and it was illustrated with photographs generously given for the purpose.

- Make use of the children's own information to produce non-fiction texts they can share with others. Themes could include When I was in hospital; How I made my model; How to play this game; My favourite poems; Sirina's food alphabet book, etc.

Using information books

It is unlikely that you will want to maintain a permanent collection of non-fiction books in the book corner. Rather you will choose a selection to provide information related to a current topic or to meet a specific interest of an individual or group. It is vital that you introduce the children to their content by reading the texts (or parts of them) aloud. This can be most appropriate when the whole class or a group has an interest or a need to know something. For example, a newspaper account of an earthquake or hurricane might lead children to wonder about the cause of such natural disasters and could be a good reason for searching for the relevant information.

A similar situation arose when Justin, a six-year-old, recently expressed surprise that people had made a landing on the surface of the moon. His teacher used the occasion to collect together some books about space travel and exploration and she modelled the skills of using information texts, namely the use of the contents and index and how to skim and scan to locate the relevant parts of the text.

Other sources of information

• Send for the leaflets, brochures or other packs produced by charitable or industrial organisations.

A class of Year Five children undertook a project on pollution recently. Finding that information in available books was limited, the teacher suggested that anyone who wanted to might write to various organisations, such as Friends of the Earth and Greenpeace, to ask for information. The writers were rewarded with replies in every case and many of the correspondents expressed great interest in their projects. Although the information they received was written for adults, the children were motivated enough by their concern for their environment to work very hard to extract what they needed to know. By asking questions of each other and of their teacher and using existing knowledge taken from their own personal experiences

they gained a great deal from their sources.
• Give the children opportunities to access information in the form of lists, directories and timetables.

A class of Year Four children were given the task of researching information to enable them to plan an outing. They had to write to various centres in order to be able to compare the facilities on offer, the costs; to ascertain what reductions would be available to a group; what places of interest there were in the locality etc. They had to work out the comparative costs of different forms of travel, taking convenience and other factors into account. Again the information they received was written for adults but these children were also able to access it because they had real questions to ask and a real purpose for finding out. This project involved using telephone directories, maps, diagrams, timetables, as well as information in prose.

Different genres

'Reading should include picture books, nursery rhymes, poems, folk tales, myths, legends and other literature which takes account of pupils' linguistic competences and backgrounds. Both boys and girls should experience a wide range of children's literature' (3).

It is important to include a wide range of genres in your classroom book collection.
• Textless books have a special place in learning to understand narrative structure. They can present very complex ideas and characterisation wherein understanding is not constrained by getting the words right. In *The Snowman* by Raymond Briggs, for example, the very expressive pictures create a personality for the central character and minute differences in the set of his mouth or the expression in his eyes portray a whole range of feelings and emotions. The challenge presented to the reader creates the perfect learning context for talk and discussion.

● A wide range of books with simple (but not simplified) text, for example, *Not Now Bernard* (David McKee), *Rosie's Walk* (Pat Hutchins), *Dear Zoo* (Rod Campbell) or *Just Like Daddy* (Frank Asch) will prove valuable. The most popular titles can be provided in multiple copies so that a group of children can read together. One or two titles can be provided in enlarged versions so that a whole class can read together. Some, for example, *The Very Hungry Caterpillar* by Eric Carle or *Peace at Last* by Jill Murphy, are produced in miniature versions which appeal greatly to some children (and teachers!)

● Alphabet books also stimulate discussion. Most children recognise some letters when they come to school – for some it may be only one or two letters from their names while others will know the whole alphabet. A good collection of alphabet books will show that one letter can stand for several sounds. Some alphabet books are art forms in their own right and worth having for the quality of the illustrations themselves. *Anno's Alphabet* is a good example.

● Counting books are also worth having. *Anno's Counting Book* is a beautiful one.

● Song books, poetry books, nursery rhyme books and books of short plays are important resources.

● Comics, joke books, newspapers, puzzle books should also be made available.

● Variety of format is also important and you should include collections of short stories, such as *Fat Puss* by Harriet Castor.

The book area

'Pupils should encounter an environment in which they are surrounded by books and other reading material presented in an attractive and inviting way' (3).

Books need to be seen so that they draw attention to themselves and invite interest. The classroom book area offers the best opportunity to present books in an attractive way and to many teachers it is the focal point of the room. It is worthwhile giving some thought to where to site it. Choose a place in the room which is bright, with natural light if possible, where shelves could be fixed to the wall. Ideally it should be in a cul-de-sac, and should be large enough for the whole class to gather in. There should be a carpet and some soft furnishings to create the right atmosphere of comfort and whatever you can find by way of comfortable seating. A few plants can make a difference to the 'feel' of the book area, as can special displays of new books, books by this week's author and books made by the children.

For young children the books should, if possible, be displayed face front so that covers and titles can be easily seen and more easily selected. This doesn't necessarily mean you need a perfect range of beautiful wall shelving. Most teachers have to make do with what can be contrived and use a variety of attractively covered boxes or baskets. (Charity shops supply an interesting range of shapes and sizes at not too outrageous a cost.) Simple plastic plate display stands will support lighter books, such as paperbacks, and can be bought very inexpensively in china shops.

The reading material should include labels, captions, notices, children's newspapers, books of instructions, plans and maps, diagrams, computer print-out and other visual displays. The non-book reading material should also include:

• Lists: written by you and the children, as well as published lists. Include shopping lists, lists of items to bring to school for an event such as an outing, lists of children who have had conferences, are waiting for conferences, have had a turn to cook, have used the computer etc.

```
 _____
|     Weather Chart                  |
|                                    |
| Monday       Rashid                |
| Tuesday      Sam                   |
| Wednesday    Ruth                  |
|_____|
```

• Captions and labels all around the room: some will relate to instructions for the use and care of equipment, to make storage of equipment clear, or to protect pieces of work or describe and explain how something was made.

pencils
Our trip to the farm
Remember
Stop: Look! Listen!

• Notes: writing and receiving messages in the form of notes is a popular activity. One teacher started a rash of note writing when she sent a child to the headteacher to show a piece of good work. The head was out of the office so the teacher suggested Roland should write a note to leave on the desk. The communication was successful – the head responded by visiting the classroom and for weeks notes were sent on every possible occasion.

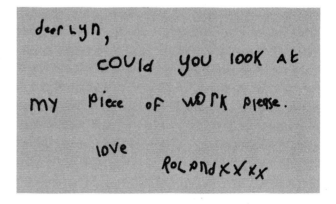

dear Lyn,
could you look at my piece of work please.
love
Roland xxxx

Rebecca Hind Leigh
Fred did Not Have tea

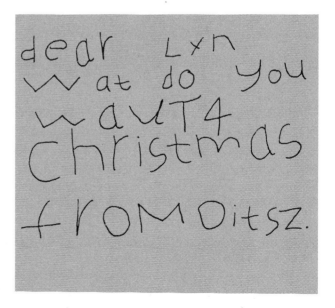

dear Lyn
wat do you
wauT4
christmas
from Oitsz.

Children's writing

'Pupils' own writing – either independently written, or stories dictated to the teacher or composed in collaboration with other pupils – should form part of the resources for reading' (4).

Pupils' own writing dictated to the teacher can be a lost resource to the class if it is written in an individual's book when only that one child participates in the dictating and watching the teacher scribe. As a class or a group activity, it has a wider audience and becomes a more social event. Write the story on the inside of a large folded piece of paper with the whole class watching, participating and helping, so that the author can later illustrate it and produce an attractive cover.

If you also provide sets of ready made booklets or, better still, teach the children to make their own books, the author might produce a mini-version to take home. This would encourage copying from your writing for a real purpose.

I have always felt some anxiety about children copying under teacher's writing because no matter how hard some children try, they will not get the match of word to word and space to space right. Their version will sit side by side with yours looking inadequate! Then if it is written to be read, which line does the reader focus on to read? If the answer to that is 'the teacher's print', then what purpose is there for the child to copy?

The class books can be individual stories told to the class, shared stories where many children contribute to the text, individual accounts of experiences or class or group accounts of experiences.

One teacher took a hand puppet of a lion into her reception class as a stimulus for shared storytelling and her class produced an exciting adventure story to which every child contributed something. Illustrations were drawn (one child drew a picture at home and thought up the next section of the plot ready to include the following day and his work was duly incorporated into the book). Almost every child in the class subsequently published a personal adventure story about the lion character in an individual book.

If offered the opportunity and the encouragement to write without the pressure to get spellings or handwriting absolutely accurate in the first draft, your children will want to experiment and commit their ideas to paper without your help as scribe and these pieces of writing too will be a resource to be shared by the whole class.

Home-school links

'Teachers should take account of the important link between home and school activity encouraging parents to participate and share in their child's reading, and supporting pupils where this is not possible' (5).

Much has been written about the value of parent involvement in helping children become readers. The Plowden Report of 1967 recommended that parents should be involved in their children's education and many research projects following publication of the report focused on the impact on children's progress when their parents played an active role in helping with reading at home. Studies in Haringey and research in ILEA (by Tizard et al, 1982) indicated that parent involvement had a powerful influence on their children's progress.

In Coventry about a thousand children in eight schools situated in Educational Priority Areas were studied over a period of two years. During this time parental support was actively encouraged. Reading scores on the Hunter-Grundin 'Reading for Meaning' scales rose from 94 to 107 – a dramatic increase from well below average to well above. Teachers also reported improvements in oracy and writing. (See *'Progress in Coventry EPA schools during a two year period of parental collaboration in reading'*, Widlake and McLeod.)

As a result of some of these studies, many schools have introduced home-school partnership schemes. It seems to be important in such schemes to:
• Have a consistent approach to the teaching of reading throughout the school, that is, a whole school policy subscribed to and understood by every teacher;
• Be absolutely clear that it is still the school's job to teach reading and that you are not handing the responsibility over to the parents, but that their role is to provide extra support;
• Make the parents aware of the whole school policy so that they are empowered to help (invite parents in during the school

day so that they can see how you teach reading or make a video that they can watch at evening parents' meetings or borrow to take home);
• Ensure that the books the children take home are the same books that they use in school (if you use a reading scheme but send home 'real books' you will be reinforcing the idea that children learn in school but not at home);
• Remember that maintaining a written dialogue with parents could be a very time-consuming task for you and it is probably sensible not to over-commit yourself (it could be reasonable to write a comment or a note once a week. You could make this part of the individual reading conference time. Most schools maintain the dialogue through sending home the child's reading log which contains a message or a commentary by the teacher. Parents are encouraged to respond to the child's reading of the text by giving their own views about the choice of book, the fluency of the reading and the child's pleasure and enjoyment);
• Remember, too, that not all parents will feel comfortable at first placing their thoughts and feelings about their child's progress in writing. Don't assume that because they don't respond they are not interested.

Involving parents

Certainly, whatever your view of parent involvement, and according to Tizard et al (*Young Children at School in the Inner City*, 1989) some teachers and headteachers still feel anxious about certain aspects, at the very least parents have a right to know about the school's general approach to the teaching of reading. They surely have a right to be consulted about their own children and to be kept informed when any developments or changes to the school policy are taking place. It is reasonable to assume that if they know what you are trying to do in school, they will be in a stronger position to help at home.

Parents may need encouragement to come into school. Many will need gentle persuasion that they can make a contribution to the work of the school. Some may simply be very busy people. Others may remember their own schooldays with less than delight.

They may well recall learning words out of context in preparation for a reading scheme and will feel that nothing should have changed. Probably they will feel most comfortable with a graded scheme; if that is not how you work, they need to know in advance.

Many schools have found effective ways of getting parents involved.

● Some have prepared leaflets for parents which explain what the school is trying to do. One school which had reviewed its writing policy produced a brief paper showing the stages of development children were likely to pass through, with examples, and the kinds of teaching the school would be employing to see that steady progress was being made. It contained explanations about the strategies children were to be given to help spelling development, such as 'look, cover, write, check', that parents could employ at home. Another had a display of similar information for parents in a central area of the school.

● Many schools have parents' evenings when parents can hear a speaker from outside the school talking about aspects of

literacy development. Before you organise such an event be sure your speaker supports your school's approach. It would be counter-productive to invite someone who will extoll the virtues of learning to read with picture books if you are firmly attached to your graded scheme and your parents will be puzzled and confused by conflicting messages.

● Displays and exhibitions of work, with explanations; slide tape programmes or video programmes; pieces of work taken home – again better if accompanied by a brief explanatory note – will all help to keep parents in touch.

● School bookshops or occasional book fairs are another way of keeping parents informed and involved. Some schools have found parents only too willing to run a bookshop. Furthermore, it is a good

opportunity to let parents know your criteria for what makes a good book.

- Some schools have organised workshops where parents and children write together and produce books about their lives to share with others.
- The practice of holding individual discussions with parents is gaining popularity. Who better than parents to know what kinds of reading experiences their children have had at home and what their children enjoy doing? They may know better than you do what aspects of reading are disliked or feared and they will tell you about these things if you ask them to.

The ILEA Primary Language Record requires that at the beginning of each school year teachers hold individual discussions with the parents or carers of each child in the class. The record has now been in use in a large number of schools in London (and in a number of other LEAs) for several years. Teachers report very positively about the parent/teacher conferences and seem to value highly the information parents give. They frequently report that parents seem to be pleased to be able to participate in the record of progress kept by the school, to see it and to make a contribution to it. They acknowledge that it takes time to do properly, but feel that it is time well spent.

One teacher whose practice has been greatly changed since she has been holding regular discussions with parents says that her children know that there is genuine communication between her and their families and that this has an effect on their work at school. She has found that they are more ready to bring drawings and writing from home because she has learned to appreciate their significance and values them more. The starting point for discussion with parents is likely to be the child's previous experience either in school, in nursery or at home. The child's ongoing school record is a good basis for talking about progress as seen by the school. The parent's aspirations and expectations form an area for discussion, as do all of the literacy events of the home.

Children with special educational needs

If a child is not making the amount of progress parents expect her to or if they do not know how they can help, they will feel extremely anxious. I have never yet met parents who did not care about their child's progress in reading, but few worried parents feel confident about how to help. There was a time when the concept of 'reading readiness' prevailed in some schools and parents were fobbed off with statements about their child not being ready but they were not advised as to how they could help the child to 'get ready'. They may even have been told to leave it to the experts and that it would be all right in the end. In the end, of course, such children did not make the sudden leap forward into literacy that their teachers hoped they would and their parents were angry to discover too late in the day that their child had not enough facility with reading to be able to participate fully in the curriculum.

For these children who have special needs, open dialogue with parents is all the more vital. Early identification of learning difficulties is also vital, so that a diagnosis can be made and a special programme of intervention prepared. Parents must be kept informed and consulted about such procedures.

Welcoming parents

Lastly it is important to try to look at the school through the eyes of parents (and indeed other visitors to the school) as they enter through the gate. Is the way clearly indicated? Are the signs accessible to parents whose first language is not English? Are the signs genuinely welcoming to parents? Could children undertake this as a project, conducting a survey of the opinion of parents and producing the necessary signs in each of the school's languages? And when they do come, is there always someone available to meet them when they drop in at school? Do you know whether they are always made to feel welcome?

Shared and independent reading

'**Activities should ensure that pupils:**
● **hear books, stories and poems read aloud or on radio, tape or television and take part in shared reading experiences with other pupils and the teacher, using texts composed and dictated by the pupils themselves, as well as rhymes, poems, songs and familiar stories (including traditional stories from a variety of cultures) (6a).**'

The purposes for reading aloud to children have already been discussed in the General Provisions, but the Detailed Provisions consider this in greater depth.

The term 'shared reading' has several different connotations for teachers and it is probably helpful to consider some of these and the different ways in which you can organise for them.

Sharing an enlarged text
This is an opportunity for the whole class or a group to enjoy following the printed text while the teacher reads it aloud. Enlarged texts were first described by Holdaway as a process whereby teachers produced big versions of a class's favourite stories so that all the children could comfortably join in the reading (*The Foundations of Literacy*, 1979). Holdaway suggests an alternative of using an overhead projector to enlarge the text. The opportunity exists to 'model' or demonstrate the reading process for the children – page turning, following the print from left to right, highlighting conventions of print and so on. He suggests teachers use a pointer to mark the one to one correspondences.

Sharing multiple copies of a text
In this situation two or more children might read as a group in different ways. For example:
● One reads while the others follow the print;
● Each reads in turn;
● The children read a section silently then discuss it with help;
● An adult reads while the children follow the print.

Reading with a partner
This is another example of text sharing, sometimes between a child and an adult. The adult generally reads the whole text, encouraging the child to join in or to take over entirely as appropriate. Alternatively, the partner can be another child.

Organising reading time

As your children are supported into taking on reading in these ways, they will want to 'have a go' themselves. It is very important though, that they do not have to read aloud in a one-to-one situation until they are ready to take over the reading entirely. It is crucial to provide daily opportunities for supported and independent reading to take place. Many teachers organise a regular time each day when everyone, including the teacher, reads. Others prefer to use the precious time to observe their children's interactions with books. For example, which children flip through the books without much interest unless an adult is present? Who seems to pore over every detail of the text? Who is visibly engaged with books?

You will need to organise a regular time each day so that children can take part in a planned way in these experiences. One of the benefits of having a regular, organised reading time where the main purpose is to enjoy books, rather than to show how well you can read, seems to be that it promotes independence and a willingness to move earlier into silent reading as the preferred mode. (This surely has to be a good thing since it is what real readers do.) It is important to distinguish between reading aloud to the teacher, which is essentially a performance or assessment activity, and the young child's vocalising as she reads to herself.

Useful strategies

- At first keep the time short, especially with a class of reception or Year One children, then build up gradually to about twenty minutes or half an hour.
- See that the children who find it hard to settle take three or four books or that they sit near the book area or listen to a recorded story through the headphones.
- Keep to the time each day – that way, parents who are interested can drop in when it suits them. Some teachers choose the first session of each day so that parents who bring children to school can stay on and join in.

- Start the session by reading aloud to the children to set the scene, to introduce any new books to the class or to refresh their memories for a forgotten favourite.
- Make sure that the children are spread about the room and that they are comfortable. They are then less likely to distract one another.
- Make sure they know the ground rules of the session in advance – that they should be as quiet as possible so that all can read in relative peace. Silence, of course, is impossible! Some children will need to vocalise. You should discuss with the children beforehand what arrangements you wish to make for sharing the experience at the end of the session.

Sharing time at the end of class reading

Reading aloud as a performance activity is something children will want to engage in when the time is right. One way of affording them this opportunity is to provide a time for sharing at the end of the independent reading session. For the teacher there are benefits in that you can make the same kind of observations as you would in the one-to-one reading aloud situation. You will learn as much about an individual's stage of development as you would if you heard her read to you.

Time is at a premium in a busy classroom and most teachers have always found it difficult to hear as many readers as they would wish. But there are fundamentally sound reasons why the process of reading to the peer group is a more appropriate one:

- The audience is genuine and is not testing the reader.
- The reader has prepared in advance during the class reading time, so reading aloud follows silent reading which is a more natural procedure.
- The reader has chosen the text and it will therefore be more likely to be within her area of competence.

In this kind of sharing remember to:

- See that the pieces to be read aloud have been carefully chosen so that the

listeners actively enjoy the readings as
much as the readers;
● Encourage the readers to choose short
pieces which sustain interest;
● See that there is variety, for instance,
jokes as well as prose passages, or a short
play in which several children can take
part;
● Make sure all children are given the
chance to read;
● Encourage the reading of books made
by the children themselves.

Dramatic play

**'Read in the context of role-play and
dramatic play . . . For pupils working
towards Level 1, the settings should
include individual letters . . . and
individual words . . . which pupils can
be encouraged to recognise' (6b).**

Different home corner or role-play areas
will offer different opportunities for
reading.
● A chemists shop could be set up with
labels, instructions on medicines,
prescriptions and so on. Discuss the safety
and the dangers of medicines and only use
empty containers. It is a good adjunct to a
hospital or a doctor's surgery.
● A hairdresser's could be organised
with magazines, price lists, invented
shampoos with specially designed labels
and an appointment book.
● Construct a building site with safety
notices. This is a good way of combining
construction play with role-play.
● Make a café with menus, price lists,
order pads, bill pads, labels for displays of
cakes or sandwiches and advertising
posters ('Try our delicious . . .').
● Organise a 'take-away'. Most Chinese or
other take-away shops will give you their
menus and maybe a selection of
containers. Alternatively, get the children
to design their own containers as a link
with the technology programme.
● Link the role-play area with a story you
have all enjoyed. See the example given
earlier of the Sorcerer's kitchen (page 12).

Familiar stories

'Retell, re-read or dramatise familiar stories and poems' (6c).

(See the section on shared reading, page 96.)

The reading and re-reading of a core of known texts is the basis of growth towards independence as a reader. Confidence is increased when the material to be read is familiar. Poems and rhymes that the children already know should form part of the material to be read in the early stages. Features of the print will gradually acquire significance and patterns will emerge in the same way as the features and details in a familiar landscape can be noticed more readily than they will in an unfamiliar one.

'Make their own books about particular experiences, areas of interest or personal stories' (6d).

(See the section on writing for a full discussion about making books and also previous pages of this section.)

Discussing reading

'Talk to the teacher and each other about the books and stories they have been reading or listening to' (6e).

Hold individual 'conferences' and use the time to discuss the child's reading in a general way. Conferencing is becoming an established way of giving a child an opportunity to talk about reading and is an occasion when:

● Recent reading experiences can be recorded;

● Personal tastes can be discussed;

● New authors can be introduced or other books by a favourite author;

● Selected oral readings can take place, preferably chosen by the child;

● Enthusiasm can be shared and the enjoyment of reading fostered;

● Any problems or difficulties can be explored and ironed out;

● Encouragement and positive feedback can be given.

Start the conference by surveying a selection of the books read recently and try to ask very open-ended questions so that you probe gently rather than take an inquisitorial stance. Encourage the children to hold similar conferences with one another. Encourage parents who want to help at home to talk about books and stories.

In the conference you will also be encouraging the pupils to:

● Widen their range of reading, turning readily to books, choosing those which they would like to hear or read and explaining their choice;

● Ask and answer questions about what has been heard or read – how characters feel, their motives, the endings of stories.

Recognition of words

'Talk about the ways in which language is written down, in shared reading or writing sessions or in discussion with the teacher, identify words, phrases, patterns of letters and other features of written language which they recognise, and notice how words are constructed and spelled' (6h).

Knowledge about words and letters and the patterns of letters in words will not develop fully if left to chance. In addition to the shared reading and writing experiences you provide and the informal way in which you discuss the features of print, you should also:

● Organise collections of words with similar initial letters, words with similar groups of letters, such as words which end in -ed or -ing.

One teacher puts a border of frieze paper on the wall near the writing area with a caption which reads, 'Can you add a word which ends in -ing?'. The children write up their word 'finds' together with their name and tallies are made from time to time. Participation rates are high – the children cannot resist the challenge of producing longer and longer lists. The word lists are useful as spelling aids or checks.

- Collect and display 'long' words and classify them into groups according to features, of words with three letters, four letters and so on and group them in various ways.
- Notice and record words which are palindromic, eg mum, dad, pap, Anna, rotor.
- Collect word families, eg play, played, playing, player, playhouse, playground and so on.

Information books

'Refer to information books, dictionaries, word books or simple data on computers as a matter of course. Pupils should be encouraged to formulate first the questions they need to answer by using such sources, so that they use them effectively and do not simply copy verbatim;
- **talk about the content of information books (6i, j).**

HMI reports frequently refer to topic work in schools as being of poor quality and consisting in the main of copying out chunks of text from books. It is important that children learn that information books are useful for providing answers to questions and that we usually make use of them when we need to find something out.

Significance of print

'Through the programme of study pupils should be guided so as to: appreciate the significance of print' (7a).

One example of print which has immediate significance for all children is their own name and many occasions arise in classrooms where this interest can be used purposefully, for example labelling on coat pegs, folders of work, storage trays for the child's possessions and on individual pieces of work, including paintings and drawings. Is there any reason why teachers should label for children? Perhaps you feel that writing the labels yourself gives a better model for children to emulate, but

there are ways of helping children to produce their own to a high standard of presentation such as:
- Drawing round commercially produced letter shapes directly on to a good background paper, preferably white or cream so that the letters can be decorated;
- Similarly using stencils;
- Composing with cut out sticky letters available from stationery shops;
- Composing with letters cut out from glossy magazines;
- Writing on a word processor using very large type.

The letters can be of similar size and typeface or mixed for a different kind of effect. The important thing is that the child chooses the effect. Different ways can be experimented with and informed choices can then be made. Decorating the empty letter shapes is a good art activity and adds to the personalisation of the finished product. Let the children try using fine brushes and coloured drawing inks, or fine roller-tipped coloured pens or just black and white in addition to the usual felt-tipped pens found in most classrooms.

Have a box of the children's names on cards and use them for work on sorting into sets in maths. Sort by:
- Initial letter;
- Long and short names;
- Children who like school dinners;
- Children who have brothers or sisters;
- Children who like red or green;
- Children who like kiwi fruit.

Labels can also be made by the children for the areas in the classroom or for notices eg to describe a piece of work, to ask others not to touch and so on.

Recognising words

'build up in the context of their reading a vocabulary of words recognised on sight' (7b).

Many children will spontaneously focus on the features of print and will point out to you details they are noticing. They will often say 'that's at the beginning of my name' or 'I can spell dog. Its D.O.G.'.

They might ask questions that indicate an appreciation that a word has a consistent spelling. Some, however, cause teachers anxiety that they are making no progress or that they are relying only on memory and picture cues. For these children help may need to be given so that they focus on the detail of print, of words and letters. This can be done in class shared reading from an enlarged text. As you draw attention to recurring refrains you can ask the children to join in and read along with you pointing to the words as you go along. You can ask questions (preferably at the end so that the fluency of the story is not interrupted) which will draw attention to similarities and differences in words.

• Make class versions of favourite stories. For example, one teacher made a book modelled on *Not Now, Bernard* entitled *Not Now, Children* which kept to the same pattern as the original and included the same recurring phrase. The children had repeated exposure to patterns of words in an interesting way.

• Make collections of words which start with the same letter. Get the children to write them on a large cut-out of the letter itself for extra impact. This could form a good backdrop for a display of objects whose names start with the letter.

• Make letters and words in clay either cut out from a rolled out slab or impressed. The advantage of clay against Plasticine is that firing can make it permanent.

• Let even the youngest children use 'write' programmes on the computer. They will start with experimenting with strings of letters but will soon graduate to words. If you encourage them to work in pairs at the keyboard they will spur each other on. And if you provide models of print in the computer area children will use them readily.

• Keep a class diary either for each week or month where you can write in events which are significant for the class or for individuals to ensure constant exposure to the names of the days of the week.

Every shared writing experience is an opportunity to talk about words and letters and where we put capital letters and full stops. It really would be difficult to write anything without constantly using a basic vocabulary of words such as 'the, is, was, we, went, my, they' etc. In the context of

November

Monday	Tuesday	Wednesday	Thursday	Friday	Saturday	Sunday
		It is Marissa's aunt Elaine's birthday 2	3	we are going to the library 4	It is bonfire night 5	6
7	8	Paul went to see Father Christmas 9	10	11	12	13
14	15	16	17	18	Kelly's cousin's birthday 19	20
21	22	23	Terence's birthday 24	Dania's birthday. 25	Kelly went to her Nan's 26	Claire and Gavin are getting christened. 27
Dean's dad is decorating his bedroom 28	Rummy went to the park 29	Akmal's dog is going to have puppies 30				

What is happening today?

pieces of writing composed by the children themselves these function words acquire significance; they will be repeated frequently and as you scribe you can remind the children about them.

Using cues

'use the available cues, such as pictures, context, phonic cues, word shapes and meaning of a passage to decipher new words' (7c).

In some kinds of poetry meaning is less important than the pleasure experienced from the sound of the language and the way in which the words are put together. This is particularly so in nonsense verse and some nursery rhymes. The same is often true of playground rhymes and chants. Apart from those exceptions, that which has been written generally makes sense and it is the sense of the story or the instructions for making something or how to do something that the reader should be searching for. The fundamental skill of being a reader is to be able to bring meaning to a text.

When a reader meets an unknown word the meaning will often be the best source of help in deciding what the word might be. Look back to Simone's reading of *Red is Best* on page 84 where she had difficulty with the word 'weather' and substituted the word 'winter'. While this did not make sense in syntactic terms, ie the parts of speech did not quite belong together ('Your red boots are only for rain winter'), it did make sense in terms of meaning and was supported by the picture on the facing page of a child clearly dressed to go out in the snow.

Simone's letter knowledge helped her here too. She was looking for a word in context beginning with 'w'. It could be accidental that the word she substituted was almost the same length and also ended in 'er'. This is an example of a child using the whole range of complicated cueing systems described above.

In contrast, Sharon, a nine-year-old described by her teacher as a 'remedial reader', does not possess the same range of cueing systems as Simone but relies almost exclusively on her limited known sight vocabulary, letter sounds and combinations and as a last resort appealing to an adult for help. She read 'We went to the supermarket to buy a cake for mum. It was to be a surprise for her.' as, 'We went to the sep . . . sep . . . the boy . . . came . . . In was to be a shop of her'.

Sharon did not expect that which she read to make any sense at all. For her, reading was a matter of getting the words as near right as possible. She rarely, if ever, self-corrected. For some reason she had learned that it was not appropriate to do so. She was reluctant to take any risks with print and had lost the confidence to allow herself to make mistakes and learn from them.

The teacher who was to give Sharon extra help with reading listened carefully to a tape of her reading and decided to teach her how to use meaning, to develop stronger use of semantic and syntactic cues and add those strategies to her existing ones.

She offered Sharon a few picture books to choose from and asked which Sharon would most like to hear. Sharon chose *Peace at Last* by Jill Murphy. The teacher was aware that Sharon still needed the support of having a text which was new to her read aloud to her first. She read the book aloud to Sharon and they discussed aspects of the story. Sharon was enthused by the story and even pointed out features of the pictures that the teacher had never noticed although she had thought she knew the book well! On the second reading they read aloud together with Sharon joining in where she could. At the end of the session Sharon asked if she could take the book home. The next time they read together Sharon brought *Peace at Last* and asked to hear it again. She then offered to read it to the teacher which she did with a quality entirely missing from her earlier reading of the book described above. She read in meaningful chunks, substituting appropriately, self-correcting and rarely appealing for help with words. Success for Sharon as a reader followed the teacher's careful analysis of her strengths and weaknesses and the realisation that Sharon did not possess enough strategies to read entirely independently and that she still needed to be helped into books. While she could tackle a known text with great confidence she was reduced to stumbling and hestitating with an unfamiliar text, even though it was a very 'easy read'.

Guessing and correcting

'be ready to make informed guesses, and to correct themselves in the light of additional information, eg. by reading ahead or looking back in the text' (7d).

Guessing unknown words is often regarded as uninformed reading behaviour and unless you take the time to analyse a child's substituted words you may not be sure whether they are informed or not. Return to Simone's reading of *Red is Best* on page 84 and look at her substitutions. Socks for stockings; high for higher; and so on. All of her substitutions could be described as guesses but none could be said to be wild guesses. Every one is an informed guess based on the information Simone has at her disposal. She uses a smooth combination of prediction and checking and self-corrects when she recognises a mismatch with her expectations.

Self-correction is a strategy for word-solving which few of us realise we possess. It is only when we read something we regard as ridiculous that we realise we have misread and automatically self-correct.

While some children like Simone seem almost automatically to use these strategies, others need to be taught how to. In one-to-one reading sessions as well as during the reading of a big book with the larger group you can model ways of reading on or re-reading to solve unknown words.

Intonation and phrasing

'develop the capacity to convey, when reading aloud, the meaning of the text clearly to the listener through intonation and phrasing' (7e).

It is through being read to and continuing to be read to even after they have begun to read independently that children learn to read in meaningful chunks rather than word by word in a stilted fashion. Children will certainly model themselves on you, taking on almost identically your intonation and phrasing. Just think of the almost universal way in which young children read or pretend read 'Then I'll huff and I'll puff and I'll blow your house in'. It surely comes from hearing others.

It therefore seems obvious that the wider their experience of listening to others read the more likely they are to develop the skill of reading aloud well themselves.

• Learning poetry by heart is a good support for modelling good phrasing and intonation and demonstrating the creation of mood and atmosphere by the use of tone of voice, loudness and softness, pausing and so on.

• Puppets and other visual props help children to develop the appropriate use of their voices when reading or telling stories.

• Give the opportunities to tell rather than read a story to the class. It could be a story the children have read or heard themselves or one they've made up, or about an event or something that has happened to them.

Having an audience creates a purpose for reading in such a way that the meaning of the text is conveyed clearly. If they only even read to an adult with the purpose of showing how well they can read or for assessment it will not be evident to children that they are reading for someone else's pleasure and enjoyment. That has to be made explicit. Reading a play with a group of friends is a favourite activity and one where there is a need to read with expression.

Silent reading

'develop the habit of silent reading' (7f).

There is no one age at which children move into silent reading. Indeed occasionally you may work with children who actively prefer right from the start not to read out loud but who pore over familiar books clearly intent on sorting it out for themselves.

Terry was an active friendly boy in a Year One class who enjoyed school. He was in a class where reading was given the highest priority by the teacher. She had at least two quite lengthy sharing book sessions each day; she herself loved children's literature passionately and could not resist telling and reading stories of all kinds, reading and learning poetry and rhymes and she passed her enthusiasm on to her class. Most of the children loved to read out loud but Terry was very reluctant to do so no matter how secure the situation. During whole class quiet reading times the teacher made a particular effort to spend some time observing Terry from a distance. She saw that he spent quite a while watching and listening to his peers every day and that when he did pick up a book he indicated by his head movements and finger pointing that he was looking closely at the print and trying to match word for word. He continued in this way for some time. It was apparent from his expression that he very much enjoyed hearing stories though he never audibly joined in! The teacher felt certain that he was learning and sensibly did not pressure him to read to her. Then one day he offered to read her the Tony Ross version of *Three Pigs* and he did, almost perfectly. If you know this book you will also know that it is just too long and complicated a text to learn by heart. Terry was an almost totally independent reader who had become so without vocalising audibly. He continued to prefer to read silently.

In silent reading a child can make use of a better range of cues. She can read as fast as she can but can vary the pace as she needs or wishes. She can read on, miss whole sections out if they don't affect the sense, read back, turning back several pages if need be to check on something. The constraint of having to make the meaning clear for the listener has gone. The reader can stop and think about it or wonder what the author meant. It is of course the preferred mode used by adults and other efficient readers and one we should encourage early by giving extensive opportunities to practise and extend the range of texts in the child's repertoire.

Early on you can encourage appropriate reading behaviour in preparation for reading silently by an expectation that your children will survey a book before reading and by encouraging browsing before choosing a book. As you introduce a new story you can model this kind of approach, looking at and talking about the illustrations and asking questions which will highlight some of the likely possibilities in the story.

Key Stage 2

At this stage some children will have proceeded to true independence as readers. Others will not and these are crucial years for the ones who have just struggled to acquire a developing literacy. Every opportunity has to be provided for them to accelerate their progress into real fluency and ease as readers.

The DES Circular 10/89 (included in the folder for English) states that; 'the working assumption, which will need to be tested in practice, has been that pupils should typically be capable of achieving Level 2 at or near the end of Key Stage 1 . . . Levels 1 and 3 will be achieved by a minority of pupils only' (paragraph VI. 18).

In the following paragraph we read: 'Much of what is taught for Levels 1-3 will in any case continue to be taught to pupils at higher levels, though with different emphases.' The assumption is that the majority of pupils at the beginning of the

Key Stage will be working towards Levels 2 and 3 and a significant proportion will be following schemes of work directed towards these levels at the end of the Key Stage.

In the Detailed Provisions teachers are reminded that they 'should refer to relevant material in the Programme of Study for Key Stage 1'. Teachers should, therefore, continue to provide all the materials, activities and support outlined in the preceding section for Key Stage 1. This will certainly be most true in relation to knowledge about words and letters, the patterns of letters in words and the development of cueing systems which are not referred to in a specific way for pupils in Key Stage 2.

Most of the pupils at this stage will need careful and planned teaching of these skills in order that they continue to grow in competence.

Developing reading

'Pupils should read an increasingly wide range and variety of texts in order to become more experienced readers. They should be encouraged to develop their personal taste in reading with guidance from the teacher and to become more independent and reflective.' (8).

Range and variety

It is implied that reading development will come from reading for an increasing range of purposes. There is no suggestion that children will become more competent readers by completing exercises in grammar or comprehension. Neither are greater levels of challenge offered as the single key to success. The key elements are seen to be range and variety of reading. It is worthwhile remembering here that those of us who think of ourselves as readers, who enjoy reading and read for personal pleasure and fulfilment, read all kinds of things depending on our mood and on the occasion. No-one tells us what we should be reading though our friends may recommend good reads to us. A small proportion of the things we read represents major challenge or very hard work or is especially 'improving'! Indeed if 'good literature' were all we were ever allowed to read we would not persist very long with it. Our reading material represents range and variety – thrillers and detective stories for the beach, where total concentration isn't required and the magazines we browse through while we pass the time waiting for appointments at the dentist or hairdresser. Sometimes we return to old favourites and re-read them. Certainly for us as adults, moving onwards and upwards to harder and harder books isn't what makes us read.

Like us, children need different and sometimes very easy reads. Donald Fry (*Children Talk about Books: Seeing Themselves as Readers*) recounts conversations with several children, among them a twelve year old boy called Karnail, who was 'not an experienced reader' and who has difficulties in beginning to read a story. Karnail 'had dipped into books, looked at opening pages, studied illustrations . . . but these were brief forays, not the excursion itself.' He had tried many books yet was still at first base as a reader. Fry says of Karnail, 'I do not believe that Karnail was reluctant to read; it was rather the books that resisted him'. It was the *Secret Seven* books by Enid Blyton which reassured Karnail and made him feel like a real reader. Blyton made reading easy for him. Our job as teachers is to make reading easy for children and it will help if:

- We acknowledge children's popular culture and provide materials we would not necessarily approve of, for example, My Little Pony, Asterix and Teenage Mutant Hero Turtles or any other current craze;
- We encourage active participation through books like the *Choose Your Own Adventure* series, in which the reader has to make decisions at different points in the story about the next move to be made in reaching a solution to a quest or search;
- We invite them into books by reading aloud the first chapter or so and stopping at a gripping point.

Developing personal taste

Talk to children about their reading and you will gain insights into their personal taste and be able to recommend what they might read next. For example, Ben's teacher asked him in discussion about Roald Dahl's *Danny the Champion of the World* what he particularly liked about Danny. Ben replied, 'I like stories where there's a lot of detail – when they describe a lot – and when things actually happen and lots of things happen quickly. I like the detail and that he doesn't only do poaching . . . things he actually spends his time doing that are interesting – instead of just playing with plastic toys . . . he makes . . . his dad helps him to make things like balloons and go-carts and things that are exciting'.

When asked about Danny's dad, Ben replied, 'He's a nice person – he spend all his attention with Danny really and does everything for Danny. He's not that rich, but he's a clever man'.

The teacher went on to ask what Ben would read next, and when Ben seemed uncertain, suggested, 'Well . . . I think you could try *Tod's Owl*. It's a bit sad at the beginning, but there's a lot about how this boy looks after the owls. I know you like animals and you'd like the detail. As I said, it's sad to begin with, but it's what really happens to people sometimes and . . . well . . . try it and see'.

Becoming more independent and reflective

Drama encourages reflectiveness and helps children focus on characters and their actions. Vital issues relating to attitudes and behaviour, eg kindness, unkindness, anger, racism, sexism, justice and injustice can be explored. You can:
● Work 'in role' yourself, participating in the drama and largely shaping its rules and the course of the events. You can 'turn the tables' and create an environment through drama where females are more powerful than males and are able to deny them rights. This could be a school playground in the future where only girls play football, for instance, and through discussion about the drama the rights and wrongs of such behaviour can be questioned.
● Set up drama situations in which well known characters can be extended or developed or story outcomes changed. For example, a Year Six class arranged a mock trial of Jack who had been charged with the manslaughter of the giant by wilfully cutting down the beanstalk in which the innocent giant had his home! Children in role as witnesses for the prosecution alleged that Jack was a lazy good-for-nothing who would do anything rather than an honest day's work. The Jack character was carefully reconstructed by the children in their prosecution role which aimed to prove his guilt. The whole class participated and the children were so involved that they continued to debate the rights and wrongs of the case in the playground at break. In addition this drama involved the children in a good deal of writing, in that statements had to be taken, eye-witness accounts written and journalists' reports and headlines compiled. Opportunities to use and develop talking and listening skills were also many and varied.

Reading materials

'The reading materials provided should include a range of fiction, non-fiction and poetry, as well as periodicals suitable for children of this age. These should include works written in English from other cultures. School and class libraries must provide as wide a range as possible. The material available must pose a significant challenge to pupils; for example, poetry should not be confined to verse written for children; folk tales and fables might include translations from original sources. Pupils should discuss with others and with the teacher what has been read' (9).

Range has already been discussed in some detail in the Programme of Study for Key Stage 1 and the appropriateness and

place of challenge for inexperienced readers in the preceding section. You should add to the collection:
● More of the longer stories and more complicated novels that will stimulate and prompt children to question, ranging from Ted Hughes' *The Iron Man* and *Charlotte's Web* by E B White to C S Lewis's *Narnia* series and *Black Jack* or *Smith* by Leon Garfield.
● Harder picture books, some for the quality of the artwork alone such as *The Bluebird* by Fiona French;
● Science fiction such as *Grinny* by Nicholas Fisk;
● Classics such as Mark Twain's *Huckleberry Finn*;
● Historical novels by authors such as Rosemary Sutcliff or Leon Garfield.

Poetry for children and adults

Ian Serraillier's poem 'The Visitor' (and it is hard to know for which age group he wrote this poem) was for many months the favourite poem in a class of infants whose teacher I worked with. There was only one copy of *A Second Poetry Book* (Oxford) on the classroom bookshelves so many children copied it out carefully to take home for their parents, their siblings and friends. It was recited in unison, read to the whole school at assembly and borrowed by every class in the school. There is plenty of evidence in *I Like This Poem* (Puffin Books

ed. Kaye Webb) that children enjoy poetry written for adults as much as they like that written for children. Among the poems chosen by nine year old children are 'Night Mail' by Auden, written as a rhythmic commentary for a film about the Post Office and John Betjeman's 'Harrow on the Hill'. Ten year olds' selections include Gerard Manley Hopkins', 'Pied Beauty', Robert Frost's 'Stopping by Woods on a Snowy Evening' and 'The Calendar' by Barbara Euphan Todd.

Poetry can simply be read aloud by one child to the class or spoken aloud by the whole group, as well, of course, as read aloud by the teacher. You can also:
● Use poetry as an accompaniment to movement and dance. For example, contrast the movement of:
   'With a dive and a dip
   it snaps its tail
   Then soars like a ship
   With only one sail'
with the last four lines of Harry Behn's The Kite (in *Hi-Ran-Ho* published by Longmans)
   'But a raggeder thing
   You never will see
   When it flaps on a string
   In the top of a tree'.
Try Michael Rosen's 'Over my toes', Dahlov Ipcar's 'Fishes Evening Song' and others which just ask for movement in Raymond Wilson's *Poems to Paddle In*.

Reading opportunities

'Pupils should:
- **hear stories, poems and non-fiction read aloud;**
- **have opportunities to participate in all reading activities;**
- **select books for their own reading and for use in their work;**
- **keep records of their own reading and comment, in writing or in discussion, on the books which they have read;**
- **read aloud to the class or teacher and talk about the books they have been reading;**
- **be encouraged to respond to the plot, character or ideas in stories or poems, and to refer to relevant passages or episodes to support their opinions;**
- **be encouraged to think about the accuracy of their own reading and to check for errors that distort meaning;**
- **be shown how to read different kinds of materials in different ways;**
- **learn how to find information in books and databases, sometimes drawing on more than one source, and to pursue an independent line of inquiry' (10).**

Listening to reading

The importance of reading aloud to children and continuing to do so throughout the whole of Key Stage 2 and indeed beyond has already been stressed in the Programme of Study for Key Stage 1. All of the activities described in the section for Key Stage 1 are equally appropriate for Years Three to Six. These will include:
- All kinds of shared reading and the activity of collaborating, planning and writing pieces of shared writing (see also Attainment Target 3, Writing on page 136);
- Listening to stories and poems read aloud by adults and other pupils;
- Discussing what has been read.

It is essential that developing readers continue to be familiarised with the language of books and with the increasingly complex structures they are going to meet in their own reading.

Participation

Children learn from one another and benefit from working with their peers and from sharing their different competences and interests. Reading can easily become a lonely and isolated activity, especially for the child who is making slow progress. These children in particular should not always be assigned to special groups which may cut them off from the benefit of working with their peers. The same is true of bilingual pupils. They need the opportunity to demonstrate their own competence and also to learn from the experience of others.

Personal choice of books

From the beginning children should be learning how to select their own books but, obviously, they will at first need guidance. They will come to have favourite authors and themes if you ensure that you always make connections for them right from the early stages.

Records and reviews

Having to write about every book you read would be a sure way of putting you off reading for ever. This is an activity which has to have a genuine purpose. Try to give it a relevant context:
- A contribution to an assembly about books;
- A review slot in the class or school newspaper;
- Assessing the recent additions to the class collection;
- A recommendation for others to read.

Making a record of what has been read, with dates, is a satisfying activity for most children and one for which teachers can demonstrate usefulness.

Encourage your children to list titles they have read and those they would like to read in future.

Reviewing such a record provides information and a basis for discussion in the reading conference. The following extract is from one teacher's notes based on discussion of a child's own reading record: 'Nicole has chosen nothing but picture books for ages: she devours them at the rate of one a day. I'm delighted she enjoys them but I must get her to try a few longer stories. I notice she misses a lot of detail. She doesn't like books with "lots of description . . . They're boring." Slower paced writing seems to stop her getting into the story which is what she wants. In their subsequent reading conference they discussed Nicole's reading of Roald Dahl's *Dirty Beasts*. The teacher suggested Nicole tried *Flat Stanley* and said, 'Emma's just finished it and she enjoyed it. I think you might'.

Later in the reading diary the teacher records: 'She's read *The BFG* . . . She thinks it's wonderful – its got her back into longer stories. She's read almost all the Dahl books. But her reading log is failing – she doesn't like writing about what she has read, even one sentence. She has talked about it at great length and has had lots of perceptive comments to make, about the BFG's feelings and loneliness'.

Reading aloud

Reasons for reading aloud to the class or teacher and discussing books have been given above. See the Programmes of Study for Key Stage 1 and earlier paragraphs in Key Stage 2.

Responding to literature

When you talk to children about their reading you need to be able to ask evaluative questions about plot and character:

- What sort of a person is . . .?
- How did she help the family to escape?
- Why did he do that?
- How do you know his dad was a kind man?
- Where did you read that the farmers were wicked?

Looking for accuracy

In the Assessment section on page 117 we see Darrell analysing his own reading as he listens to himself on tape. Tape recording and listening to the playback is one way of encouraging readers to respond to their own accuracy. Talking about the reading is another way. Ask questions which invite reflection:

- Do you remember what you read there?
- Can we go back and look at that page?

Organise a cloze procedure as a group activity. This will encourage accurate and considered response as children justify their suggestions to fit the blanks. Any text can be 'clozed'. Words can be deleted either randomly or according to word type if the teacher wishes to focus on a particular kind of word (eg adjectives, prepositions etc). Usually the first part of a text is left intact so that the readers can get a feel for it before attempting to find words to fill the spaces. Cloze procedure is often used to construct tests of reading ability, but a far more valuable use is as a group activity when children are invited to discuss the possibilities before agreeing on appropriate words to fill the gaps. They should be shown that there are often several equally valid alternatives and that, if it makes sense, it is not wrong.

An alternative to 'cloze' is 'maze', where two or three other words are added to the one used by the writer and readers have to discuss and select one of them. Children enjoy finding out, after they have made their choices, which were the author's words. Often further discussion will ensue if they have chosen a different alternative.

Activities like cloze which invite reflection and discussion, are more valid ways of developing 'comprehension' than any comprehension exercises, where the questions generally test only surface understanding and can often be answered by simply juggling with the syntax, without any necessity to understand the passage.

Different reading materials

Children need to develop many different kinds of reading skill apart from those they use to read continuous prose or narrative. They need to be able to read in order to learn about something new, or about how to do something or to find out a specific fact. Each of these requires a different kind

of reading. Sometimes simply browsing will reveal interesting information and this can lead to the production of posters or other material drawing attention to interesting facts. One teacher gets her children to compose 'Did you know that . . .? posters as they work on topics. These encourage others in the class to join in and take an interest.

Topic work has been the traditional means of introducing children to information texts. Sadly HMI continues to report that children spend quantities of time copying chunks of information into their topic books without either purpose or understanding. It is important that children are helped to formulate questions to which they would like to find answers and that you help with strategies for this:
● When you use collections or anthologies show the children that you use the contents and the index;
● Show them how you skim for the relevant part of the text;
● Make notes as you prepare for a visit;
● Provide real situations for real information to be collected;
● Provide real activities which provoke real questions, such as hatching chicks or visiting a farm;
● Make tape-slide sequences about events, activities or visits.

Examining characters

'In order to achieve Level 5, pupils should be helped to:
● **look in a text for clues about characters or actions, and to use these clues to reach conclusions, evaluate and predict what may happen;**
● **distance themselves, when appropriate, from a text' (13).**

Clearly talking about texts after reading aloud is one way of encouraging pupils to think about characters and actions, as are:
● Preparing accounts for class newspapers eg for the trial of Jack for slaying the Giant;
● Writing diaries for characters, for example after reading *Grinny* which is written in diary form;
● Writing modern versions of folk tales, or anti-sexist versions (see page 156);
● Writing 'in character' or from one character to another.

Assessment

The TGAT report recommended that there should be a national standardised system of assessment of children's progress, in order that schools can compare their performance with other schools and also compare their levels of achievement in one year with those of previous years.

The report recommended that children's achievement should be measured at the end of Key Stages in their education for these purposes and for the purpose of reporting to parents.

Assessment for these purposes will be by Standard Assessment Tasks or SATS undertaken by seven and eleven-year-olds.

Running alongside the nationally prescribed assessments, TGAT advised that schools should adopt their own methods of internal teacher assessment. Such internal assessment procedures would be essentially formative in nature, ie they would be ongoing, would inform teachers

about a child's learning so that future teaching could be more precisely matched to the child's needs.

In reading, some schools have traditionally made use of published tests, particularly diagnostic tests, to help in this process. We have become increasingly aware, though, that every time we read or talk about reading with a child we are in a position to acquire better insights into her ability as a reader. We become more skilled in making informal assessments of progress in the context of the everyday learning activity.

Informal assessment takes place whenever you notice anything new or different in a child's reading. For example, when you become aware that she is focusing on print or is carefully matching word for word as she retells a familiar story, you have acquired evidence that a significant shift has been made in progress.

You need to have a clear view of what constitutes progress and development in becoming a reader so that your observations and assessments are consistent and the notes you make prove useful to you in planning your future teaching. The ILEA Primary Language Record sets out two very useful scales of progress which can be used to:

- Identify where a child is on a learning continuum on a scale of one to five;
- Map progress from year to year through the whole primary range;
- Help identify new strategies to be taught.

The first scale charts progress from 'dependence' to 'independence', ie from the very earliest stages to real fluency. The second describes an older child's growth as a reader from inexperienced to exceptionally experienced. Both can be used by teachers as part of their ordinary work and do not require any special materials. They have special advantages for teachers of bilingual pupils in that they can be used to identify what a child is able to do in her community language. Principally they help you to sharpen and make consistent your observations.

Observing children using books

Watching and listening as a child interacts with a text can tell you a lot. In the very earliest stages Marie Clay (1972) suggests we look for evidence that a child has early concepts of print such as:

- Knowing where the front of the book is;
- Knowing that print carries the message;
- Knowing that we follow the print in English from left to right to the end of the line then sweep back to the left at the beginning of the next line;
- Knowing that we read the left hand page before the right.

There would be very little point in attempting to teach a child to decode or learn words if she didn't possess these fundamental concepts. Similarly, if the teacher always holds the book and turns the pages for the child there is no opportunity for the child to demonstrate the skills she has.

Sampling reading

Sampling a child's reading in an informal way on a regular basis should provide all the information you need to plan effectively for her development. As an assessment process it can be used with children of all ages and levels of ability; it has the advantage that familiar materials can be used and that there is no need for special or different contexts to be set up. Children are enabled to perform at their usual level and are not disturbed by being 'tested'. It is, therefore, more likely that the child's true ability will not be distorted by the 'test' situation.

To make the most of the opportunity it helps if you are clear in your mind what you are looking for. At the early stages you may well be looking for evidence about the child's concepts about print. Later on you will be trying to identify which strategies she uses strongly and which, if any, need specific teaching. You will want to know about letter knowledge and phonic skills. You may also want to check for the deeper kinds of understanding of the subtleties and nuances of the text as well as the reader's response to it. You will want to assess the degree of confidence with which she approached the reading and whether or not she enjoyed the style, the illustrations or that particular genre.

Assessing the silent reader

Although part of the sampling procedure might be listening to reading aloud it does not have to be. A child who normally prefers to read silently can do so and the assessment can take place as you discuss the text afterwards or as she retells it to you. You might ask her to select a part of the book to share with you. For very fluent or avid readers who rarely make mistakes or 'miscues' as they read this is probably the best way of assessing reading development.

Where children keep their own log of titles read with dates, a quick survey of the log can equally provide a basis for discussion about reading preferences.

Bilingual pupils

If your school has a community language teacher she too can carry out informal assessments of a child's reading either in English or in the community language or in a combination of the two. The child might read the text in English but discuss it in the first language. This gives you a fuller picture of a bilingual pupil's progress.

A further advantage of informal assessment over a published test is that the choice of reading material is less likely to put children from other cultures at a disadvantage. You can select texts which you are sure are not culturally biased.

What to look for

With beginning readers you will be looking particularly for the first of these indications as a sign that they are moving closer to becoming 'real' readers.
● Are they successfully 'playing' at reading and making sense of the text?
● Are they using 'book language'?
● Are they reading the pictures?
● Are they focusing on the print?
● Is directionality consistent?
● Do they have one-to-one correspondence?
● Do they recognise any words at sight?
● Do they use initial letter cues?
● Do they notice and try to self-correct miscues?
● Do they predict?
● Do they use graphic and phonic cues?
● Do they use semantic and syntactic cues?
● Do they use a combination of cues or rely more heavily on one or two?

Note how confidently the reader approached the reading; did she make it flow, trying to read in meaning units,

pausing appropriately or was the reading jerky and with long hesitations? How involved was she in the story? Note whether and how deeply she understood. Lastly, try to note what you plan to offer next. Often this will be more of the same but at times you might decide that more challenging texts would be appropriate or that a particular author would appeal.

Miscue analysis

Sometimes you will be concerned that a child is making insufficient progress and you will want to take a closer look at a sample of her reading. The miscue analysis procedure devised by Kenneth and Yetta Goodman in the USA in the 1960s is often found to be helpful by teachers. Over time the original procedure has been modified and adapted by others but the process essentially enables you to identify the strategies which a reader ordinarily uses and those which she uses less or not at all, so that you can plan a structured programme for her. You use the following procedure.
● Choose a text the child is not familiar with. At first this may present difficulties as it is important that the text is not so challenging that the reader cannot make sense of it because she is making too many miscues or that it is insufficiently challenging and she makes too few to analyse. Try to choose something you know she will enjoy. Ideally the text should be one that supports the reader by flowing well when read aloud. In general, aim for something where the child is likely to miscue about one word in ten, and of a length of about 150 to 200 words.
● Make a tape recording of the child's reading. This is important if you have not used miscue analysis before because you do not have to be as totally adept with the marking conventions as you would if you were trying to do the scoring while the child is reading. Other advantages of taping are that the child will not be distracted by what you are doing, the tape can be

replayed if you mishear the first time and it can be kept as a record.

• Then ask the child to retell the story on tape and record the discussion you have about the text.

• Make a copy of the text (preferably typewritten with double line spacing).

• Mark the miscues on the copy using the conventions described below and score for balance of positive and negative miscues.

You can vary the procedure to suit yourself and your children. Some teachers see that the reader surveys the book first or reads it silently before reading all of it or a suitable section of it aloud.

Example of miscue analysis: Darrell

Darrell is a child in Year Three who chose to read *Lion* by Betty Root (*Animaland* series, Jolly Learning Ltd). He enjoys stories and reading and often chooses reading as a preferred activity. His teacher felt he was at a stage in his reading development when he should be making more rapid progress and wanted to see what she could learn from a closer examination of his responses to a text.

The marking conventions used are no more than a convenient shorthand for identifying each kind of miscue. It is helpful to stick to these forms so that colleagues can make sense of your marks. The numbers in brackets on the script refer to examples of these particular kinds of miscue in Darrell's reading.

• Substitution: where a word has been substituted for the word in the text – write the miscued word, or attempted word immediately above (1).

• Self-correction: draw an elongated 'L' round the miscued word and mark with the letter 'c' to indicate correction (2).

• Omission: circle the word(s) omitted (3).

• Insertion: use the normal inverted 'v' you would in drafting writing (4).

• Repetition: draw an elongated 'L' round the repeated word(s); mark with an 'r' (5).

• Reversal: use a continuous line round the words eg 'she said'. There are no examples of reversals in Darrell's reading.

LION

"Out of my way everyone," roared the lion as he wandered down to the lake. (3) The other animals soon (scampered) off when they heard him coming. When lion had finished drinking he looked at his (2) reflection in the water. "Why am I so ugly?" he thought.

He moved his head from side to side. Then he climbed on to a rock to get a better (view) of himself. (5) The (sky) became dark. Spots of rain (splashed) on the water and soon lion could not see his reflection. This was too much for him and he roared as loud as he could. Then he sat down in (a) puddle. All the other animals gathered round. They asked if there was anything they

could do to help, for lion was after all the king of the jungle. "I'm so ugly." cried lion as he (buried) his head in the bushes. "Why don't we give him a bath?" said pelican and make his mane curly. "All right," said lion, "but please don't hurt me." Lion sat very still. Hippo washed him and the monkeys tied up his mane with reeds and grass. When it was dry they put a crown on his head. Lion ran to the water. "Just look at me. I'm much better looking than I thought," he said. Of course all the other animals agreed. For (several) days lion was kind to Everyone but then it started to rain. It rained so hard that everyone got very wet. "Look at me. I'm ugly again," roared lion

and his crown fell off into a puddle. The other animals were frightened and hid in the trees. "Come back, come back," cried lion. "I won't hurt you." Gradually (they) (returned). "This won't do," said monkey. "Every time it rains lion gets angry. Every time we make him beautiful we risk being (eaten)."

"I know what we can do," said (pelican). "Lion is our king and he should live in a palace. (We) will build him one by the lake so that when it rains he can keep himself dry. When it's fine he can look at his reflection in the water." So they built him a fine palace and made a roof with large green leaves. They put flowers in the window and dry leaves on the floor. Lion became the happiest animal in the forest.

Darrell's re-telling of *Lion*

D. It's about this lion . . . No . . . When the rain falls this lion gets very very angry and . . . and . . .

T. Why was that?

D. Because the rain makes him very angry and horrid . . . and . . .

T. So what does he do about it?

D. He axes the animals to help him get beautiful . . . and . . .

T. And what happens?

D. And when the rain falls again . . .

T. Did the other animals help him to get beautiful

D. Yep.

T. How?

D. They . . . um . . . a hippopotamus washed him. The monkeys . . . I've forgotten now . . . (looks at the pictures) . . . The monkeys put leaves on his curly hair. I don't know what that is.

T. A pelican.

D. Well the pelican curled his hair and they put a crown on his head and he looked in the water and he was beautiful. The rain started to fall again and he got very very VERY angry and the hippopotamus and the monkeys and the pelican helped him again and made a place for him not to get wet. And when the rain doesn't fall he can look at his reflection.

After re-telling the story Darrell asked to listen to the tape. As he listened he followed the text in the book and quite spontaneously corrected some of his miscues such as kind/king, weather/water. By re-reading to gather the sense he read some of the words he had omitted originally, such as 'several', 'returned' and 'eaten'. He asked for some words, such as 'gradually' and 'gathered' and said he had never heard them before.

Analysis

All the self-corrections were positively helpful in that they contributed to Darrell's understanding of the text. He made a quite high number of omissions and rarely looked back or ahead in the text to help himself gather meaning. His substitutions were generally helpful and made as a result of his phonic knowledge.

Over all, Darrell showed that he was reading for meaning. He expected what he read to make sense and his re-telling shows that he did understand the gist of the text. He needed some help in sorting out the detail of the story in his re-telling (this may be because it was an unfamiliar activity). He did not appear to realise that the animals helped the lion because they feared for their lives!

His positive response to hearing himself read on tape and his spontaneous review and further self-correction would lead me to offer this to him as a future learning experience to increase his involvement in self-assessment.

He should be shown that reading ahead and re-reading are useful strategies in utilising context effectively and should be encouraged to tell and re-tell stories more frequently. His own language experience would be broadened by more opportunities to hear stories read aloud or on tape.

Previewing a book with an adult would allow him to ask for information before reading.

We might now wish to look at what this one sample of Darrell's reading tells us about his achievement in terms of the Statements of Attainment in Attainment Target 2. Clearly we would wish to have a great deal more evidence than we have about Darrell from just one look at his reading of just one text. However, we could be sure that this particular sample provides some evidence of several attainments at Level 2.

● Darrell demonstrates his knowledge of the alphabet (2b).

● He uses picture and context cues, recognises words on sight and phonic cues in reading (2c).

● He can describe what happened in a story (2d).

● He can read with some independence, fluency, accuracy and understanding (2f).

We could be sure that he meets at Level 3 the need to 'read aloud from familiar stories . . . fluently and with expression' (3a).

Summative assessment

To make the kind of summative assessment necessary at the ends of Key Stages in order to assign pupils to a level of achievement in reading, we need a much greater range of evidence than we can expect to find in one reading sample. This evidence has to come from a range of observations and samples over a period of time. The following is an extract from Ben's teacher's record of reading conferences with him (Ben was aged nine at the time).

September
He is very keen on the Navy, space and all things military. His concentration in silent reading is absolute.

November
He reads more at home than at school. He was reluctant at first to read anything other than books with solid writing. He is now sharing picture books. He especially likes Charles Keeping and brought his own copies to show the others the illustrations.

March
He has read several poetry books and written some poems of his own with a real feeling for words. Especially likes poems about feelings (wrote a very good one about being afraid, and about being old).

Did some excellent research about the space shuttle. Located what he needed in the library and selected appropriately. Supplemented with newspaper accounts. Talked about it to the class.

July
Is reading longer novels without any difficulty (eg *Machine Gunners*). His concentration shows complete involvement. Talks about reading, showing real understanding of motivation of characters.

Diary of observations
Angry Arthur. Talked about the pictures and about being angry. Wrote poem called 'Seeing Red'.
Machine Gunners. Saw this on TV. Knows every detail of the story. Talked a bit about war and what happens to people in wartime.
You Tell Me and *Mind Your own Business*. Says Rosen writes about 'just the things children like to say'.
Oliver Twist (abridged). Had a long talk about Oliver and what life was like 100 or so years ago. Very sensitive to others' suffering.
Flat Stanley. Liked the idea and thought up several more situations where it would be useful to be flat.
Stanley Bagshaw and the Fourteen Foot Wheel. Read this very fluently with accents for characters . . . made us all laugh.

Ben's achievements
We can see here plenty of evidence that Ben is well on the way to achieving all the statements for Level 4, ie he can:
- 'read aloud expressively, fluently and with increased confidence from a range of familiar literature' (4a);
- 'demonstrate, in talking about a range of stories and poems which they have read, an ability to explore preferences' (4b);
- 'demonstrate, in talking about stories, poems, non-fiction and other texts, that they are developing their abilities to use inference, deduction and previous reading experience' (4c);
- 'find books or magazines in the class or school library by using the classification system, catalogue or database and use appropriate methods of finding information, when pursuing a line of inquiry' (4d).

Chapter three
Writing

The teaching of writing

Attainment Target 3 of the National Curriculum for English is 'a growing ability to construct and convey meaning in written language, matching style to audience and purpose'. In working towards this aim children will also be developing spelling and handwriting skills (Attainment Targets 4 and 5). The separation of writing from handwriting and spelling signals very clearly that there is much more to learning to write than becoming a good speller and producing legible script. The distinction made between what Frank Smith (1982)

has called 'transcriptional' or 'secretarial' skills and 'compositional' or 'authorial' competence reflects our growing understanding of what is involved, for all writers, in the creation of written texts. So, Attainment Target 3 is about children's growth as composers of texts of many kinds, in a range of contexts and for different audiences.

Traditionally the teaching of writing has emphasised more heavily the young writer's ability to spell and to write clearly, than their ability 'to construct and convey meaning in written language' and to 'match style to audience and purpose'. The emphasis in the National Curriculum means that classrooms must provide many different contexts for writing across the whole curriculum, and will need to be resourced so that children are able to write frequently, independently and relevantly in the course of their work in all subject areas. The Non-Statutory Guidance for English (page C13, 10.1) has this advice to offer for the planning of writing: 'Every piece of writing produced in the classroom is the culmination of a series of decisions by the child and the teacher. Effective plans provide for a classroom where activities take account of:

- the reasons for which children have chosen or been asked to write;
- the support and advice they might need;
- the audience for which they are writing;
- their knowledge of varieties of written language.'

Organisation and resources

'Teachers should make decisions about the materials which they need to make available' (NCC Non-Statutory Guidance: English Key Stage 1, page C14, 11:2). Before any scheme of work can be planned and implemented, the class teacher must look at the resources for writing offered in the classroom. We cannot expect children to use writing for learning, to produce written work of a high standard or to take a pride in their writing if we offer them limited, uninspiring resources. If the only writing that is ever done is in an English exercise book, the only tools available are blunt pencils and the only audience is the teacher, we shall be offered writing which reflects this.

Writing should take place for many purposes and in many situations and appropriate materials must be provided.

The writing space

A quiet, possibly screened, area should be created so that children can work on individual or personal writing, free from interruption. In this space they need to have access to reference materials including:

- Alphabet books;
- Reference posters;
- Word banks;
- Dictionaries;
- Thesauruses.

Writing materials should also be provided including:

- Ready made-up booklets of different sizes;
- Scrap paper;
- Good quality paper of different sizes and colours, card, line guides, borders;
- Pencils, pens, felt-tipped pens;
- Rulers, pencil sharpeners, erasers, staplers;
- Envelopes, post-cards, home-made stamps, labels;
- Typewriter;
- Word-processors.

These materials will also be required in other areas of the classroom. Therefore, storage of booklets, various paper, pens, pencils etc, will need to be in a central position, well-organised and labelled so that children can find for themselves the materials they need when they need them.

The word-processor

Most classrooms will have micro-computers available on a regular basis; some may have one permanently in situ. However, it is likely to be used for many purposes, such as data-retrieval, mathematical activities or games, in addition to word-processing. It is important that time is allocated for the computer to be used as a word-processor as this is a powerful aid to writing for many children. The computer 'should be seen not only as a means of publishing text but as a way of composing, drafting and editing . . . Children should be encouraged, when composing, to use word-processors, together and independently' (NCC Non-Statutory Guidance, page C15, 11:5).

Making books

Materials will be needed for children to make their own books. In the earliest years these may be zig-zag books, stapled booklets, or simple hard-back books. Any printing, painting, cutting or sticking needs to be done away from the writing area, if children's finished versions of pieces of writing are to be kept clean and tidy. If they are to make books, children will need to be taught the processes necessary, to be given the skills to enable them to select the most appropriate format for publication.

The NCC Non-Statutory Guidance, in stating the need for teachers to 'provide resources and opportunities for children to make a variety of books' (11:7), has this to say about authorship: 'Consideration will need to be given to providing opportunities for the child to:

- identify the audience for the book;
- understand the needs of the audience;
- compose the text;
- make decisions about the organisation of the text;
- share the writing with peers to gain another viewpoint;
- have opportunities to reshape the writing;
- have a choice of published format.'

Instructions for making a variety of books can be found in the Appendix, on page 183.

Key Stage 1

Frequent opportunities

'Pupils should have frequent opportunities to write in different contexts and for a variety of purposes and audiences, including for themselves' (2).

If provision is made and children are given time beyond teacher-directed tasks, they will write for their own purposes, whether in play or because they are interested in a particular kind of writing. They may want to write notes or invitations to their friends or to take home, reminders or instructions for themselves. Much writing will be at a teacher's suggestion and some will be done in collaboration with other children, but some time must be allowed for children to write for themselves on topics of their own choice.

For very young children the provision of a writing area with a variety of materials is often enough to inspire writing. If 'writing' is one of the activities teachers value and make time for, the habit is easily established. Whenever an adult, whether an ancillary helper, parent, nursery assistant or teacher, can be available in the writing area to take dictation, children can be encouraged to take advantage of the situation to compose at greater length. The demonstrations or models provided by adults writing alongside children are immensely valuable.

One way of encouraging slightly older or more competent children to write on topics of their own choice, is to establish a 'writing workshop' as part of the classroom routine. The operation of such workshops had been well documented by Graves (1983), Calkins (1984), Newman (1985) see Bibliography, page 189. Children new to this activity will need to discuss possible topics, perhaps keeping a list of ideas, and will need in advance a clear explanation of how it will work. Once they understand that they do have genuine choices regarding what to write about, that they can discuss on-going work if they wish and that they can choose which pieces, if any, they wish to publish for a wider audience, children are usually enthusiastic about these sessions. To begin with, it is often easier settling down together to write. Once established, this kind of writing can be taken up and put down whenever children feel there is something important for them to write about.

For all children the example of the teacher writing alongside them can be a confidence booster. When they see that even teachers need to think, cross things out, re-write, and, most of all, that adults have things they want to write about, they are seeing a valuable demonstration of one of the uses of writing.

Different contexts and purposes

The writing children do will take different forms and will not always appear to be part of the English curriculum. When they are writing stories, letters or poems, English as a curriculum area is easy to identify. But they will also use writing across the curriculum, just as they will read for mathematics, history, science, geography, technology and RE.

● A group of children making biscuits may be investigating the effect of heat in cooking (ie science) but they will undoubtedly want to list the ingredients, describe the way to make the biscuits and probably record an account of the activity either in a journal or for a wider audience.

● A group of children collecting and sorting data for mathematics may be

undertaking a survey of traffic. They will need to list vehicles, record their observations and possibly write an account of how the survey was carried out, in order to inform other children or for display.

● A group of children involved in a local history project may wish to compile a list of questions to ask a visiting tradesman or an older member of the community. While they talk they will need to take notes. The information from the interview might then be written up in the form of a broadsheet, an article for a class newspaper, as an account to go with photographs for a display or as a section in a book they are making.

A variety of audiences

Both children and teachers need to know who is the intended audience before a piece of writing is started, as this will affect the way in which they write. The wider the range of audiences available, the greater the variety of forms of writing they will be able to undertake. Within the school, possibilities might include:

- Notes to each other;
- Notices for the class notice-board;
- Instructions to users of equipment (eg the computer or tape-recorder);
- Instructions to those caring for class pets;
- Instructions for games children have made up;
- Labels, captions and commentaries on displays;
- Reviews of books for display in the reading area;
- Invitations to other classes to visit or to see an exhibition or performance in their class;
- Information books related to topics, stories, photographic accounts of activities, recipe books and collections of poems;
- Charts or graphs recording observations or surveys;
- Newspapers, for the class or school;
- Posters or information leaflets.

Outside the school, different forms of writing could include:

- Letters home to parents;
- Letters to authors or illustrators;
- Letters requesting information from local shops, firms or agencies;
- Letters of thanks (for information, to visitors);
- Letters to children in other schools;
- Surveys (such as those organised by wild life organisations like RSPB);
- Newspapers, leaflets for parents;
- Posters advertising school activities.

Teachers should not, however, 'regard most writing as needing an audience. Writing may be in an unfinished form such as notes, and some which is finished may not be intended for any reader, other than the person who has written it.' (NCC Non-Statutory Guidance, 12:6, page C16).

'Writing used to organise thinking is perhaps one of the most personal forms and is frequently left incomplete and rarely published.' (Non-Statutory Guidance, 12:7, page C16). Such writing may be done in a working journal or a rough note book and will not be corrected by a teacher. The value of the writing lies in its use as a way of organising and sorting out the child's ideas. Teachers of older primary children will often respond in writing themselves to the ideas or thoughts expressed, but will not correct spellings or comment on handwriting. One of the teacher's responsibilities is to explain the purpose of such writing to any parents who might see it, in order to prevent their thinking that 'teachers do not mark the work'.

Collaborations

Many schools have successfully involved parents in writing with and for children. Some of this writing has been done in school 'workshops', some at home. Families have written accounts for local history projects or stories about their own childhoods. Where there are members of the community with differing cultural backgrounds, collections of traditional stories have been made and published in other community languages as well as English. Close liaison and collaboration like this can be very positive as it results in adults sharing with their children the problems of writing for others to read and appreciating the necessity for re-drafting and editing. Other forms of collaboration are dealt with further on page 136.

Writing activities

'Pupils should write in a wide range of activities. Early 'play' writing, *eg in play house, office, shop, hospital*, should be encouraged and respected' (3).

Children, we know, are great observers and imitators. Before they have come to school they have seen writing being used for a great variety of purposes and will have imitated many of these in their play. In role-play of this kind young children develop their understandings of the world and learn about their own place in it. Recognising the way in which print permeates our lives, teachers need to plan literate home-corners, cafés and shops so that children are encouraged to use these materials as imaginatively as they use the dressing-up clothes.

For 'play' writing to take place they will need to have various reading and writing materials provided.

- In the play house or home-corner they should have notebooks, pencils, pens, stationery, cards, message pads (as well as the complementary reading materials such as directories, magazines, TV programmes, newspapers, recipes, books of all kinds).
- In the class shop/hairdresser's/café there should be paper and pencils to make stock lists, take orders, write price lists, price labels and bills, and large paper to make posters.
- In the office, post office or travel agent, provide an endless supply of paper and envelopes for letters, carbon paper, date-stamps, forms, typewriter, as well as pens and pencils.
- In the hospital/clinic provide paper, pens, pencils, clipboards for nursing notes, charts, cards, stationery and notelets for patients to use.

Writing done by young children in the course of play may not always be readable to adults, but children will often have devised symbols and ways of recording that they can 'read' back themselves, as well as using elements of a conventional writing system.

In play, children will experiment and try out activities of which they may not be fully in control. If teachers respect writing like this, not only will the children be encouraged to believe in themselves as writers and continue to produce quantities of writing, but teachers will be able to observe what children know, understand and can do.

Pre-school writing

'Pupils will have seen different kinds of writing in the home – their names on birthday cards or letters, forms, shopping lists and so on. Those whose parents are literate in a language other than English may have observed writing in their own first language, for which there may be a different writing system. Such awareness of writing in any form can help pupils to understand some of the functions of written language and should be used to promote their understanding of the functions of the English writing system' (4).

There is an increasing amount of evidence about children's pre-school learning which reveals that very young children, growing up in an environment where they are surrounded by print, have absorbed a good deal of knowledge about its purposes and have developed logical hypotheses about how the system works. Teachers who are interested in this early development might like to look at the work of Glenda Bissex (*GNYS AT WRK*), Shirley Payton (*Developing Awareness of Print*), Ferriero and Teberosky (*Literacy Before Schooling*) and at *Awakening to Literacy*, ed Goelman, Oberg and Smith. Details of all of these are given in the Bibliography on page 189.

In our society print is part of our everyday lives. It is in the street on advertising hoardings, signs and notices, in the supermarket on packaging, shelves and posters, on the television screen in advertisements and as part of programmes, as well as in our homes.

Many people buy newspapers, magazines or books, but even if we do not choose to bring these into our homes ourselves, a huge quantity of printed material arrives unsolicited (free newspapers, advertising material, etc). In some communities the scripts of languages other than English may be even more visible: children growing up in such multilingual communities may bring to school a knowledge of and ability to write parts of other scripts as well as English.

Most children will have seen adults writing for a multitude of purposes, such as birthday cards, letters to keep contact with families and friends, shopping lists and reminders, filling in forms and ordering goods from mail-order catalogues. Children may have done many of these things alongside adults or on their own in play. All of this valuable knowledge is the foundation for children's learning in school and should not be disregarded. Liaison with parents and other care-givers will enable teachers to gain information about what their pupils do and are interested in at home. They may already visit a library regularly, 'help' with shopping lists, find things on supermarket shelves, be able to locate particular items or particular shops, make and write birthday cards for brothers and sisters, write letters to their grandparents, be able to write their names and much more. All of this is valuable information for teachers if they are to build on what children already know.

To build on children's existing knowledge of writing, teachers should consider the following points.

• Nursery and reception teachers can visit children and their families at home before the children start school. During these visits families could be invited to talk about their children's interest and involvement in literate activities like those mentioned above.

• Discussions with families can be initiated as an annual event as the children move through school, when discussion of current interests and enthusiasms can be included in reflection on wider issues.

• The children themselves, given the opportunity, will talk readily about their writing and reading at home, especially when it is related to popular toys and cartoons (eg Transformers, Teenage Mutant Hero Turtles, Batman). They will also, when encouraged, bring books and writing from home.

• Much information can be gained from observing children's play in the home-

corner, shops, cafe etc.

'The knowledge parents have of their child's development is indispensable in planning for further work.' (NCC Non-Statutory Guidance, 1:3).

Writing with children

'Pupils should see adults writing. Teachers should write alongside pupils, sharing and talking about their writing *eg. in journals, notes and diagrams*, **so that the range of uses of writing is brought out. Pupils should be made aware of how pieces of work they have produced relate to adult uses of writing' (5).**

Very often conscientious teachers spend hours of their time preparing beautiful displays in classrooms. Labels are written, captions and questions placed on the displays, so that when children come into the classroom the next day, it is all completed. If writing of this kind is carried out with the children, an enormous amount of discussion is generated about written language, about the way individual letters are written, about the things children notice.

Most labels and notices can be written with the children. Their comments and suggestions about what to write reveal much about their current understandings and knowledge and enable teachers to develop these within the context of writing for a real purpose.

An infant teacher writing a simple notice with which to label the book corner, was surrounded by a group of five-year-olds. The range of comments was very wide. 'That's my name,' said Brian, as the teacher wrote the first letter. The group then looked at all the names on the children's trays and found five 'B' names; they looked closely at the other letters and discovered that there were differences. Other children then identified letters in these names that were in their names.

When the teacher got as far as 'Boo . . .' one boy said, 'You did that already', pointing to the second 'o'; the teacher explained that sometimes there are two letters together like this and asked him if he had noticed another word in the room that had two 'o's. Very quickly he found 'look' on a notice inviting the children to 'look at these pictures'. When the teacher

reached 'o' in 'corner' the same boy spotted yet another 'o' and commented on it. Whilst she wrote, the teacher said the name of each letter, which many of the children repeated. At the end she read the notice and asked each of the children if they could read it; all, of course, could do so.

Later on that day the boy with an interest in 'o' insisted on showing his teacher other notices in the room that had the letter in: quite clearly he had been noticing throughout the day. He would probably not have done this had he not been one of the group writing the book corner notice.

Making labels and captions with the children not only saves time after school but also provides a relevant context for talk about letters and words. Situations like the one above capitalise on the children's curiosity about writing and allow the teacher to extend their knowledge, as well as to note what they already know. Perhaps most positively, having shared in the writing, children will be aware of labels and be able to read them.

Other forms of writing which are part of classroom business can be done with children.

- When they see their teacher writing a note to a colleague, and the teacher explains what she is doing, children will frequently begin a spate of writing notes to their friends.
- Teacher and children can work together on writing a letter of invitation from the whole class and in doing this another important aspect of writing is demonstrated. If children see an adult re-drafting, crossing things out, changing her mind, they will come to realise that 'mistakes' are not a crime, that they can be put right and that the final version may be the only one that is 'correct'.
- Other writing that is part of a teacher's job, such as recording observations and assessments of children, can often be done alongside the children. The teacher should explain what she is doing and discuss the contents with the child involved.

● Teacher and children can collaborate on making a poster to advertise a class or school event. This will lead to discussion about layout and about how important information can be emphasised.

● Price lists for a shop or café can be written collaboratively: this will also provide a context for talk about money and about appropriate items to include.

'Write alongside pupils'

If older children are involved in a 'writing workshop', a time may be set aside for the whole class to write on self-chosen topics. Often, within these sessions, the teacher will be involved in discussing pieces of writing with individual children, preparing them for publication, or simply encouraging the less confident writers. It is a good idea, especially if several children are writing on a similar topic, to join them occasionally and write something yourself. It is a salutary experience for teachers to write like this, to struggle with the first few sentences, to spend time thinking, to cross sections out and insert others, to make errors of spelling or punctuation, even to abandon the piece if it is not going well, and also to share their thinking and difficulties with the children, who can be extremely supportive and helpful. Watching their teacher write like this demonstrates to young writers that adults have many of the same difficulties and concerns as they do. The teacher's final version can be published or displayed alongside the children's and will certainly be read avidly.

Adult uses of writing

Author visits

Inviting a professional writer or illustrator into the classroom to talk about his work can be a particularly positive way of promoting writing. Some schools hold regular book events or book weeks when authors are invited to talk and this invariably has the positive effect of raising the children's level of interest in books and reading as well as writing. But author visits at other times can be just as positive and sometimes permit more extensive and deeper reflection on the role of the writer than is possible in the excitement of a book event. Both are certainly worthwhile and demonstrate to children one of the 'adult uses of writing'.

Many writers are prepared to bring with them earlier drafts of their writing to show how changes have been made and to explain why. They will often talk about how they set about writing (the physical situation as well as the tools they use), the time it takes to produce what seems a short text and the difficulties they sometimes experience. Some will also explain the stages and processes involved in publication and will show lay-out sheets, proofs etc. The children's interest will be particularly intense if the visiting author is one whose books the children are familiar with.

Not all professional writers write fiction or poetry and it can be fascinating to invite an information book writer to explain how such books are written and compiled and the particular demands of writing informational texts which are clear, concise and interesting. Children often find themselves that writing of this kind is more demanding than writing stories or poems and there is much to be learned from discussing their problems with a real writer.

The Children's Book Foundation (see Resources, page 192) which organises the National Children's Book Week, also produces a list of authors and illustrators who are willing to visit schools, together with details of what they will talk about or do. Local writers may be willing to visit a school regularly on a more informal basis and be prepared to work alongside children, helping them to produce their own books. The School Bookshop Association's Journal, *Books for Keeps*, also reports regularly on book events, author visits and book publication (see Resources, page 192).

Writing books for publication is one adult use of writing, but there are very many others. Often many of the activities children undertake in school are purely school uses of writing, for example, doing comprehension exercises, writing about a topic so that the teacher can check on what appears to have been learned. It is important that the writing we ask children to do has a real purpose and that we demonstrate the ways in which school writing relates to the real world. There are so many real reasons to write that artificial ones should rarely be needed.

Many adult uses of writing will be experimented with in play – in shops, home-corners and other role-play activities. Many others will arise from the business of the classroom – notes, letters, journals etc.

Children will often need to discuss with adults the best ways of doing particular pieces of writing and teachers will need to make explicit the need for clarity in writing that is intended to communicate something to a reader.

● Examination of instruction leaflets for equipment or for games in the classroom can lead to discussion of the need for clear explanations and about the best way to present information. Children will then be able to write their own instructions, for example, for games they have made up.
● Looking at recipe books or 'how to make' books will help children write their own recipes or instructions more clearly, especially if time is given to discussion about order, sequence of steps or explicitness.

Media issues

One of the most important contemporary adult uses of writing is for advertising, news, television, radio, and film. *English for Ages 5-16* stresses the importance of media education 'to increase children's critical understanding of the media'. Topics such as the selection and presentation of news and persuasive advertising will be dealt with in much more depth in the later stages of the English curriculum, but even young children can begin to see how writing can persuade as well as inform.

Children and teachers can bring printed advertising material and perhaps also video taped advertisements into school. They can use these to promote discussion about the language of advertising and how advertisements persuade.

● One class of top infant and first year junior children had made up their own board games on a wildlife theme. As well as writing instructions for how their game was to be played, they made advertising posters and scripted television commercials to promote them. Before they did this they looked at advertisements in magazines, talked about commercials they knew and discussed how the writers attracted attention and how their choice of words to describe the game could make it sound exciting. In doing this, they began to see how written and spoken language can achieve a desired effect and can persuade readers and listeners. Many of their own advertisements reflected accurately the methods of professionals. The activity certainly raised their awareness of the ways in which language can be used to create particular images.

• Some older junior children (Year Four), working on their own newspapers, looked at the way in which different newspapers reported the same event, an incident that had occurred locally but which was reported nationally. They analysed the way reporters had selected different aspects of the incident to emphasise, looked at the accuracy and truth of the reporting and at the headlines used to introduce the item. This group was more critical, thereafter, of reports in newspapers and they spent much time discussing their own reports before agreeing what would be published.

• A group of first year junior children (Year Three) had great fun making up their own advertisements for well-known products. They selected the products and produced a recommendation from famous users of the products. These included footballers, television and pop stars, politicians and cartoon characters. Some advertisements were produced as written material, others were performed as on television.

Other methods of composition

'Pupils should be encouraged to compose at greater length than they can manage to write down by themselves, by:
• **dictating to their teacher or another adult, or into a tape recorder; or**
• **working with other children; or**
• **using a word processor. Pupils should be able to produce copies of work drafted on a computer, and be encouraged to incorporate the print-out in other work, including displays' (7).**

Dictating to an adult
When a teacher is working with a class of 25 or more young children, it is often difficult to find time on a regular basis for this invaluable activity. This is one area in which other adults could become involved. Ancillary staff and parents working in the classroom will usually be pleased to

undertake the role of scribe for children.

We often under-estimate what children are able to achieve in the composition of texts, because the sheer physical effort and concentration required for young writers to write down a long story or account stifles their creativity. Young children's ability to compose narrative texts is often overlooked. When they are given the opportunity to dictate, they show that they know much more about the construction of stories than they are able to demonstrate through their own transcription. Through dictation they can be given the chance to experience the satisfaction of producing a completed story, which can itself act as a spur to further composition and writing. The author of a story is usually able to read her own text because she knows what it says, even if she is at the earliest stage of reading and would not normally be able to read a text of similar length or complexity. This, too, will give beginner readers confidence in themselves as readers and will support their efforts to tackle published books.

Dictating into a tape recorder
Dictating into a tape recorder can be both a preparation for writing and a way of composing a finished text, which can be written or typed up as a book, either by a teacher or a volunteer.

A version of a story or an account can be dictated on to a tape as a first draft of the piece. This version can then be discussed and edits or additions considered before the composition is committed to paper.

A group of seven-year-olds had become fascinated by ghost stories and spent a story-telling session one afternoon telling each other ghostly stories. The following day the teacher invited them to dictate their stories on to tape. These second versions were already better developed, contained more detail, more explicit setting and description. The children played these taped stories to each other and they commented on each other's stories. Finally, each child wrote down a version of his story, to make a class book of them. These final versions, incorporating many of the listeners' suggestions, were carefully crafted and showed a more conscious build-up towards a climax. A great deal had been learned about what was needed in a good 'scary story' from this whole undertaking, which lasted several days. The children were learning about writing and learning to be writers, but they did not put pen to paper until the very last stage.

Another context in which the use of a tape recorder can be invaluable is the composition of play scripts, for a puppet play, for example. A script can be tried out on tape before a final version is decided upon for performance. Young children can compose far longer, more complex scripts working in this way, than they can do if they have to write it all down.

Working with other children
Collaboration with other writers can be a most powerful spur to the creation of a written text. As Smith (1983) says, 'The ability to write alone comes with experience and is not always easy or necessary.'

Working with others enables some children to share in the composition of a text which they could not possibly have completed alone. Sometimes children need the opportunity to discuss their on-going work with others. At other times the whole composition may be a collaborative enterprise, when the children each make suggestions, extend each other's ideas and discuss the composition as they proceed. They may take it in turns to write down what they want to say, so that the sheer physical effort required does not become too great for one partner.

Partnerships between young children and older pupils can be particularly fruitful, especially if the older ones are encouraged to be supportive and listen to their younger partners, rather than impose ideas on them. Some schools have developed the idea of writing workshops, when older juniors regularly spend time writing with younger children. The

satisfaction and enjoyment experienced by both age groups has stimulated much excellent writing which is published within the school for all to read (see also Shared writing on page 136).

Using a word-processor
The use of a word-processor releases all writers from the tiring physical effort necessary for writing by hand. When young children are beginning to write, the concentration and physical control needed to put ideas on to paper are so great that it is surprising that most of them do persevere! The use of word-processors in classrooms will encourage hesitant, anxious writers to take risks with their writing, knowing that it can easily be changed or corrected later, leaving no trace of the original errors, as well as to compose at greater length. First drafts can be worked on, lines or words removed or inserted, before a print-out is made. It is also possible to print out a first draft which can be worked on away from the computer. Children can work alone or collaborate at the keyboard to produce their writing.

Although initial production of writing in this way may be slow, as the children become more familiar with the keyboard and with the functions of the program, they will be able to work faster. Because working at the word-processor keyboard is more exciting and interesting than struggling with their own handwriting, children are prepared to persevere with it and the slow pace does not seem to hinder creativity. In fact, young children, who have fewer anxieties about using computers and who are strongly self-motivated, learn very quickly to master the keyboard, provided they are given plenty of opportunities to use it.

None of these suggestions for enabling children to compose at greater length than they could do unaided is meant to imply that children should not be taught handwriting. There is a separate Attainment Target for Handwriting and it does need to be taught and practised, though this is better done at a time when

the child can concentrate on the skills of handwriting and not when she is also working on the task of composition.

'Pupils should be able to produce copies of work drafted on a computer and encouraged to incorporate the print-out in other work, including displays' (7c). Work drafted on a word-processor does not need to be 'copied out neatly' as it is already legible. Printers can produce multiple copies of the texts created, allowing children who have worked collaboratively to have individual copies and allowing easy publication, either in books, of which several copies can be made, or in displays.

Class or school newspapers can be compiled from print-outs of short individual items, then laid out, as a real newspaper would be, by an editorial team. There are several newsdesk-type programs available now which enable a more professional appearance to be given to school newspapers, but it is possible to obtain very effective results using only a conventional word-processor program.

Displays incorporating well-placed computer print-outs, both as integral parts of the display and as labels or explanations, are not only easy to read, but also demonstrate publicly children's skill as word-processor users and one aspect of the school's commitment to information technology.

A range of writing

'Pupils should:
• **undertake a range of chronological writing including some at least of diaries, stories, letters, accounts of tasks they have done and of personal experiences, records of observations they have made,** *eg. in a science or design activity*, **and instructions,** *eg. recipes*;
• **undertake a range of non-chronological writing which includes, for pupils working towards Level 2, some, at least of lists, captions, invitations, greetings cards, notices, posters and, for pupils working towards Level 3, plans and diagrams, descriptions . . . and notes for an activity . . .**
• **play with language, for example by making up jingles, poems, word games, riddles, and games which involve word and spelling patterns' (9).**

Playing with language

From a very early age, long before schooling begins, children love to play with language. Listen to a toddler playing with sounds and words in a cot, prior to going to sleep; listen to a two- or three-year-old, engrossed in play, repeating phrases, words, patterns of sounds; listen to a four-year-old struggling to make up a rhyme and resorting to nonsense words which retain the sound pattern, or the four-year-old attempting to make up a joke or pun; listen to the playground rhymes and songs and the endless 'Knock-knock' jokes of school-age children. All of these demonstrate children's natural inclination to play with language. Much of this enthusiasm is ignored in school, which emphasises the seriousness of learning about written language. But this interest could be channelled and capitalised on in the classroom.

Jingles and poems

There are not many children who do not know at least some of the advertising jingles from television, for they are usually easily memorable.

• Discussion about those that they know will help children see how they are made up of rhyme, rhythm and repetition. Given the opportunity and purpose children can make up their own, to act as reminders of class activities, or to 'advertise' class entertainments or activities.

• Making up rhymes and songs is an enjoyable activity and a way of focusing on patterns in language. Many children's books are written in rhyme, so there are many models available.

A group of five-year-olds made up these rhymes about a mouse, following the model in one of their favourite books, *My Cat Likes to Hide in Boxes* by Eve Sutton:

The mouse from Japan,
Met a man.
The mouse from India,
Rode a reindeer.
The mouse from Berlin,
Loved to sing.
The mouse from Wales,
Liked to pick up shells,
But Freddie (the mouse) likes it in our classroom.

Their teacher wrote down their compositions and made them into a classbook that all could read. In the process of composing, much discussion was generated about rhyming words as well as about spelling. The teacher pointed out letter combinations that were the same, such as Japan/man, Berlin/sing, and that were different, such as India/reindeer.

Poems do not have to rhyme, but they do need a rhythm or a pattern, and children need to hear poetry read to them often if they are to appreciate this for themselves. Familiarity with other writers' poems frequently inspires young writers to compose their own. They will try out not only the form but also the subject-matter. Hundreds of children have been inspired to write about incidents or people in school after they have read Allan Ahlberg's *Please*

Mrs Butler, or about brothers and sisters, things people say, their rooms, quarrels etc after reading Michael Rosen's work. Rosen himself has recently written about getting children to write poetry in *Did I Hear you Write?*, which has many valuable suggestions for starting points, for word games, riddles, jokes, shape poems etc.

Word games and riddles

The simplest forms of word games, like I-Spy, can be an enjoyable means of learning about initial letters and sounds:

• Extensions of this kind of activity are the creation of tongue-twisters or comic alphabets. For example, a group of six-year-olds made up an alphabet using their names, seeking the most unlikely and amusing activities:

'Ali asked Aunty Ann for apples,
Becky brought baby a big balloon,
Carly carried crispy Christmas cakes,
Donna danced on dented drums,
Ewan eats eleven elephants every evening.'

The finished alphabet was illustrated and displayed delightedly in the corridor for all to see.

• Written word games like search-a-word, crosswords, jumbled names and hangman are fun to make up for friends and require a good deal of thought and checking of spelling.

• There needs to be frequent discussion about words, constant drawing of attention to curiosities, word families and patterns in words to sustain and encourage children's interest in language. Children who are fascinated by words will be adventurous with them. For example, a class of first year juniors made a collection of all the words that could be used instead of 'said': cried, shouted, whispered, answered, replied, hissed, bellowed, argued, sobbed, joked. Having been made aware of the new variety of possibilities, this group were constantly on the look out for new ones in their reading. At the last count over 50 had been entered on the chart on the wall and many children were trying them out in their writing.

Shared writing

'Pupils should write individually and in groups, sharing their writing with others and discussing what they have written, and should produce finished pieces of work for wider audiences (eg stories, newspapers, magazines, books, games and guides for other children)' (10).

Although children need to write on their own sometimes, not only to produce texts that will be read by others, but also so that they can use writing as a way of organising their thinking (as in journals, writing to plan, to record observations), they also need to work regularly with others. As Smith (1983) says: 'Especially when writing is being learned, there is often a great need for and advantage in people working together on a letter, poem or story.' The advantages are many:

● Collaborative writing requires discussion, ideas and suggestions will be challenged and discussed with the group, so children will need to explain and justify a point of view so that others can understand.

● The requirements of a particular piece of writing are often made explicit during discussion.

● Writers can draw on each others' knowledge and strengths.

● Working together, children will often be able to produce longer, more complex texts than they could do alone and thus experience great satisfaction from their achievement.

● Transcriptional problems can be shared and spelling, expression or punctuation discussed.

There are many contexts, too, in which collaboration can be fruitful. Shared writing sessions, either with or without a teacher or other adult, can provide a supportive context for young writers.

The adult scribe
One way of introducing shared writing is for an adult to act as scribe for a text

which is composed by a group of children. This may be a retelling of a familiar story, a development of a story, a letter, an account of a visit or an activity or a response to a story or TV programme. It is easiest to use large sheets of paper placed on an easel, the floor or a table where the whole group can see what is written down.

A session may begin with a general discussion about what is to be written, or a brainstorming of ideas. The focus of a particular session will depend on the teaching points the adult hopes to include. It may be that the teacher wishes to make explicit the characteristics of a particular genre (eg fairy story, factual account, report), to encourage the forms of written rather than spoken language; to demonstrate that texts can be edited, revised, changed and improved; to show how ideas can be organised into a cohesive whole; to demonstrate transcriptional details (eg directionally, the use of full stops, question marks, inverted commas) or to focus on particular spelling patterns. There may be considerable overlap between any of these, but it is unlikely that any one piece of shared writing will be used for all of them simultaneously.

By writing with an experienced writer children take on the role of apprentices, contributing what they know and can do and receiving support and encouragement in areas where knowledge and skills are still developing.

Several sessions may be needed to complete a text and the re-reading and reviewing as each session begins may, in itself, lead to revisions and changes as the children listen and respond as readers to what has been previously written. Obviously shorter texts such as lists, plans or letters will usually be completed in one session and will not require as much revision.

Completed stories and accounts can be published as either large or small format books and these provide material for children to read which is both accessible, in the sense that those who wrote it know the text, and relevant to the readers.

As well as 'teaching' in these sessions, teachers are able to observe individual children and note competencies, as well as take note of those children who seem to need support with particular aspects of writing. Teachers are able to encourage the less confident children to make a contribution and ensure that they are heeded by others in the group. Occasionally a group may be set up for a particular purpose, such as a group of less confident writers or a single-sex group, so that the teacher or scribe can offer support.

After working in this way with an adult, children will often be able, depending on their age, experience and level of confidence, to work in groups on their own. Certainly, as they gain more experience of working collaboratively, they will become more capable of working without a teacher present all the time.

Group conferences
Sessions involving sharing individual writing with a group and inviting comments and suggestions from peers will need guidance to begin with, but as children become used to listening to each other's work, they can be very supportive to one another. This approach is one used by teachers who worked with Donald Graves and there are useful strategies for helping children offer positive comments in accounts of this work (Graves, *Writing: Teachers and Children at Work* and Calkins, *Lessons from a Child*).

Response partners
This is an idea which developed during the work of the National Writing Project. A pair of friends who trust one another can regularly share their on-going writing, inviting each other to respond as readers and to suggest improvements or places where the writing needs to be more explicit or something made clearer. They may also use each other to check spelling, punctuation and expression prior to publication of a final version.

Responding to stimuli

'Pupils should be asked to write in response to a range of well-chosen stories, poems, plays or television programmes' (11).

Writing in response to a teacher's demand for a response can be both tedious and unproductive. How often has it been said to children, after they have enjoyed a visit from a TIE company, or watched a TV programme, or been on a successful visit outside school, 'Now . . . I want you to write about it'? This, for some children, is so much a part of the routine, that they will actually ask, in the middle of the experience, 'Miss, have we got to write about it?'. Not only does this diminish their enjoyment of the activity, but the resultant writing is frequently a mundane listing of events with no real response at all.

As with all other forms of writing, children are likely to write best if they have a clear idea of the purpose and audience for the writing. A 'response' does not have to be 'an account of': a response can take many forms:

• Many children keep a record of responses to books they have heard or have read themselves as a matter of routine. However, if there is a real reason for responding in writing for an audience, and if they are not required to write about every book they read, their writing is likely to be much more lively and to be fuller. Reviews of books that have been particularly enjoyed might be written in order to recommend them to others: a folder of these, kept in the book area, or changing displays on the wall near the books, serves a real purpose. If professional reviews are collected, they can be used alongside the children's as reference points for those choosing a new book or seeking out another they think they will like.

• A response to a story, play or poem may not be a straight review. It could be a reflection on the reasons why events in a story happened, or on some of the characters. It could be an alternative version or ending or an account of events that might occur after the end of the published story. It could even be a re-casting of the events from the point of view of a particular character.

• Enjoyment of a play or TV programme might encourage children to write a script of their own.

• A response to a poem might be to write a poem yourself on the same topic or theme – or even to respond in another medium altogether, in a painting or drawing.

• Visits from professional writers or performers can inspire particularly vivid writing. For example, Michael Rosen had visited this six-year-old girl's school and she was keen to write this account for the school magazine about the Book Week:

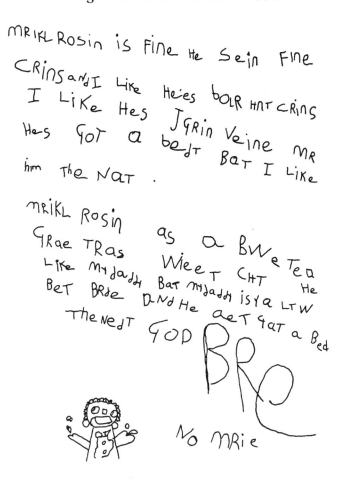

Translation: Michael Rosen is funny. He sings funny songs and I like his bear hunt song I like his juggling very much He's got a beard but I like him.
The end.
Michael Rosen has a blue T (shirt) grey

trousers white shirt He (is) like my daddy but my daddy is a little bit bald and he aint got a beard.
The end
Goodbye
No more

This was the longest piece of writing she had so far done, and it was completed in a short time immediately following the experience.

Children in another school were also producing a magazine about their Book Week, which included a performance, by ten- and eleven-year-olds, of 'Alice in Wonderland'. Some of the responses included these:

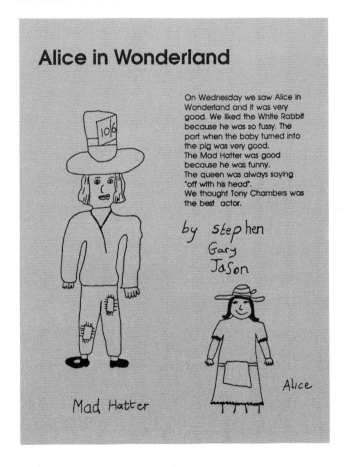

Alice in Wonderland

On Wednesday we saw Alice in Wonderland and it was very good. We liked the White Rabbit because he was so fussy. The part when the baby turned into the pig was very good. The Mad Hatter was good because he was funny. The queen was always saying 'off with his head'. We thought Tony Chambers was the best actor.

by stephen
Gary
Jason

Mad Hatter

Alice

These responses to the same event reveal some of the differences between the writing of seven-year-olds and that of an eleven-year-old.

The younger children reflect their involvement and appreciation by saying 'it was good' and selecting their favourite parts. Each of these is commented on in a short sentence. The organisation of the text is chronological in that the events

BEHIND THE SCENES

"SHUT UP!"

Was the pleasant reply to an very loud conversation between a gardener, a caterpillar, a mouse, a Royal child and a Queen of Hearts.

A varied conversation, yes, but since there were only a few members of W_____ School dressed and ready for the Brown Area's performance, it is not so unusual. Alice, played by ten year old Sophie Walker, nervously held out her hand to her sister, played by Lyn Walker, and impatiently waited for her cue. Soon the door to the dining room opened and in marched a row of doors, they came and went and to replace them came a crowd of animals, mostly extinct, led by a dodo played by Jonathan Novelli, all taking no notice of Mrs L., who was jumping up and down shushing everyone as quietly as she could manage without loudly exploding.

From then on all went smoothly. The end came, "Wake up Alice dear, what a long sleep you've had."

Then came the applause which, as any actor can tell you, makes it all worthwhile.

commented on appear in the order that they did in the performance, but the individual statements are discrete and do not produce a cohesive text.

The eleven-year-old has produced a more consciously crafted response. She has written an arresting opening which shows an understanding of the way to capture your audience. The whole text, constructed in complex sentences, reveals an awareness of the style of a review and a reflectiveness absent in the first piece. It makes no attempt to relate all the events but makes a judicious selection and tries to re-create the atmosphere 'behind the scenes', from the point of view of the actor. This account has cohesion and reaches a satisfying conclusion which reinforces the writer's viewpoint.

All of these children had an audience other than their teacher and something they wanted to say about an experience they had enjoyed.

There is no doubt that some stories, poems, plays and TV programmes will invite more enthusiastic responses than others. Literature offered to children must be carefully chosen by the teacher, building on their previous experiences, and judging the right time to introduce a particular writer. The teacher needs to be aware of what children have already encountered and to be knowledgeable herself about the wealth of children's literature that is available, including that from other cultures and from writers from a variety of ethnic groups. *English for Ages 5-16* stresses this latter point: 'Today, literature in English in the classroom can – and should – be drawn from different countries . . . English teachers should seek opportunities to exploit the multicultural aspects of literature' (7:5) and: 'The concept of "range" extends also – and very importantly – to social and cultural diversity . . . critical thinking about existing stereotypes and values can be stimulated by studying literature which expresses alternative points of view' (7:4).

Punctuation and grammar

'Pupils should discuss their writing frequently, talking about the varied types and purposes of writing, *eg. list, poem, story, recipe*. Teachers should talk about correct spelling and its patterns, about punctuation and should introduce pupils to terms such as punctuation, letter, capital letter, full stop, question mark' (12).

'Pupils should be taught to help the reader by leaving a space between words and by ending sentences with a full stop or question mark and by beginning them with a capital letter' (13).

'Pupils working towards Level 3 should be taught to recognise that writing involves:
● decision making – when the context (the specific situation, precise purpose and intended audience) is established;
● planning – when initial thoughts and the framework are recorded and ordered;
● drafting – when initial thoughts are developed, evaluated and reshaped by expansion, addition or amendment to

the text.

They should be taught to look for instances where:
● ideas should be differently ordered or more fully expressed in order to convey their meaning;
● tenses or pronouns have been used incorrectly or inconsistently;
● meaning is unclear because of insufficient punctuation or omitted words;
● meaning would be improved by a richer or more precise choice of vocabulary' (14).

'They should be taught, in the context of discussion about their own writing, grammatical terms such as sentence, verb, tense, noun, pronoun' (15).

All of these sections direct us to think of ways in which children can be encouraged to review, re-draft or 'correct' their writing, to discuss its spelling, punctuation and grammar. The least intimidating and most positive context for encouraging reflection is a writing conference: 'Teachers have found that pupils' understanding and use of style, form, presentation, vocabulary, punctuation and spelling are best developed through discussion of the pupils' written work.' (*English for ages 5-16* 3:14).

Writing conferences

Teachers of the youngest children will be used to talking with their pupils both while writing is being done and afterwards, and the children will be used to talking about what they have written. In the earliest stages the talk is most likely to be about the child's intentions and about how her meaning can be represented. If, at this stage, children's confidence in themselves as writers is boosted, they will continue to share their ideas and be ready to develop suggestions from teachers. But, if they are told only about their 'mistakes', they can become reluctant to say much and will wait passively for corrections. It can be difficult to rebuild confidence once children have learned to expect this latter response.

One strategy for beginning a discussion about a particular piece of writing is to invite the child to talk about what she has written before the writing is referred to. Often more detail will be offered orally than has been committed to paper, so the child will be able to see for herself where improvements might be made or detail added.

In responding to a piece of writing it is important to begin with what the child has said or tried to express and then to invite expansion of ideas, discuss clarity of expression, the need for explanation and explicitness, related to the writer's intention. It often helps to make a note of places where amendments might be made, so that the writer is reminded of the discussion when re-drafting a piece.

Consideration of clarity and 'helping the reader' may lead to discussion of punctuation, appropriate use of full-stops, question marks and capital letters. Teachers should be aware of when a child is ready to understand the need for demarcation of sentences in written language. Spoken language, however fluent, does not emerge in sentences and, until a young writer begins to appreciate some of the differences between spoken and written language she will not be able to 'hear' sentences.

Discussion of spelling will certainly arise as writers reach a final draft of what they want to say. Most children are remarkably adept at identifying where their spelling errors are, even if they cannot correct them without help from a teacher, a word-list or a dictionary. Even at the earliest stages children are aware of what they know, and can prepare for discussion about spelling by marking their text in some way.

This six-year-old has followed the suggestion of his teacher to underline words he thinks he needs help with:

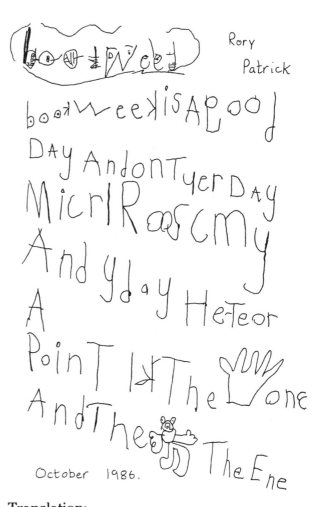

Translation:
Book week,
Book week is a good
day and on Thursday
Michael Rosen came
And yesterday he told
a
poem. I like the HAND one
and the BEAR.
The end

This seven-year-old has been asked to circle those words he is unsure about:

Both are remarkably accurate.

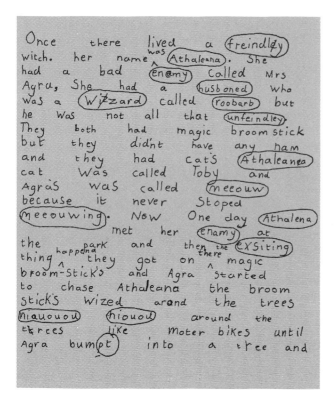

It is inevitable that, in discussion of writing, teachers will gradually introduce more of the terminology required to talk about written language. At the very earliest stages they will use vocabulary such as 'letter', 'word', 'space', 'capital letter', and 'alphabet'. Later, terms such as 'sentence', 'full stop', 'question mark', 'heading', 'word ending', 'tense', 'noun', and 'verb' are likely to be required. Teachers will need to observe and judge carefully when it is appropriate to introduce terms to children. There is nothing to be gained from attempting to teach definitions of terms like 'noun', 'verb' or 'adjective' outside any context: 'Terms should not be introduced through drills' (*English for ages 5-16*, 5:16).

Clearly not every piece of writing can be discussed in detail with every child: indeed such discussion of writing that has been done for planning purposes, journals or notes, would be quite inappropriate.

'Teachers should encourage children to bring different expectations to different tasks. Notes made during a scientific

investigation may not need sharing or drafting.' (English for Key Stage 1, Non-Statutory Guidance 12.9, page C17).

Often ideas, and even transcriptional details can be discussed between the children themselves.

It is important, however, for teachers to discuss writing with children on a regular basis, and to record observations of children's learning, knowledge and developing skills from such conversations. These notes will form the basis of planning for future writing activities to extend the children's range of writing.

Sometimes discussions may be of a more general nature. They will depend on the stage the child has reached and may include:
● The child's feelings about writing;
● What she sees as her strengths;
● Where there are difficulties;
● What kinds of writing she most enjoys doing;
● Whether she likes to work alone or with others and why;
● Which particular piece of writing she is most proud of;
● How she would like the teacher to help;
● Where she most likes to write – at home or at school.

These responses too, need to be notes as part of the teacher's formative record.

Attainment Target 4: Spelling

'As they become familiar with the conventions of writing, pupils should be introduced to the most common spelling patterns of consonants and short vowel sounds. Pupils should be taught how to spell words which occur frequently in their writing, or which are important to them, and those which exemplify regular spelling patterns. They should be encouraged to spell words for themselves and to remember the correct spelling, *eg. by compiling their own list of words they have used. They should be taught the names and*

order of the letters of the alphabet' (8).

Learning to use the conventional spellings of words is clearly an important part of learning to write. It is significant, however, that the National Curriculum for English designates a separate Attainment Target for Spelling up to Level 4 and 'Presentation' after Level 4. This separation of 'Writing' and 'Spelling' serves to remind teachers that learning to spell is only a part of the process of learning to write.

Children who are taught with a heavy emphasis on correct spelling often believe that learning to write is about learning to spell. When they are asked whether they are good writers these children respond with comments such as:
'Bad – my spellings are wrong.'
'Yes – I can spell hard words.'
'I get the words in my head and spell them wrong.'
'I can't do hard words.'
'The easiest part of writing is the words you can spell.'
(Source: 'National Writing Project')

If young writers become over-anxious about spelling, they will often try to avoid writing 'in case it's wrong'. There can be nothing more discouraging for a child, who has spent a long time writing a story or account, than to have her work 'marked' and returned for 'correction' covered in the teacher's crossings out, corrections of spellings, or underlinings accompanied by 'Sp' in the margin, and with little or no comment on her ideas. When children's writing is evaluated in this way they learn quickly that they cannot spell and begin to perceive themselves as poor writers. They may avoid being 'adventurous with vocabulary choices' (Programmes of Study for Key Stage 2) and stick to words they think they can spell correctly.

It is far more positive and encouraging for the teacher to focus on how near the child has come to the conventional spelling, on how much the child does know, rather than to cross things out. For example, the seven-year-old child who wrote 'fling sorser' for 'flying saucer' was very close to the conventional spelling of

'flying'. He may have omitted the 'y' because of its proximity to the 'i' of '-ing'. The teacher helped him by pointing out how close he was to 'flying', reminding him that he could spell 'fly', 'cry' and 'spy' and that '-ing' was simply added onto the end.

'Sorser', too, revealed a mastery of some letter patterns: he knew that one way of writing the sound in the first syllable is 'or'. He knew also how to represent the '-er' ending and he had used the most logical representation of 's' sound in the middle of the word – the soft 'c' is a much less frequent spelling than 's'. All of this the teacher pointed out to him and then helped him to learn the rather unusual spelling of 'saucer' by the 'Look, Cover, Remember, Write, Check' routine (see Non-Statutory Guidance 12:10, page C17).

Much has been revealed recently of children's hypotheses about spelling (see Clay, 1975; Temple, Nathan, Burris and Temple 1988; Bissex 1980; Read 1986 in bibliography) and 'Teachers will need to be aware of the steps which can be identified in learning to spell correctly . . .' (Non-Statutory Guidance 12:10). It does appear that most children move through observable stages as they progress 'from invented spelling towards conventional accuracy', if they are allowed the opportunity to try out their hypotheses.

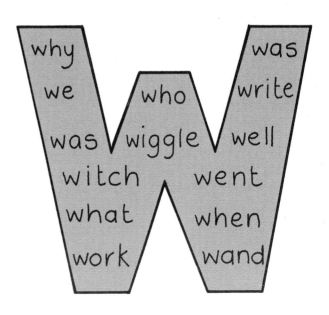

At the beginning their interest in letters, especially the letters in their names, needs to be encouraged. It is at this point that alphabet games, funny sentences, endless talk about letters and words, pointing out of letters, making links with the print all around them (eg 'M' of Macdonalds', 'S' of 'Safeway', 'BBC', 'BMX' . . .) need to be a regular part of classroom activity. The children's growing repertoire of letters and the sounds associated with them will then be used as they try to write things down. They are likely to concentrate hard on representing what they hear, referring mentally to the sounds of words in their attempts to write them. They can be heard muttering to themselves as they write. At the earliest stages children will often use letter 'names' as well as 'sounds' to represent words.

Transcription:
A letter to the headteacher:
Dear Mr Griffiths
Mrs Torrino says can we read to you. She is very proud of us.

They may also, if they have been helped to see the shapes of words, be developing a 'sight vocabulary' of frequently used words, such as 'is', 'my', 'mum', 'and', 'the'.

Spellings like this provide much information for teachers and it is important that children are encouraged to 'have a go' at spelling, so that teachers can observe something of their thinking and of the strategies they are using.

'The invented spellings of the young child are usually quite simple to interpret because they show the use of logical and not conventional rules. Teachers can assess the child's level of understanding of the spelling system and give appropriate help.' (Non-Statutory Guidance, 12:10)

If children habitually copy the teacher's writing, or individual words given by a teacher, they will not have the opportunity to reveal what they know. They are also less likely to think about the way words are constructed or to pay attention to the patterns of letters in words. One of the problems associated with personal word-books in which teachers write words on request (apart from the time wasted in queueing for the teacher!) is that they encourage thoughtless copying, letter by letter, rather than helping children to see words as wholes. Of far more use is the strategy of the teacher writing the requested word, which the child looks at and attempts to memorise before going back to her writing and trying to write the word from memory. Teachers need to help children to see patterns in whole words by looking at word families – groups of words with similar spellings – and letter strings. The link should be the appearance of the word rather than its pronunciation, such as 'one – gone, bone, done, honey, money . . .'.

144

The aim should be to replace the 'sounding out' strategy with visual references.

There is considerable evidence (Cripps 1978, 1983; Peters 1985) that good spellers rely on visual memory, so it is visual strategies that must be encouraged and taught.

The Look, Cover, Remember, Write, Check routine (see Non-Statutory Guidance 12:10) has helped many children to learn conventional spellings:

- First the child looks at the written word.
- The word is then covered over.
- The child then attempts to remember the word.
- The word is then written from memory.
- This version is then checked against the original written word.
- If the word is correct, the child writes it once more to help establish the pattern.
- If the word is spelt incorrectly, it can be helpful to point out where the error lies before repeating the whole procedure, until a correct, remembered spelling is achieved. Usually not more than two or three attempts will be needed.

In classrooms where teachers and children are interested in words, where words are a source of fascination, children will learn to spell more readily. There are those who 'catch' spelling almost effortlessly, but others will need to be taught helpful strategies for learning.

Children need to be able to perceive likenesses and differences in things around them if they are to be able to perceive likenesses and differences in words. They can be helped to develop this skill through activities which encourage observation.

- Finding words within words. If there is print around them in the classroom, children will often initiate this for themselves. For example, a five-year-old girl noticed in the label for a display 'Our Favourite Books', that 'Our' at the beginning was in 'Favourite'. If the children do not notice such things by themselves, the teacher must start to point out such observations herself. The children will soon be finding examples too.

- The children's names are always of interest and are usually amongst the first words they recognise. Trays or drawers labelled with names will often be the focus of comment. For example, two children, aged five and six, were observed poring over the names on a pile of books. When their teacher asked what they were doing, they told her they had found a 'the' in Matthew and an 'and' in Sandra.
- Teachers can use name cards in many games. These could include grouping together those with the same initial letter, those with the same number of letters, or those with the same final letter. Other possibilities are putting words in order of length, looking for little words in the children's names (eg 'my' in Amy, 'am' and 'in' in Shamina, 'are' in Hareshi and Karen), and talking about unusual spellings (eg 'ph' in Joseph).

Once such activities have been initiated, children will start to look and to notice for themselves and will point out their observations to each other. Teachers need to point out similarities and differences whenever the chance arises. Every possible opportunity should be taken to develop and nurture this interest in words.

Supporting development

The Non-Statutory Guidance for English Key Stage 1 lists 'a variety of techniques (which) will support children's development towards mastery of spelling conventions'. These include the Look, Cover, Remember, Write, Check routine already described, and:

- 'reading with teacher and referring to print such as captions and lists in the classroom, in order to learn a range of words and practice them in their writing;
- composing stories with groups of children using large books providing examples of 'spelling in action', and discussing the words and their patterns;
- grouping words and looking for common letter clusters in books and magazines;
- encouraging children to recognise that there are strategies for learning to spell

words and that they should try to identify the word by the initial letter and look for the word in an alphabetical word bank or dictionary, or in a book where they know it appears, or ask another child;

• using 'spell checker' computer programmes to draw children's attention to the need for accuracy'.

Many of these activities link with others suggested for other aspects of the Programmes of Study and there will often be overlap between the focus on spelling and the other purposes of the activity.

Publication of their writing for wider audiences will help young writers see the need for standardised spelling. Most work on spelling will inevitably take place within the context of the children's writing and is therefore unlikely to be identifiable merely as 'spelling'.

The teacher's response to a piece of writing should, firstly, be to the content, to the message being communicated and not to the surface details of spelling, however inaccurate. Above all, it is important to encourage children to believe that they can write, that they will gradually learn more about spelling words in the conventional way and to offer support and useful strategies as they do so.

Attainment Target 5: Handwriting

'Pupils should be taught the conventional ways of forming letter shapes, lower case and capitals, through purposeful guided practice in order to foster a comfortable and legible handwriting style' (6).

The separation of handwriting as an Attainment Target, like spelling, reflects our growing understanding of the different processes involved in creating a written text. The surface features (orthography, punctuation and handwriting) must be attended to and taught, but they can only be developed if children have something to express in writing. Historically, emphasis has been on developing 'a good hand':

indeed, writing in English Elementary Schools at the beginning of the nineteenth century consisted only of copy-writing. Pupils were not expected to compose texts, merely to copy them out neatly, and were ultimately judged on their ability to write legibly and accurately from dictation. Despite the 'creative writing' movement, this view has persisted in some infant schools, where children have been taught more about the mechanics of writing than they have about its composition and purposes.

Vygotsky, writing in the 1930s, questioned this emphasis: 'until now, writing has occupied too narrow a place in school practice as compared to the enormous role that it plays in children's cultural development. The teaching of writing has been conceived in narrowly practical terms. Children are taught to trace out letters and make words out of them, but they are not taught written language.' Increasingly, teachers are striving to redress this balance. Writing is now less frequently viewed as just a complex motor skill; the practice of handwriting skills is generally separated from the task of composition, and many handwriting schemes have been revised in the light of this growing understanding.

Handwriting continues to be an important skill which should not be ousted by the growing use of modern technology: typewriters and word-processors are not always the most conducive medium for the expression of personal thinking.

There is also considerable evidence (Peters and Cripps, op. cit) which suggests that there is a link between the quality of a child's handwriting and spelling attainment. Some suggest that spelling is learned as much through the hand as through the eye and advocate that a cursive script is taught from the begining, so that joined letter patterns are established in a 'running hand'.

Clearly there is much to be considered when a school's handwriting policy is being constructed, but there can be no doubt that a cohesive policy providing

continuity and progression as children develop, is essential. 'Teachers should appreciate, however, that over-emphasis on formation is not effective and can damage children's confidence to write.' (Non-Statutory Guidance 12:11, page C18). There is a need to provide for 'purposeful guided practice'. Whether this is provided on an individual basis, in groups or with the whole class, will be a matter for teachers to decide, taking into account each child's level of development and control. It is important for teachers to be confident themselves in demonstrating the formation and joining of letters. Especially at the early stages, children will need to practise where teachers can observe the way in which they are writing so that mistakes can be corrected. If they are left to copy without supervision, pupils may establish habits which will be difficult to eradicate later. 'Teaching of handwriting can only be done effectively when the teacher can observe exactly what each child is doing, with an individual or in a small group.' (Non-Statutory Guidance 12:11, page C18). This is particularly so for left-handed children who are likely to need considerable assistance in positioning of paper, pencil grip, and the angle of their writing, if they are not to develop idiosyncratic ways of holding a writing implement in order to see their script.

Attention will also need to be given to the range of implements available for children to write with and paper for them to write on. Rosemary Sassoon (1983) suggests using small pieces of paper for both pattern practice and writing practice for small children, in order to ensure 'the writing arm is neither unduly stretched or cramped'. She also points out that both the point and the handle of the writing implement should be appropriate to the size of the child's hand: the habit of offering fat pencils to infant children makes it harder for them to write with control. 'Ordinary pencils, or extra-thin ones are far easier to manage at 5 years old.' (Sassoon, op. cit). In many respects fibre-tipped pens are more suitable implements for beginner writers because they move more smoothly over the surface of the paper.

The question of whether children should use plain or lined paper for their writing invariably provokes disagreement. Certainly, in the early stages, the use of lines introduces an additional difficulty for the beginner and most teachers feel that plain paper is more appropriate. As children acquire greater control they can be expected to use either kind of paper or line-guides, depending on the purpose of the writing.

These examples of handwriting from third year junior children (Year Five) were done as part of their regular handwriting practice. In their school, from Reception right up Year Six, all children spend a short time each day on handwriting practice. Teachers try to suggest interesting formats and contexts for this, so that practising does not become a meaningless chore.

These two pieces were written inside leaf and fruit shapes, on plain paper over line guides, using fibre-tipped handwriting pens. They were beautifully mounted and formed part of a display of work for the harvest celebrations. In this way status is given to good handwriting without the children having to concentrate on it whilst they are attempting to compose texts.

After some years of neglect, the National Curriculum has placed handwriting firmly back on the agenda for primary schools, but has equally firmly separated it from the composition of written texts. Children do need to be helped to develop a legible personal handwriting style and time needs to be set aside for them to practise and to develop an interest and pride in the appearance of their work. Many, given encouragement, will develop a real interest in calligraphy and will spend many hours attempting to perfect a style. For older children investigating the history and development of different scripts, the ways in which handwriting has evolved through the use of different implements and encouraging calligraphy as a craft skill, may not only create enthusiasm for handwriting but also contribute to the children's interest in and knowledge about language.

Key Stage 2

According to the Programme of Study for Key Stage 2 **'Pupils should continue to have varied and frequent opportunities to write. They should know for whom they are writing, *eg. themselves (to help in their thinking, understanding or planning of an activity), their classmates, their teacher, younger children in the school, their parents or other trusted adults.* In writing for others they will learn that writing for a public audience requires more care to be taken with the finished product than writing for oneself as an aid to memory'** (16).

This requirement makes clear that the practices developed in Key Stage 1 should be continued into the junior or middle years. Children will have begun in Key Stage 1 by 'writing for a variety of purposes and audiences . . .', developing understandings about 'the range of uses of writing . . .' and 'talking about the varied types and purposes of writing'. This understanding and ability to differentiate and gear the writing to a particular audience will be refined in Key Stage 2. Here they will be able to consider quite carefully, for each piece of writing, its purpose and audience, and they will be aware of the differing requirements.

Many contexts will lead to a range of different kinds of writing. For example, a group of children recording observations of their pond-dipping will need:

- To keep notes and jottings as aids to memory for themselves;
- To order and expand the notes to use

149

them to repeat discoveries to their classmates;
- To write up an account to be included in either a display or a book being made to document changes in pond life or activity through the seasons, or an information book about a particular species;
- To refer to their notes in composing a letter to an outside body to request detailed information.

A class of eleven-year-olds made a study of the canal which ran alongside their school. The writing they undertook included:
- Notes, for themselves, of observations;
- Informal letters inviting parents to accompany them on a longer excursion on a canal boat;
- Letters to book the canal boat;
- Letters to the local historian requesting information about buildings observed in old photographs;
- Letters to the natural history museum asking for help in identifying an unusual plant;
- Individual and collaborative factual accounts of different aspects of their observations (eg commercial transport on barges and life on canal boats);
- Poems relating to the natural environment, to change over time and life in the past;
- Imaginative writing about life in earlier times in the area;
- Lists of questions they wanted to ask older inhabitants about changes in the area;
- Factual accounts relating to what they learned from their interviews and their information searches;
- A collaboratively produced guide-book to the area, drawing on all they had learned and incorporating their photographs and drawings.

In each context the children knew the audience for the writing and demonstrated that they appreciated that care needed to be taken over writing for public audiences. The presentation of the finished products was of a very high standard.

Selecting topics

Extended topics or studies like the one above provide contexts for many of the elements of Detailed Provision 18: **'Pupils should use writing to learn, and to record their experiences in a wide range of classroom activities across the curriculum.'**

Many contexts for such a range of writing have been described for Key Stage 1. As they move into Key Stage 2 and are able to work more independently across the whole curriculum, children will need to be offered an increasing range of experiences and activities. As they become more able to undertake research independently, both from books and through first-hand observation, teachers will need to create a stimulating environment rich in possibilities, from which writing for real purposes arises and can be developed.

Teachers must plan for many kinds of writing in their selection of a theme or topic. The Non-Statutory Guidance for Key Stages 1-4 (June 1990) gives several examples of topics or centres of interest to show how teachers might plan work which crosses the boundaries of both the language modes (speaking, listening, reading and writing) and curriculum areas.
- Storytelling (Key Stages 1 and 2);
- Folktales (Key Stage 2);
- Names and terms (Key Stages 1 and 2);
- Local community (Key Stage 2);
- Taking photographs (Key Stage 1);
- The local area (Key Stage 2);
- The visit (Key Stage 1).

A variety of chronological writing, as well as non-chronological writing will arise from all of these topics, and from a multitude of other themes.

Non-chronological writing

Children should: **'be helped to understand that non-chronological types of writing can be organised in a variety of ways and so, generally,**

require careful planning; this might include the presentation of information or imaginative prose' (18c).

One of the difficulties for young writers in creating texts that are not accounts of events (fictional or factual), which follow each other chronologically, is that they have no set framework. They have to devise a way of organising what they want to say as well as make decisions about what to include. Very young writers often write down everything about the topic in no particular order and thus produce texts that jump around from one aspect to another and lack cohesion.

Analysis of the following piece of writing shows some of the problems teachers will observe.

This factual, non-chronological writing from a boy in Year Six is an account, arising from his research relating to the topic of 'Sight'. It accompanied a labelled diagram of the eye.

> The human eye
>
> The eye is one of the most important things in your body : part of your eye is the cornea which protects the eye. The iris is the coloured part and the pupil is an empty hole in the middle of your eye. It lets in light which goes through the lens and focusses on to the retina. The retina is at the back of the eyeball. The message is sent to the brain through the optic nerve and the brain makes sense of it. When you close one of your eyes the other pupil gets bigger because it lets in more light. When you look at some thing it looks upside down: the picture goes to your eye upside down and the brain turns it up the right way. There are different coloured eyes in the world. Blue eyes have less coloured pigment than brown eyes. There is a blind spot where the optic nerve is. There are muscles holding the eye in it's right place. The eye is being washed all the time: when you cry the water comes so fast that the eye can't handle it all so it lets it out. The eye is shaped like a ball.

The writer has been fairly successful in organising his factual information. He has used correct terminology and has attempted to organise the writing by recording a piece of information about each named part. However, he has not maintained this throughout the piece; the information relating to eye colour interrupts his 'listing' and after this he adds further information about previously mentioned parts.

Teacher intervention would help him to understand and to try out one particular organisational structure. He could be shown how to use headings and sub-headings as a way of grouping together his statements.

After the opening sentence, the general points about the eye could be collected together (ie its shape, the muscles holding it, the tears washing it and the colour).

Then, using the heading 'Parts of the Eye', sub-headings could be used to keep related information together logically.

It is not the topic or factual writing as such that causes the problems, as this short piece by a boy in Year Three recording his experiment with a candle clock, shows. As this account is chronological (literally!) he has no difficulty in structuring his writing.

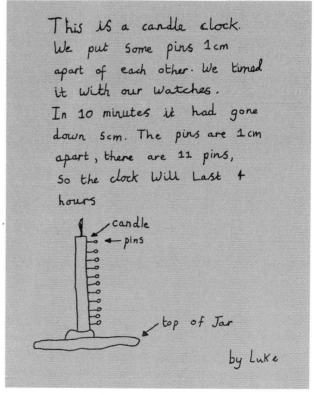

> This is a candle clock. We put some pins 1cm apart of each other. We timed it with our watches.
> In 10 minutes it had gone down 5cm. The pins are 1cm apart, there are 11 pins, so the clock will last 4 hours
>
> candle
> pins
> top of Jar
>
> by Luke

Descriptive writing

'Children should read good examples of descriptions, explanations, opinions, etc and be helped to plan and produce these types of writing by being given purposeful opportunities to write their own' (18d).

This explicit linking of reading experiences with children's ability to compose particular kinds of texts reinforces the notion of 'modelling' or 'demonstrations'. The most experienced readers will absorb from what they read, ways of organising and structuring particular written forms. It is vital, therefore, that the written examples they read or hear being read, are of good quality.

Many information books offer inadequate models of explanations or descriptions. Older children, if they have encountered good models are able often to rewrite such texts more effectively.

This writer, a boy in Year Five, has located clearly written information to answer his queries about a bottle he found on a country walk. He is able to use this in his own piece most effectively.

Hamiltons

On our walk we found an old bottle with a rounded bottom. Mr Laverty thought it was a baby's bottle but I didn't think it was so we argued. When I got home I got out a book about bottles and from our bottle collection a bottle the same as the one found in the woods. I looked it up and found out some things about it. They had rounded bottoms as they could not be stood up as the gas would shrink the cork. These bottles were called 'Hamiltons'. Later Mr Codd developed another bottle, also for lemonade, but this had a flat bottom and there wasn't a cork, instead a marble. Not many of these survived as children smashed them to get the marble out.

An extremely rare type had an oval marble. The name 'codd swallop' came from these bottles and their maker.

F. CHITTY

CHICHESTER - BRIGHTON

The writer of the following explanation, another boy in Year Five, has imitated the language of a guide book:

'Blackgang is a small village on the South West coast of the Isle, and it gets its funny name from the smugglers who based themselves there in olden days. The bay below has always been dangerous to shipping and over 180 vessels have been wrecked there since 1750. Even in the last 10 years there've been eight ships stranded on the coast, ranging from a 10,000 ton cargo vessel to small yachts.

The word 'chine' is of Saxon origin and means 'a gorge or chasm leading to the sea.' From the entrance at the top of the chine there are paths going straight to the famous Observation Peak. That's 400 feet above the sea. From here you can get the best views in the island . . .'.

The same writer shows his ability to handle another form in this description:

'It took us about an hour to get to where we went today, which was the Brecon Beacons.

Fortunately when we woke up it was sunny so we were all very happy as we got ready for breakfast. After breakfast we got our things, found the coach and got on it. The sun was still shining when we arrived at the Beacons. They are called 'beacons' because, like other hilltops, all over the country, people used to light beacon fires to signal from one community to another. The Beacons are formed of old red sand stone and the area is high moorland which is only suitable for sheep.

While we were walking we saw quite a lot of sheep and I collected a bag full of lovely soft sheep's wool. There were no people on the hills – except us – and it was all very peaceful. We saw several different birds and flowers, especially violets, which were everywhere. One part was all purple because there were so many all together.

We stopped half way to have a picnic lunch and then carried on. About 15 of us went on to the top ridge – I think it's called a 'saddle' – with Mark, and he said we would get a certificate to say we had got there. I'm glad I got so high, even though I sprained my ankle again on the way back down.'

He is able to select parts of the whole experience (a walk on the Beacons) to convey both the visual appearance of the place and his response to it. He is drawing on his own reading experience of how professional writers create an image of a place through their descriptions.

A more elusive skill to develop in young readers and writers is the ability to distinguish between fact and opinion. Many older information books present the writer's opinion as fact. Discussion of books like these will help young writers differentiate between the two in their own writing. Newspapers are a useful source of opinion, as are professional reviews of books. Discussion of these kinds of texts will help to make explicit what is opinion and will provide models for the children's own written opinions.

The following example is of a book review written by a Year Five boy of *Holiday with the Fiend* by Sheila Lavelle.

'This book is funny because Angela always sees the funny side of life. Everything she describes is funny. The funniest thing in the book, I think, is when Angela wires drippy Julian up to cure his static problem and they left him there for over an hour. It started to rain and he got electrocuted (an electric shock). This book is exciting because of the tricks and the vocabulary is easy to read.

Each chapter is about Angela getting other people into trouble and the book is hard to put down because you want to know what the next chapter is about.

I recommend this book for 6-11 year olds.'

Writing letters

'Pupils should write personal letters to known recipients and be shown how to set them out' (18e).

There will be many opportunities for children to write letters in school, especially if they are asked to write on those occasions when a letter may previously have been sent by the teacher or headteacher:
● To give parents information about school events;
● To invite parents, families and other members of the community to school events or to be part of some class activity (eg to come and talk to them and share experiences).
● To firms, businesses, organisations for information (for example, a group of Year Three children wanted to know how the lead got into the middle of pencils, so they

wrote to a manufacturer for information. They received not only answers to their questions, but samples showing the whole process of manufacture, for which they then wrote letters of thanks);

• To children in other schools to compare experiences (for example, some children (Year Four) in an inner city school made contact with children of the same age in a small rural school through their teachers who knew each other. Exchanges of personal letters eventually led to reciprocal day trips);

• To authors or illustrators commenting on books they have enjoyed, asking questions about books or inviting an author to their school (for example, as part of a book week, formal arrangements had been made by a teacher for a visit from author/illustrator Caroline Holden. Two children then wrote to make the arrangements and received a delightful reply in response).

• When opportunities for real letters are not available, imaginative letters can be written. A class of Year Three children had been delighted by the letters in *The Jolly Postman* by Janet and Allan Ahlberg. Their teacher invited them to pretend they were story characters and to write to other story characters. Some children wrote in role, others wrote as themsevles. Dozens of letters were written commenting on the events of a story or asking questions.

Some of these were responded to by the teacher, also writing in role, to the children's further delight.

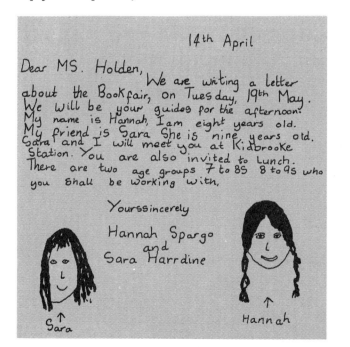

Dear Cinderella

I am sorry your sisters hit you, I bet they swore at you, too. I am happy you married the Prince.

Love
Rosna

14th April

Dear MS. Holden,
We are writing a letter about the Bookfair, on Tuesday, 19th May. We will be your guides for the afternoon. My name is Hannah, I am eight years old. My friend is Sara She is nine years old. Sara and I will meet you at Kidbrooke Station. You are also invited to Lunch. There are two age groups 7 to 8s 8 to 9s who you shall be working with.

Yours sincerely

Hannah Spargo and Sara Harrdine

Sara

Hannah

Dear BaBa BlackSheep,
            I thank you for your wool. I made my mother a nice jumper. It was black. She liked it very much, thanks to your wool. My mother think her jumper is very warm. I hope my jumper is a warm one, too ooo. Sorry about doing to many o when I writ too. I am not a good writer you can see that. I did a word wrong So thats why that big mark is there.
            Love from,
                        the Boy down the lane.

Dear B.F.G.,
            I would like a dream about abolition. I would like a nice dream. In My dream I would like to be on Holiday In Jamaica, with my mum and dad and my brother Jason. We are all sitting on the beach and it is sunny.
            Please can you send me this dream?
            Love from
                        Natasha.

155

Story form

Pupils should: **'be helped to increase their control of story form, through their experience of the stories they have read and heard, recognising, for example, that the setting and the outcome need to be made explicit to the reader'** (18f).

Children's familiarity with different story forms will almost always be reflected in their writing. Readers who have read many stories of a particular sort often unconsciously imitate their style. Older children are able to discuss the characteristics of particular forms of writing.

A Year Four class had been investigating the characteristics of well-known fairy stories (ie poverty to riches, three sons, magic, tests of worth, princesses etc). They contrasted these with some of the lesser known stories in which the central character was female (eg 'Clever Gretchen', 'Cap o' Rushes', 'Woman in the Moon'). They also read some of the more modern stories where the female characters are shown as having more initiative and resourcefulness (such as *The Paper Bag Princess* by Rober Munsch, *The Practical Princess* by Jay Williams, see Bibliography on page 189). Then they wrote their own story of each kind. One girl in Year Four wrote as follows:

'Not long ago there was a Spanish King and Queen. They had two daughters but they wanted one more daughter and their wish came true. They were so happy that they decided to give a splendid christening. The King and Queen were so excited that they couldn't keep it a secret, so they told the two beautiful older daugthers, Angela and Rosalie. But Angela and Rosalie were jealous so they made a plan. They worked all day trying to think of a plan, but they couldn't think of anything. The King and Queen didn't even notice because they were too busy getting ready for the christening.

Then it was the day for the christening and all the important people came. But someone unexpected came. It was Lucy, the Sorcerer. When it was time for the presents the Sorcerer, Lucy, went up to the baby and said, 'When she is 13 she will turn into a cat, because your grandmother, long ago, went into my garden of lovely fruit and took my fruit and she promised me that I can have her grand-daughter.

This is the spell I want to cast on her. And remember that I can see the future.'

And with that she disappeared, and it was followed by a laugh, 'Ha . . . Ha . . . Ha . . . I win this time'.

It was all silent and the first one to move was the Queen who fainted. Then the noise began to grow like this, 'Oh no . . . The Queen . . . What a shame . . . Bring the smelling things . . .'. And they all gathered round the Queen. The baby, whose name was Josie, cried gently. When the Queen came round she started crying, and then everybody was crying. There was a 'Sniff, sniff . . .' and a 'Boo . . . hoo' and a 'Woo . . . woo . . .' and a 'Sigh . . . sigh . . .'.

Josie grew up happily and beautifully. But when she was 13 she started to grow whiskers. Then she started to grow fur, until she looked like a cat. The King was very upset, so the story went all around the world and many Princes came to try and help the Princess Josie . . . .'.

In the rest of the story Josie asks all the princes a riddle: those that cannot answer correctly get their heads chopped off. Eventually one arrives who can answer and he is given three tasks to complete, one of which is to overcome Lucy the Sorcerer. He returns and is told to chop Josie's head off. Unwillingly, he does so and Josie changes from a cat back into a beautiful princess. They get married amidst great rejoicing.

The same writer produced a second story:

'Long ago there was a Princess called Grenda, but no ordinary princess. She was beautiful, of course, and she was intelligent, helpful and strong. And she had common sense. Now, she was going to marry Prince Perry, who was young, handsome and strong. But one day Prince Perry got kidnapped by the Princess of Strength. The Princess of Strength was beautiful as well as strong and Princess Grenda was cross. She rode off to see Maureen the Fairy.

When Grenda was at Maureen's palace she went inside to find Maureen. Grenda opened a big door and there was Maureen dressed in a silver gown all covered with jewels and Grenda was only wearing a plain grey dress.

At the palace, Grenda's father the King put an advert around the Kingdom saying, 'Whoever finds Princess Grenda can keep her. As the old legend says – Finders keepers, losers weepers.' . . .'

Grenda explains to Maureen the Fairy that she wants to get Prince Perry back and Maureen explains that she will have to overcome 'The Devil of Hotness, Fritter the Troll', that she must get 'a piece of the Snow Queen's Chair' to get herself into the 'Kingdom of Strength'. Once there, she had to defeat the 'Dragon Tod' to rescue her

Prince. Maureen gives her three wishes to help her when she is in difficulties. Grenda, of course, rescues her Prince from her rival and they marry and live 'happily ever after'.

These two very different stories reflect this young writer's understanding of the requirements of the different kinds of fairy story. She has absorbed the conventions and is able to use them in her own writing.

Many young children, if they are familiar with a range of stories, either through reading themselves or hearing them read aloud, are aware of what needs to be made explicit in a story. In dictating stories, they show understanding of the needs of the reader by providing details of setting, action and outcome. Because they are dictating they are able to concentrate on the creation of the story. At a later stage, when they are trying to write it all down for themselves, some of this explicitness seems to be lost. This is, perhaps, because they have to grapple with transcribing their ideas, as well as composing the story.

It is certainly true that often much of the setting and the action remains in the young author's head and does not get written down. It is usually not that they haven't thought about the details, but that they simply have not written them down. Answers to questions about where an event is happening, how characters got there, about loose ends at the conclusion of the story, often show that the necessary detail has been filled in, in the writer's mind, though not transferred to the page.

One way of showing children the need to make such settings and outcomes explicit, is to encourage them to work with response partners, who can ask questions when they do not understand and prompt inclusion of greater detail. Teachers can also do this, of course, but there is not likely to be the time available to spend long periods with each individual child, so it is a good idea to facilitate such collaboration and support amongst the children themselves.

Poetry

Pupils should:

'have opportunities to write poetry (individually, in small groups or as a class) and to experiment with different layouts, rhymes, rhythms, verse structures, and with all kinds of sound effects and verbal play' (18g).

Before children can be expected to write poetry, they must have had experience of reading or hearing a wide range of poetry forms. They will also need to have talked about rhyme, rhythm and alliteration. There are now many books available to teachers with ideas for introducing children to poetry. These provide many practical ideas for teachers who feel less confident with this form of writing themselves (see Bibliography, page 191).

Sometimes the starting point can be the children's reflections on their experiences, both in school and out, their fears, families and the environment. 'Angry' was written by a Year Four boy and 'Writing' by a Year Five boy.

> ## ANGRY
>
> Angry, Angry, Angry,
> throwing things around,
> ~~sp~~ staping hard as thunder,
> shouting very loud.
>
> Throwing out tantrums,
> Thumping on the Door,
> Pulling funny faces,
> Not very nice at all.
>
> ~~Pepo~~ People think I'm funny,
> laughing out aloud.
> But I'm feeling terrible,
> and burning hot inside.

These next two examples, both from the same writer, a Year Five boy, reveal a willingness to experiment with different forms and subject matter.

> ## Writing in the classroom
>
> I hear noises of
>
> shoving of chairs.
>
> The tapping of a type writer.
> Banging of doors
>
> The quiet chatter of boys and girls.
> Bleeping of watches.
>
> Scratching of a sharpener.
> A car zooming up Bannock Burn Road.

NOVEMBER NIGHTS

Leaves hang limply on branches,
Their colours still exotic in the street light.
Swish, swish.
Someone walking in the fallen leaves.
Standing in the street, everything is wet,
The leaves smell mysteriously sweet.
Even now rain softly falls,
Puddles form in hollows.
Cats curl up under parked cars,
Silhouettes of people move against
  the warm yellow light indoors,
As I reach the gate,
Grey November evening turns to black winter night.

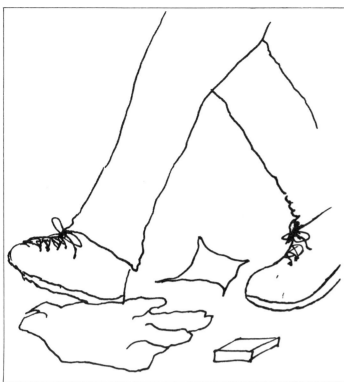

Litter

Litter litter litter,
Strewn in the street
Walking in the high street,
With litter at your feet!
Oh what a pity,
It's not just in the town
That this stuff is thrown down.
Skinheads sit in murth, IT DEFACES THE EARTH!
Flittering, Fluttering,
Down to the ground,
Fish and chip wrappers make a rustling sound.
One of these days,
There will be a huge mound,
Of litter, litter, litter.

They were part of a collection of his poems, *A Whole Heap of Poems*, written and published in the classroom. He commissioned his teacher to illustrate them for him!

Collections of children's writing, now being published regularly, demonstrate most powerfully what is possible. Children will often be encouraged by other children's writing to have a try themselves (see Bibliography, page 191).

Another starting point is to introduce a poem that has an easily assimilated form and then to invite children to write using that particular structure, such as limericks. Nonsense verse or funny verse will always appeal. By the time they are seven, children are capable of quite sophisticated verbal play and will relish punning. Michael Rosen's short verse, 'Down Behind the Dustbin' inspired a group of Year Three children to compose extra verses:

Down behind the dustbin
I met a dog called Mike.
I said, 'What are you doing there?'
'I'm riding a bike.'

Down behind the dustbin,
I met a dog called Nelly.
I said 'What are you doing there?'
'I'm playing with some jelly.'

Down behind the dustbin,
I met a dog called Bill.
I said, 'What are you doing there?'
'I'm having a meal.'

Down behind the dustbin,
I met a dog called Sam.
I said, 'What are you doing there?'
'I'm fixing the van.'

Some children wrote several verses; each child contributed the one she liked best, illustrated it and mounted it onto a page of the book made to hold the collection. When this was added to the book corner it was read avidly and many more verses were composed orally.

Extended texts

Pupils should: **'have opportunities to create, polish and produce individually or together, by hand or on a word processor, extended written texts, appropriately laid out and illustrated,** *eg. class newspapers, anthologies of stories or poems, guidebooks etc'* **(18h).**

The opportunity to work on extended texts is particularly important in Key Stage 2. Really worthwhile pieces of writing may take several weeks to complete, especially if they are being re-drafted and polished. Children in Key Stage 2 will develop the stamina to persist with a long term project, the ability to plan over a period of time and the patience to take up and put down their work whenever necessary. If writers undertake only one-off, 'completed-this-lesson' pieces of writing, the opportunity to reflect upon the way the writing is going, to polish and perfect the finished product, to mull over their ideas, will be denied them.

Sometimes the end-product will be an anthology of individual pieces around the same theme. A collection of original fairy tale stories was produced by a class of Year Four children as a result of discussion about this kind of writing. Each child contributed a story to be put into a hardback book. This was added to the other books in the book corner and proved to be a very popular read.

A second collection of 'modern' fairy stories was produced to complement the first and was just as popular as reading material.

Making a newspaper

Collaboration on a newspaper will lead to a variety of different kinds of writing (reports, articles, letters, comic strip, comment, interviews, reviews) being undertaken by different pupils. A group of children may form an editorial board responding, as readers, to first drafts, discussing with the writers, making suggestions for changes, editing and even précis-writing. If several editions of a class or school newspaper are produced, then different groups can take turns in the editorial role. Working on the word-processor enables printed final versions to be obtained easily (see Key Stage 1, pp 133); the school photocopier can be pressed into service to make a print run, which might be sold to pupils and parents to cover costs.

Autobiography

Autobiography is another form of writing which lends itself to extended writing. Children enjoy recalling and relating events from their own lives and can spend many weeks writing and selecting before a final version is ready for publication. Children's experiences are often very different, perhaps including memories of life in another country, and make fascinating reading in a published volume.

These two Year Four children's experiences were very different; both were included in a class collection.

Dai's autobiography

'As far as I can remember I was born in Vietnam on April 6th. I was born at the end of the Vietnam war. I can remember the Americans giving me and my brother sweets and toys. My mum owned a sweet shop and she was proud of it. When I was two I was in bed and I could hear my mum talking to my brothers about the Vietnam war. She could remember the American troops coming in boats and aeroplanes and they had to go underground to shelter and take cover.

She could hear bombs exploding . . . bang, bang, bang. My mum said she was terrified. We were lucky that we did not die.

One night my dad said to my mum, 'We have to get out of Vietnam.' So the next day

Ben's autobiography

'When I was born, I think I weighed 7 or 8 pounds. I was born at home, not in hospital. When my sister came and said, 'Hello, baby', I pulled her hair. But I can't remember that.

The first thing I can remember is when I was two. My dad was away and my mum decided she would take me and my sister to Greenwich Park. When we got there we went to the part that had swings in. In that part there is a wall that has bricks sticking out of it. At one end there is a ladder which I climbed up. I thought it was for walking across, so I walked across. When I got to the middle there was something like a step. I decided to stand on it. Then a boy that was trying to go across it, came along with his hands out by his sides. Can you imagine what would happen when he passed me? He would knock me off. And he did. Me, a child of two being knocked off a wall about 12 feet high! I cannot remember exactly what I felt in mid-air, but I was very scared. When I landed, I split my head open. I screamed very loudly. After a few minutes my mum came. The next thing that I can remember was that I was in a room that was round. My mum was there and there were two other people. One was bathing my head. My mum took my sister and me to the hospital. We went to Brook General. I can remember my mum sitting on a chair with me on her lap whilst a nurse stitched up my head. I screamed very loudly. The door was open and I could not see my sister anywhere.

The next thing I can remember is when my dad came back from Paris. He brought me a French fire-engine which I have still got.'

me and my brothers went on a small boat. A policeman came with us because he was our friend and he wanted to get out of Vietnam, too. My dad came late and we'd already set off. My heart was beating. I was only four years old and I was crying because daddy was not on the boat.

We were a speck on the ocean when he came. My dad dropped his bags and started swimming. He swam as fast as possible and he reached us in time.

For the rest of three days we went sailing and I got sea sick twice. Luckily we saw a ship. It was a food carrier and they picked us up and we were safe. One day later there was a huge storm and my mum said that we would have been smashed to pieces and we would have been drowned.

We had to use sign language to speak to the sailors. On the ship we had spaghetti and I thought it tasted horrible, so I didn't eat it.

Soon we were in a harbour and my brother got his photo taken. We stayed in a house which was broken. I had my tooth taken out and my mum gave me some money. I remember walking by my brother and there was an ice-cream man. I bought an ice-cream but I couldn't eat it because my teeth were aching, so I gave it to my older brother.

We waited two weeks for an aeroplane. The aeroplane came and we went off. ZOOM . . . we had taken off. As we flew away I looked down and I could see Singapore as a little speck. We flew to England and it was cold and misty. It was nearly Christmas and we were greeted as homeless people. We had to wait for the Council to find us a place to live . . .'

Responding to stimuli

Children should be able to: **'Write in response to a wide range of stimuli, including stories, plays and poems they have read and heard, television programmes they have seen, their own interests and experiences, and the unfolding activities of the classroom'** (18i).

A response to a story, poem or play may be in the form of a review, but more often enjoyment of one of these will be reflected in a version of the child's own.

This Year Three girl had read *The Lion at School* (Phillipa Pearce) and was captivated by the idea of what would happen if a lion appeared in her classroom. Imagination is given free rein in her story.

'Elizabeth and the lion finally got to school. When they got there all of the children were sitting on the mat. They came in.

"And what are you doing with that clockwork toy?" Mrs Spring said.

"It's not clockwork, Miss."

"If you will just let the air out I will put it in the drawer."

"It's not blow up."

"Well, what is it?"

"It's real!"

"Help, help," said all the children.

The teacher was standing on her desk. The lion was just standing there looking at all the hustle and bustle. Now the teacher was running round the room. She was rounding the children up into a corner of the room. She shouted, "Get that lion out of here."

"Oh, I can't do that, he will eat me up," cried Elizabeth.

"What does he want to do?" the teacher asked.

"Work," said the Lion.

The teacher slipped out of the way. Elizabeth said, "Don't be scared. He's my friend." She said, "Be a good boy. Don't growl. Be a good boy."

Then it was play time and all the children went out to play and the lion was giving them all rides on his back. The teacher was telephoning the zoo people to get the lion out of school and take it back to the zoo. They came and took it away.

But now the lion has it's own little school to play with, only it's a toy, not a real school.'

Sometimes events which receive a great deal of public attention can be responded to in writing. The television and newspaper coverage of a major earthquake in California prompted this response from a girl in Year Five.

'Screaming everywhere. Terrible havoc. In San Francisco there is havoc everywhere. There is widespread damage. What shall we do? This is the worst earthquake we have known. More than 272 people have died. The collapsed highway must be a highway to the Pit of Terror . . . as motor bikes crashed through Bay Bridge. Terrible sadness, confusion and terror. Only fifteen seconds and look what the earthquake has done! "I am so sad", said President Reagan, "but I will give my full assistance."'

One can see the influence of the language of newspaper reports in this response.

The events of the classroom, or class visits will usually be starting points for some kind of response, whether drawn, painted or written. As part of their study of rocks, one Year Four class had received a visit from a local geology enthusiast, who had shown them slides. The slides of a volcano eruption had particularly impressed this child.

'Volcano
Volcano, volcano, you look like a mountain,
Bumping, crushing, running, screaming, scared.
The lava is hot inside you,
You let out bombs,
You let out sparks.
Houses collapsing, people are dying.
The lava that comes out of you is burning hot,
The lava is runny, and showers sparks like fireworks.'

School trips and school journeys, of course, often prompt writing that is not only a record of the events, but is also a vehicle for the writer's feelings about them. This account of a Year Four girl's first-ever experience of camping on a school trip shows this mixture. It was written to accompany photographs the children had taken to form part of a display.

'We went camping at Thriftwood and I shared a tent with Beverly and Dai. We were right in front of a tree and when we went out of our tent we had to walk under the washing line we put our tea towels on. When we first got there it was a bit cold, but we still had to put up our tent.

After that Miss B. showed us how to use the trangia and then we went for a walk in the woods. We saw some cows and we thought the smell was terrible – in a few days, though, we didn't notice the smell any more! In the woods we saw a hut and we all went up to it and went in. All the windows had been broken and it was all dirty inside. The boys were messing about in it. Dylan climbed in the back window and he said there was a bogey-man inside, but there was not. We went up a lot of hills and my legs were tired. We saw some badger holes.

When we got back we cooked tea on our trangias. Then we played 'run-outs'. I chased first and then we changed over. After the game we had to get ready for bed. We had cocoa and biscuits and then got into our sleeping bags in the tent. It was funny in bed, but Mrs L. came to the tents and said "Good night and sleep well." We didn't go to sleep for a long time, so we told stories . . .'.

Further development

Pupils should:
- 'be encouraged to be adventurous with vocabulary choices;
- be taught how to use a thesaurus;
- be introduced to the idea of the paragraph and encouraged to notice paragraph divisions in their reading;
- be shown how to set out and punctuate direct speech;
- be introduced to some of the uses of the comma and the apostrophe;
- be taught the meaning, use and spelling of some common prefixes and suffixes *eg. un-, in- (and im-, il-, ir-), -able, -ness, -ful, etc*, in the context of their own writing and reading;
- think about ways of making their meaning clear to their reader in redrafting their writing;
- be encouraged and shown how to check spellings in a dictionary or on a computer spelling checker when revising and proof-reading;
- have opportunities to develop a comfortable, flowing and legible joined-up style of handwriting;
- consider features of layout, *eg. headings, side-headings, the use of columns or indentation*, in the materials they read, so that they can use some of these features to clarify structures and meaning in their own writing;
- be encouraged to find ways to reduce repetition in their own writing;
- be introduced to the complex regularity that underlines the spelling of words with inflectional endings, *eg. bead-ing, bead-ed, bed-d-ing, bed-d-ed*, in the context of their own writing and reading' (18j-u).

Each of these parts of the Programmes of Study for Key Stage 2 builds upon ways of working that are begun in Key Stage 1 and activities which develop these skills are a continuation of much that is suggested there.

Children's vocabulary is growing and developing all the time. As well as an increasing quantity of specialised vocabulary encountered through topics studied in school, children will be taking on words and expressions they encounter in books and poems. Some words will initially be only partly understood and may be used incorrectly. Newly acquired words used in writing will often be mis-spelled as well. It is important that children have the confidence to experiment with new vocabulary and that their efforts are acknowledged and praised. If, every time she uses a new word incorrectly, a child has it crossed out or it is marked wrong in some way, she will soon learn to play safe and use only the vocabulary of which she is sure. Whether it is a grammatical structure or a word that is incorrect, the teacher will need to respond sensitively, explaining where the error lies in the context in which it arises, but nevertheless giving credit for the attempt.

The use of a thesaurus follows naturally from the confident use of a dictionary, which should be well established by the time children move into Key Stage 2. Alphabetical order should be secure and the habit of checking spelling will be established. The use of a thesaurus can be introduced when individual pupils are ready, in redrafting their writing, to seek alternative ways of expressing what they mean. As in teaching the skills of dictionary use, it is better not to try to teach through exercises and drills, but through the children's own writing. The occasional game, however, using these reference materials will be enjoyed and give practice in locating words. For example, ask the children to find as many words as they can which mean nearly the same thing, in a given time. If this is played in groups, it becomes a collaborative undertaking and children who do not have fully developed skills will not be made to feel failures. Words gathered in this way can be made into charts, which will then provide a source of reference.

Similar games can be created to focus children's attention on 'prefixes, suffixes,' and 'the spelling of words with inflectional endings', though the best contexts for this will remain their own work.

Indeed the children's own writing must be the context for teaching about paragraphs, punctuation, headings and layout, when the need arises. In this example the use of columns and boxes has been suggested to the child, a Year Four girl, as a way of collating and organising her observations.

FABRIC TESTING.

Name of fabric	Hypothesis	Results
Blue denim	After ten rubs with Sandpaper it will be very hard to tear.	My Denim curled up and streched also hairs come off of it
Green Leather	Might tear if you try in one place a lot.	Rajinders leather streched and hairs went on to the sand paper. It was rough.
Gold materiel	Very easy to tear and it will all tear	Hernas material ripped ¼ of the way down and the stiches joined together
cordruoy	hard to tear and wont tear easily	My Cordruoy curled up and went fluffy It also put hairs on the sand paper
Flower materiel	Might tear a lot	Rajinders flower mate reil began to shrink and a hole came.
Shelley.		

Many of the examples quoted in other parts of this book show contexts in which teachers have intervened to help the children develop and extend their knowledge. As soon as dialogue is used in stories, the need for direct speech to be shown clearly will become apparent, so the use of inverted commas can be taught.

The need for the apostrophe may well have arisen long before Key Stage 2 is reached because children will have observed its use in adults' writing, in notices and labels, as well as in books, and will frequently over-generalise, using it indiscriminately whenever they write a word with an 's' ending, for example.

One way of helping children to remember uses of the apostrophe is to get them to identify what has been missed out in examples like 'I've', 'we'll', 'can't', and to stress belonging in 'John's', 'mother's' etc. They can then test their own uses of the apostrophe against the examples they know!

The uses of the comma are not always straightforward and teachers may need to research some of the correct usage themselves. Its use to separate items in a list is probably the one which children will need first and this is not difficult to demonstrate in labels and notices, as well as in shared writing. The next commonly encountered use is in separating the name of a person who is being addressed from the rest of a sentence ('Jenny, come here,' 'Mr Brown, can I go home?') and in separating off tag phrases at the end of a sentence (eg 'I told you, didn't I?', 'You've finished, haven't you?'). These are readily understood, as children can hear the separation. It is important that all these uses are explained when the need arises in the children's writing, in the interests of 'making their meaning clear to the intended reader'.

Development of 'a comfortable, flowing, and legible joined-up style of handwriting' will be achieved through regular practice. Alongside the practice, contexts in which children can take pride in the presentation of their work will need to be created. If writing is carefully mounted and displayed with well-presented art work or artefacts, good handwriting will be equally valued. Older children can be encouraged to take an interest in calligraphy as a craft skill, looking at its history, writing implements and styles in illuminated manuscripts.

The role of the teacher

'In order to achieve Level 4, pupils should be helped to recognise how

Standard English has come to have a wide social and geographical currency and to be the form of English most frequently used on formal or public occasions and in writing. They should be helped to recognise any differences in grammar or vocabulary between the local dialect of English and Standard English, recognising that local speech forms play an important part in establishing a sense of group identity.

They should have opportunities to write for formal or public purposes so that there are valid reasons to use Standard English in their writing.

Pupils should discuss the history of writing and consider some of the ways in which writing contributes to the organisation of society, the transmission of knowledge, the sharing of experiences and the capturing of the imagination' (20).

'In order to achieve Level 5, pupils should be helped to extend their range of vocabulary and to increase their awareness of what is suitable according to purpose and context, *eg. the kinds of topics and situations in which slang is used; the need for specialist terms and the effects of their use outside the specialist group.* Discussion should bring out contrasts in how vocabulary is used in speech and writing' (21).

Most of the pupils at the end of Key Stage 2 will be working around Level 4. A few will be at Level 5. Both of these groups will already have begun to make their knowledge about language more explicit. Items 20 and 21 of the Programme of Study relate directly to this aspect of English/ Language study and will be discussed more fully in the section entitled Knowledge About Language (pp 177-182).

A framework for writing

Learning and development in writing proceeds as a result of the interactions between the individual child, the teacher and the texts that are produced in the classroom.

In school, the foundation for all learning, including writing, is the organisation of the classroom. If both resources and time are organised so that children can be autonomous to a great extent, time wasted waiting for direction from the teacher in trivial matters (eg asking where materials are, awaiting permission to get or do something, asking what the next task to be undertaken is) can be used more profitably. Equally if children know why they are doing things, have a clear aim and a personal commitment to the task in hand, they will be actively involved in their own learning and not simply passive recipients of information or performers of tasks.

In order to build on children's literacy experiences outside school, teachers need to be aware of their interests and enthusiasms. Liaison with home is therefore necessary to provide both a background to school learning and a source of opportunities for collaboration. Invitations to families to become involved in collaborative activities (for example, by writing family stories together or by having parents working in classrooms) must be preceded by the development of shared understandings between school and home. Teachers will need to explain why things are done in a particular way and what their expectations of the children are, as well as demonstrating to parents what progress looks like. To this end samples of children's writing will need to be collected and explained.

The Non-Statutory Guidance for English Key Stage 1 summarises concisely the role the teacher should play in planning and implementing the Programmes of Study (13:1). 'The teacher should be:

● an organiser of adults other than teachers who can work alongside teachers, 'scribing' for them, or using a keyboard and enabling them to compose at greater length than they could on their own;

● an editorial consultant;

● a praiser of achievement;

● an example of adult writing behaviour;

- a setter of procedures;
- a setter of standards;
- a recorder of progress;
- a monitor of learning development.'

The focus is entirely positive – there is nothing here about the teacher as 'marker of work', as critic or as instructor.

Embodied in this summary are implications for the organisation of the classroom, of the teacher's and the children's time and of resources. If the teacher is to fulfil this role, she will need to be involved in continual interaction with her pupils.

For this to happen the children will need to be capable of working independently. They will need to know about 'procedures' and the use and location of resources if the teacher is to have time to be a consultant and to observe, monitor and record progress. The task will be made easier if there are other adults working alongside her and if they, too, can provide support and advice for the children. This will mean inviting parents and other members of the community to be a part of the classroom, which will in itself require the school to be open about its aims and procedures.

Perhaps the most significant elements of this summary are those which require the teacher to be 'a monitor of learning development and recorder of achievement'. The on-going formative assessment of children's learning is the basis of the teacher's planning of future activities, whilst the record of each child's achievement will be necessary to inform other teachers and the child's parents.

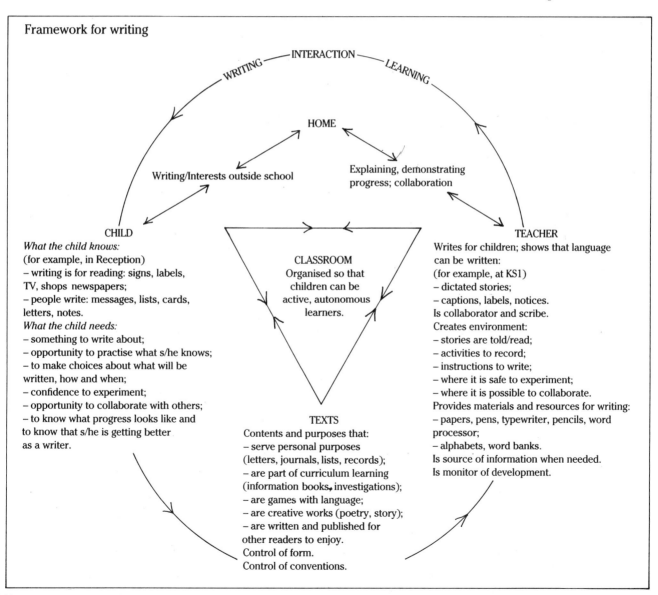

Framework for writing

WRITING — INTERACTION — LEARNING

HOME

Writing/Interests outside school

Explaining, demonstrating progress; collaboration

CHILD
What the child knows:
(for example, in Reception)
– writing is for reading: signs, labels, TV, shops newspapers;
– people write: messages, lists, cards, letters, notes.
What the child needs:
– something to write about;
– opportunity to practise what s/he knows;
– to make choices about what will be written, how and when;
– confidence to experiment;
– opportunity to collaborate with others;
– to know what progress looks like and to know that s/he is getting better as a writer.

CLASSROOM
Organised so that children can be active, autonomous learners.

TEACHER
Writes for children; shows that language can be written:
(for example, at KS1)
– dictated stories;
– captions, labels, notices.
Is collaborator and scribe.
Creates environment:
– stories are told/read;
– activities to record;
– instructions to write;
– where it is safe to experiment;
– where it is possible to collaborate.
Provides materials and resources for writing:
– papers, pens, typewriter, pencils, word processor;
– alphabets, word banks.
Is source of information when needed.
Is monitor of development.

TEXTS
Contents and purposes that:
– serve personal purposes (letters, journals, lists, records);
– are part of curriculum learning (information books, investigations);
– are games with language;
– are creative works (poetry, story);
– are written and published for other readers to enjoy.
Control of form.
Control of conventions.

Assessment

An important statement in the National Curriculum Task Group on Assessment and Testing Report (TGAT) helps to set assessment in its proper perspective (Paragraph 4):

'The assessment process itself should not determine what is to be taught and learned. It should be the servant, not the master of the curriculum. Yet it should not be simply a bolt-on addition at the end. Rather it should be an integral part of the education process, continually providing both 'feedback' and 'feedforward'. It therefore needs to be incorporated systematically into teaching strategies and practices at all levels.'

Assessment of a child's development in writing must be done through analysis of several pieces of writing of a range of types. Writing is eminently collectable and is therefore more easily analysed and assessed than more transitory spoken language interactions, or even reading. The evidence of progress is more tangible and permanent.

Example 1: Key Stage 1

In the following example, one piece of writing is set against the relevant Statements of Attainment as evidence that this girl has fulfilled the requirements for Level 2 in writing, spelling and handwriting, although this alone would not be sufficient evidence that she always performs at this level. The girl is a six-year-old with Turkish as her first language.

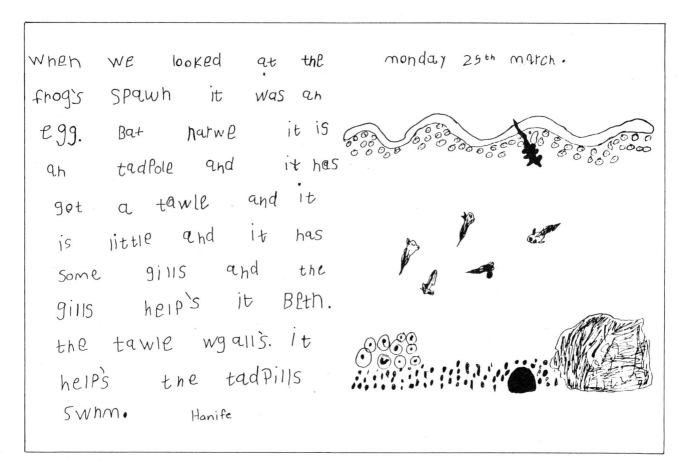

Attainment Target 3; Writing, Level 2, says that children should be able to: 'Produce, independently, pieces of writing using complete sentences, some of them demarcated with capital letters and full stops or question marks' and 'produce simple, coherent, non-chronological writing.'

This piece fulfils most of the above criteria and would therefore be placed at Level 2. Although she does not use capital letters at the beginning of sentences, she is able to demarcate sentences with a full stop. Each sentence contains a new idea.

This is non-chronological writing – the most difficult for young children to organise. Here, for example, the topic of the tadpole's tail is interrupted by the sentences about 'gills', then returned to at the end of the piece. Nevertheless, Hanife has produced 'coherent', if not perfectly organised, writing.

To know whether Hanife has achieved the other elements at Level 2, we would have to look at further examples of her writing. At least two other samples, of a story and of a chronological account of a

visit or an activity, would be needed to establish whether she had attained Level 2 in these respects.

Attainment Target 4, Spelling, Level 2, says that the pupil should be able to:
● 'Produce recognisable (though not necessarily always correct) spelling of a range of common words';
● 'Spell correctly, in the course of their own writing, simple monosyllabic words they use regularly, which observe common patterns';
● 'Recognise that spelling has patterns, and begin to apply their knowledge of those patterns in their attempts to spell a wider range of words.'

Hanife's spelling is well within the Level 2 band. All of her spellings in this piece are recognisable and all of the frequently used words (the, when, we, looked, at, was, has, little, got, it, some, helps) are spelt correctly.

She seems to be aware of spelling patterns and has used her knowledge of the double 'L' and the word 'all' in her attempt to spell 'wiggles' (wgalls). If the syllables of 'wiggles' are separated and said aloud, it is possible to see how she arrived at her spelling – 'wig-alls' – and to note that it is an intelligent hypothesis drawing on the knowledge she has.

Her spelling of 'breathe' ('Beth') reveals her knowledge of the 'th' pattern.

'Tawle' for 'tale' also draws on a pattern she has observed (the 'aw'), although it has been used incorrectly here.

Attainment Target 5, Handwriting, Level 2, says that children should be able to:
• 'produce legible upper and lower case letters in one style and use them consistently (ie not randomly mixed within words)';
• 'produce letters that are recognisably formed and properly oriented and that have clear ascenders and descenders where necessary.'

This handwriting would place Hanife at Level 2. Her handwriting is 'legible' and 'in one style'. Upper and lower case letters are not randomly mixed, though she does use a capital 'B' on both of the occasions she uses the letter. This is quite common in children of this age and sometimes it happens because the child is still slightly insecure in differentiating between 'b' and 'd'. Hanife used the lower case 'd' correctly, but perhaps she used an upper case 'B' because its shape is easier to distinguish and remember, and she is wary of writing 'b' the wrong way round.

Her writing has clear ascenders (d, t, h, l) and descenders (p, g) though the latter are not correctly orientated. This may have arisen because she was struggling to keep her writing on the line. If she had written on plain paper it might have been easier for her to orientate the letters correctly in relation to one another. It would be necessary to compare this writing with some done on plain paper in order to be sure. Both of the above inconsistencies in Hanife's writing will need to be discussed with her and she should be given the opportunity to practise correct orientation.

Monitoring progress

Although teachers will need to be aware at Reception and Year One, before the statutory reporting stage for Key Stage 1, of the level at which pupils are operating in relation to the Attainment Targets, this will not be the most important purpose for close observation of children's writing. Regular sampling and analysis of work will be needed to inform teachers' planning and to ensure that provision is being made for children to undertake activities which will enable them to develop as writers, as well as to move them towards the next level of attainment.

The Non-Statutory Guidance for English-Key Stage 1 (1:1, page D1) sets out two key principles which 'underpin the gathering and recording of evidence:
• it is an integral part of the plans for learning; teachers must provide children with the opportunity to reflect on what they have done. Material which is kept, collected and selected by the child and the teacher will help the child to review the success and progress of their learning;
• it should lead to a response; gathering and recording evidence is not an end itself but a means of informing the next stage of learning for the child and teacher.'

There are many aspects of children's writing development not assessed in the Attainment Targets that teachers will need to be aware of for their on-going records, for example:
• The way in which each child approaches writing;
• Her level of confidence;
• Her appreciation of the requirements of an audience;
• Her ability to handle different genres;
• Whether she prefers to work alone or in collaboration with others;
• Whether she enjoys writing and is developing what, in later stages, is termed 'commitment' (level 7);
• Whether she can and does write in other languages.

It is worth noting that Hanife is using English as a second language and that consideration will also need to be given to her literacy knowledge in her first language if there is to be a full picture of her achievement and ability. The National

Curriculum does not, at present, include aspects of bilingualism in either the Programmes of Study or the Attainment Targets, other than to remind teachers of the need to include 'a wide range of literature including that of other cultures'.

Teachers will need to know these things if they are to provide appropriate experiences to extend children's writing skills. Some kind of observational framework will need to be established to facilitate such recording. One very practical framework is provided by the ILEA 'Primary Language Record'. This record was recommended as 'a starting point' for the development of teachers' records in *English for Ages 5-11* – 9:20 and 10:32 – and has already been mentioned in relation to reading.

The 'Observations and samples' sheet provides useful headings which could be adapted for recording your own observations on:
- Context and background information;
- Child's own response;
- Teacher's response;
- Development of spelling and conventions of writing;
- The child's development as a writer and experiences needed.

A re-examination of Hanife's writing using this framework might look like this.

Context
Most of the children were keeping personal diaries recording the growth and development of the frog-spawn in the classroom. Hanife had spent ten minutes using a magnifying glass to look closely at the tadpoles whilst talking to her friend. As they watched, the question of how the tadpoles breathed was raised and the teacher showed them the relevant pages in an information book which explained 'gills'.

Hanife and her friend sat together to do their writing, occasionally discussing what they were doing, but writing independently. Much discussion centred around the drawing – done before the writing – and what they had noticed in the tank. There was no discussion with the teacher.

This is a complete section of a single draft from an on-going diary, showing non-chronological writing.

Child's response
She was pleased and very keen to write regularly in this diary. She pointed out proudly that she had spelt 'frogs-spawn' and 'gills' correctly because she had 'looked at the labels' by the tank and 'in the book'.

Teacher's response
Observations were well recorded, reflecting a real interest. She has integrated the information from the book quite well, though she still needs support to help her organise this kind of writing. She is slightly less confident with non-chronological writing than she is writing stories.

Development of spelling and conventions
- Most regularly used words were spelt correctly.
- Good attempts were made at 'wiggles' drawing on her knowledge of 'all'.
- 'Tawle' (tail) was consistent though incorrect.
- Good strategies were used in locating correct spellings of 'frogs-spawn', 'gills' and 'tadpole'.
- The second use of tadpoles was mis-spelt, perhaps because she had just written 'gills' and had this pattern/sound in her mind.
- 'Swnm' (swim) was nearly right.
- In 'bar narwe' (but now), the spelling of 'now' was the result of sounding out 'nar-we'.
- She used capital, not lower case 'B'.
- The use of apostrophes (in frog's-spawn) was over-generalised (ie help's and wgall's).
- The writing was in sentences but without use of capitals.

Development and experience needed
There is growing control of this kind of writing. This sample is longer than the first entry in the diary and contains fewer random statements. Talk to her about how

to organise information about the same thing into chunks. Continuing with this diary will give her more practice; it must be monitored.

Discuss with her the capital 'B'; the apostrophe (explain why, but praise her for noticing); the spellings of 'tadpoles', 'tail', 'now', 'swim'. Do look, cover, write, check to help her. Discuss demarcation of beginnings of sentences with capital letters.

Text and illustration

An additional factor not included in these headings is the inter-dependence of the written text and the illustration. Much information about the tadpoles' development is represented and recorded in the picture. Hanife has noticed the way in which tadpoles cling to the pond-weed near the surface of the water; that much of the frog-spawn lies in a black mass at the bottom of the tank; that the size of the egg in each piece of spawn varies (bottom left of picture); that the outside part of the tadpole's tail is semi-transparent while the centre is not. She had tried to represent the feathery gills in the right place after observing them through a magnifying glass.

Many young children will represent their observations through drawing, partly because they have not yet reached 'second-order symbolism, which involves the creation of written signs for the spoken symbols of words' (Vygotsky 1978). For some time, while they are learning to write, children often employ both symbol systems, sometimes inserting a drawn symbol for a word they do not know or putting most of what they want to say into an accompanying drawing (see Barrs, 1988, *Drawing a Story: Transitions between Drawing and Writing*). It is not surprising that this is so, for martialling ideas and controlling all the transcriptional aspects of writing are very hard work for the beginner-writer.

The last heading ('Development and experience needed') acts as a reminder to the teacher of the provision that needs to be made for Hanife and possibly others in the class and as an aid to planning. This is the kind of record keeping which:

• Is 'A means of informing the next stage of learning for the child and teacher' (Non-Statutory Guidance Section 1:1, page D1);
• For the child 'enables positive response and feedback';
• For the teacher 'provides reliable information upon which decisions can be made about the success of current teaching programmes and the planning of the next';
• For the parents 'provides the basis for discussion about their children's progress' (Non-Statutory Guidance, Section D1:2).

Example 2: Key Stage 2

In the example on page 174 one piece of writing at Key Stage 2 is set against the relevant Statements of Attainment as evidence that this boy has fulfilled the requirements for Level 4 in writing, spelling and handwriting. However, this alone would not be sufficient evidence that he always performs at this level. The boy is an eleven-year-old with Punjabi as his first language.

Attainment Target 3, Writing, Level 4, says that the pupil should be able to:
• 'produce, independently, pieces of writing showing evidence of a developing ability to structure what is written in ways that make the meaning clear to the reader; demonstrate in their writing generally accurate use of sentence punctuation.'
• 'write stories which have an opening, a setting, characters, a series of events and a resolution and which engage the interest of the reader; produce other kinds of chronologically organised writing.'
• 'begin to use the structures of written Standard English and begin to use some sentence structures different from those of speech.'
• 'discuss the organisation of their own writing; revise and redraft the writing as appropriate, independently, in the light of that discussion'.

This piece fulfils most of the above criteria and would, therefore, be placed at Level 4. His use of sentence punctuation is

Look out Broadstairs

I got so excited on Friday 18th my brain was about to burst. I couldn't wait ~~now~~ to get ~~jat~~ to Broadstairs. At Last we went on ~~to~~ the coach and ~~we~~ the driver ~~started~~ it up. At long Last I was ~~away from~~ going on my holiday. I was Jivan's partner he kept offering me biscuits. ~~then~~ We pack of boys were right at the back ~~and sang 99 bottels~~ the journey wasn't boring we were telling jokes and there ~~there~~ were lots of things to see ~~look~~ out of the windows. The first thing we saw of the sea was a blue patch on the horizon and a ~~so~~ river We passed an air field (Manston) and ~~o~~ when we reached the hotel ~~quite~~ I thought it's ~~was~~ quiet small ~~quiet small~~ to have 16 rooms. We went into the garden and mr and mrs Hayden who came out to meet us told us the rules ~~in~~ of the hotel ~~we went~~ The garden was ~~was~~ large and square ~~square~~ with

groups ~~and~~ we walked up steep ~~and small~~ steps I nearly ~~dr~~ dropped my suitcase down the stairs when ~~we~~ we got to our room is had one ~~a~~ double bed and one bunk bed with a lamp on either side ~~which~~ (we broke one of them later on!) We struggled to get to our wardrobes ~~we struggled to get our wardrobes~~, we had a shower in our room. In my room were Justin Jwan and Wayne. ~~which~~ Then we had a fire drill ~~which~~ (we fair got lost in the hotel!) ~~we~~ later we went to the sea half of the group ~~got~~ went the wrong way it was fun we rolled up our trousers and went in to the water. Some of the boys got wet and Jat in der fell in! We came back and had our first meal (3 courses!) soup, main course and dessert ~~desert~~. After the meal we went to the park and played football and rounders. The end of the first day's and the beginning of an exciting week.

not 100 per cent accurate, but is 'generally' so. He corrected much of the sentence demarcation in his revision.

This is a chronologically organised account – a part of his school journey diary. It is not a fictional 'story', but there is an arresting opening, 'a series of events and a resolution' and it certainly 'engages the interest of the reader'. Many sentences reflect the structures of written Standard English. Some of the amendments were made when Sadaf read and revised his writing prior to discussion with the teacher; others were made 'in the light of that discussion'.

Other pieces of writing would be needed to confirm this evaluation, at least a fictional story and a non-chronological piece.

Attainment Target 4, Spelling, Level 4 says that pupils should be able to:
• 'spell correctly, in the course of their own writing, words which display other main patterns in English spelling.'

Attainment Target 4/5, Presentation, Level 5 says that pupils should be able to:
• 'spell correctly, in the course of their own writing, words of greater complexity.' This would include words with inflectional suffixes such as '-ed' and '-ing'; where consonant doubling (running) or '-e' deletion (coming) are required.
• 'Check final drafts of writing for misspelling and other errors of presentation' (eg use a dictionary or a spell-checker where appropriate).

Sadaf's spelling was generally accurate. All '-ed' endings and '-ing' endings are correct (offering, telling, passed, reached, walked, rolled, played, struggled). Consonant doubling was accurate (dropped, beginning) and errors were satisfactorily corrected by reference to a dictionary, except 'quiet' for 'quite'.

Attainment Target 4/5, Presentation, includes Handwriting and this needs to be assessed by reference to Sadaf's final draft. This, too, is at level 5, which states that the

pupil should be able to:
* 'produce clear and legible handwriting in printed and cursive styles'.

The Primary Language Record framework, used in the same way as for Hanife's work produced the following assessment.

Context and background information

Sadaf, who is now in Year Six, arrived in England in Year Three speaking no English. He speaks Punjabi at home. He is literate in Urdu and attends Saturday classes. He reads the Qu'ran in Arabic every evening.

The children in this class, who had been to Broadstairs, were writing accounts of each day to include in the hardback books they had made to record the trip. This is a first draft, following discussion with the teacher, about what might be included in this introduction to their books. The teacher says, 'We talked of what they had expected of the journey and the reality, and they recorded notes of all that they could, though not necessarily would, include in the introduction. After writing the first draft, which Sadaf did quickly and with few problems, they paired to discuss and refine each other's work.' The teacher then met with Sadaf and read the piece, discussed the use of brackets for asides, punctuation, spelling and an interesting ending.

Child's response

He enjoyed reflecting on his first responses to the school journey experience. He was satisfied with his final version.

Teacher's response

Sadaf now tackles factual writing with little difficulty and is developing a good sense of style and cohesion in this kind of writing. He has had more opportunities in this area this year. It is an interesting account which shows awareness of the way to capture and hold an audience.

Development of spellings and conventions

Spelling is generally accurate. Errors include 'biscuits' which was a slip of the pen in writing; he knows how to spell it. 'Samall' and 'saguare' were misspellings as the result of vocalising, but both reveal a knowledge of patterns in English spelling ('-all', '-uare'). 'Desert' is a spelling he needs to learn because of the different meanings of 'desert' and 'dessert'.

Punctuation of sentences was not always present initially. This was corrected in discussion.

Development and experience needed

Sadaf is now handling this form of writing well (see above).
* Further work is needed on demarcation of sentences. He still needs reminding about punctuation.
* He is using written Standard English forms with only occasional incorrect usage (. . . things to look out of the windows . . ./ . . . the rules in the hotel . . .) His fluency in English continues to increase, and these he will correct for himself gradually as we discuss minor lapses.
* There is a need to increase the amount of creative (story/poetry) writing so that his ability in this kind of writing does not dwindle with the increased emphasis on factual writing.
* We should encourage some writing in Urdu so that he continues to value his ability to use it.

The Non-Statutory Guidance for English Key Stage 1 reminds schools of the importance of distinguishing between different kinds of evidence and provides a chart as an example of the range which may be considered.

EVIDENCE	SPEAKING AND LISTENING	READING	WRITING
	The development of the spoken word and the capacity to express themselves effectively in a variety of speaking and listening activities, matching style and response to audience and purpose (AT1)	The development of the ability to read, understand and respond to all types of writing, as well as the development of information retrieval strategies for the purposes of study (AT2)	A growing ability to construct and convey meaning in written language matching style to audience and purpose (AT3-5)
FACTUAL DETAILS	• date • location • names of talkers/listeners • purposes of the talk • teacher's role • whether speaking/listening activity was child or teacher generated	• date • location • names and roles of readers and those with whom reading is shared • purposes of the reading material being read • whether reading activity was child or teacher generated	• date • location • names and roles of writers and audiences • purposes of the writing • whether writing activity was child or teacher generated
TEACHERS' OBSERVATIONS OF CHILDREN OVER A RANGE OF ACTIVITIES	• siting or working with groups • conversation with individual children • watching a child in different grouping, activities, areas of the classroom • observation by parents on children speaking and listening • ways in which children keep 'on task'	• working with individuals and groups • reflective discussion with individual children • children's observations of own reading • observations by parents on children's own reading • ways in which children keep 'on task'	• the reading of children's writing in the process of production • ways in which children plan their work • ways in which children keep 'on task'
SAMPLES	• short transcripts of talk • particular words or moments which were revealing • observations made by others, including other children • tape recordings • the child's own observations • parents' observations	• reading records undertaken by teacher or child • tape recorded reading sessions • close observation of the child's reading of a chosen book • the child's own comments • parents' observations	• notes, plans and drafts • reflections on own writing • responses to the writing of others • a range of finished pieces • the child's own comments • parents' observations

Chapter four
Knowledge about language

'Knowledge about language should be an integral part of work in English, not a separate body of knowledge to be added on to the traditional English curriculum' (*English for ages 5-16*, 6:2).

Much has been said and written since the publication of the Kingman Report (1988), about the extent to which it is necessary or desirable for children to be taught explicitly about the English language. There can be no doubt that all children, unless severely impaired, know a great deal about language when they arrive at school at the age of five. This implicit knowledge is drawn upon whenever children speak and becomes a natural plaything whenever they make up rhymes or puns. They reveal their awareness of differences in people's use of language when they comment on the way a new teacher speaks, if her accent or dialect is unlike the local one. They show their interest in language when they become fascinated by palindromes (*English for ages 5-11*, 5:7).

Bilingual and multilingual pupils

Children who arrive in school speaking little or no English also know a great deal about language forms and functions: 'Many pupils in school are bilingual (or multilingual) and sometimes bi-literate, and quite literally know more about language than their teachers, at least in some respects' (*English for ages 5-16*, 6:11).

Knowledge of a first language supports the acquisition of a second if children are placed in contexts where they can use that knowledge and are not discouraged from doing so, or treated as though they have learning difficulties (see Hester, 1984 and Barrs *et al*, 1990, see Bibliography, page 189).

Any attempt to teach about language must acknowledge and start from the pupils' own linguistic competence, gradually making explicit some of this wealth of implicit knowledge.

Schools also need to recognise that language can never be neutral. The individual's knowledge and use of language will be rooted in his social, cultural and linguistic experience. Equally, 'it can trigger emotional responses which may spring from prejudice, stereotyping or misunderstanding' (*English for ages 5-16*, 6:7). Study of language must recognise differences and remain non-judgemental. It must be 'descriptive' rather than 'prescriptive'.

Standard English

There is a danger that the National Curriculum goal of enabling children to become proficient users of Standard English could lead to the undermining of children's confidence as language users and a return to notions of 'deficit' if schools, however unintentionally, transmit a view that only Standard English is valid. Standard English is the language of 'wider, non-regional public communication'

(*English for ages 5-16*, 4:35), and as such it is right that all children should be confident users of it, in addition to their first dialect or language. 'The aim is to add Standard English to the repertoire, not to replace other dialects or language' (*English for ages 5-16*, 4:43).

Teaching Standard English, therefore, requires senstivity on the part of schools and teachers: 'It should not be introduced at too early a stage; teaching pupils a new dialect may be confusing when they are learning many other aspects of language use. The profound implications for pupils' relationships with their families and communities should be recognised' (*English for ages 5-16*, 4:36).

Most children in Key Stage 2 will not be expected to speak Standard English, and certainly their speech will not be expected to be in Received Pronunciation. Throughout the first two Key Stages they will be developing their abilities as writers and coming to understand that spoken and written language are different. Written language lacks the support of intonation, gesture and expression and so needs to be much more explicit.

Very young children assimilate phrases and structures they have heard in books, and this is one reason why reading aloud to them from well-written books is so important. It remains an important experience throughout the Key Stage 2: '. . . we can be confident that in reading aloud from really fine books – books that would be too difficult for the pupils to read by themselves – we are helping (the children) to develop an ear for the language in a way that no textbook exercises can' (Perera, 1987).

Children's knowledge of Standard English will be developed in the early years, through their encounters with 'book language'. They are also likely to use written Standard English forms in their own compositions long before they add spoken Standard English as one of their range of spoken dialects. They will be learning to adjust the way they write according to the purpose and audience for the writing. The Programme of Study for Writing says that **'they should have opportunities to write for formal or public purposes so that there are valid reasons to use Standard English in their writing'**.

Non-Standard English

Dialect forms

In talking about this writing as they help children to redraft, teachers will certainly be making explicit some of the differences between spoken and written English, as well as between Standard and other dialects. For example, children in London may say, 'We come home' but will gradually be encouraged to write, 'We came home'; they may say, 'We got off of the bus' but accept that 'we got off the bus' is the Standard written form.

Katharine Perera (1987, pp 10-16), in a very clear explanation of what is grammatical language, uses this example: 'What are yous doing?' spoken by a Liverpool speaker is not ungrammatical, but it follows a different grammar from Standard English which makes no distinction between singular and plural forms of the second person pronoun (you).

Black English dialects (amongst other characteristics) regularly omit plural endings, as in, 'Two girl read this book'; past tense endings, as in, 'John walk to school yesterday'; and the verb 'to be' is redundant as in, 'Teacher coming' or 'The boy happy'.

The Kingman Report (1988) identified historical and geographical variation as one aspect of their 'model of English': 'Language changes over time – all forms of language are subject to change, to inception, modification and to decay, sometimes rapidly and sometimes immeasurably slowly. Changes continue to take place in our own time.'

Colloquial English

Children are sensitive to changes and interpretations of language, constantly adapting their speech to fit with that of the peer group. The language of the group culture is often incomprehensible to outsiders. For example, the use of words like 'fab', 'groovy', 'cool' in the past, and the current use of 'wicked' as a term of approval and 'bad' meaning 'good', with 'well' used as 'very', as in 'well wicked' and 'well bad'.

Derivation of words and language development

Children are fascinated by the language used by older people; their grandparents may use words and phrases which are not part of the children's own vocabulary. The reasons for the differences may be historical or geographical. For example, older people may use words like 'gym shoes', 'pumps', 'daps' or 'plimsolls', for sports footwear, depending on their regional origin. Most young people would say 'trainers', partly because the shoe itself has changed over time! Older people might refer to 'frocks' and 'jumpers' instead of 'dresses' and 'sweaters'.

The way in which English absorbs words from other languages would also be an interesting area of study for Key Stage 2 children. From the age of about nine years, they are delighted by the detective work involved in seeking the origins of words with which they are familiar as in Figure 1.

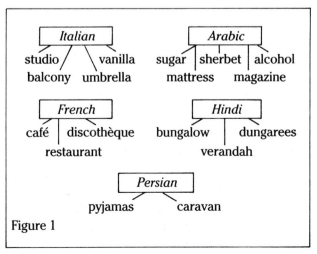

Figure 1

They also enjoy tracing the roots of words like:

- Manufacture, from the Latin, '*manus*', hand and *facere*, to make;
- Civic, from the Latin, '*civis*', citizen;
- Century, from the Latin, '*centum*', one hundred;
- Bring/brought from Old English *bringan/broght*;
- King, from Old English *cyning*.

They can find out the reasons for some of the unusual spellings, as well as something of the history of the English language.

Words which children encounter in songs, poems and stories sometimes seem rather strange to them because the meanings have changed over time. For example,

- 'Silly babe' in a Christmas carol, goes back to the Old English '*saelig*', meaning 'holy'.
- 'Awful' once meant only 'inspiring awe'. It now is more likely to be used as 'bad' as in 'awful writing', 'awful behaviour'.
- 'Quick' as in 'the quick and the dead' in the prayer, where the meaning is 'alive'; it is now more likely to be used to mean 'fast'.

Place names and their origins as descriptions of what those places used to be like, would make an interesting strand for study in a local history or environment project:

- 'thorpe' from the Danish, meaning 'a small village';
- 'thwaite' from the Danish, meaning 'a clearing in the woods';
- 'leight' or 'ley', also meaning a clearing in the woods, was often used with the name of the trees in the woods, as in '*Ash*ley, *Thorn*ley, *Bex*ley (box), *Brom*ley (broom);
- Small parts of names like Birmingham or Buckingham reveal much information; '- ing' (OE) meaning a tribal group, and '- ham' (OE) meaning a homestead or a water meadow. Thus Birmingham means, 'the homestead of Beorma's people' and Buckingham means, 'the meadow of Bucca's people'.

- 'Chester', '-caster', '-cester' (Latin) meaning 'town' from the time of the Romans, as in 'Manchester', 'Lancaster', 'Cirencester'.

The Non-Statutory Guidance (Part 2, 1990), outlines an example of a way in which children can explore names more widely to develop their knowledge about language. The 'starting point is the pupils' names, those of family, friends, pets and local names. Children can explore the names of things in and out of school' and there are suggestions for many kinds of follow-up activities appropriate to Key Stages 1 and 2.

Linguistic terms in teaching English

The strand of Knowledge About Language which is, perhaps, the most contentious is 'linguistic terminology'. The Cox Report, *English for ages 5-16*, has a lengthy chapter on this topic which includes some revealing examples of classroom practice with children talking about 'palindromes' (5:7), 'alphabetical order', 'vowels', 'spelling' and 'full stops'. Because the discussions are rooted in the context of their own interests and their own work, it is perfectly natural for the teacher to introduce the appropriate terminology and for the children to understand it. Terminology has traditionally been taught through exercises from English work books, when over-simplified definitions have often been used. For example, a verb is a 'doing word'. But what about thinking and feeling? As *English for ages 5-16* reminds us, 'Questions of pedagogy are crucial in discussions of linguistic terminology. It is often assumed that to argue for the value of linguistic terminology is also to argue for the learning and testing of such terms in exercises and drills. But these things by no means necessarily go together' (5:12) and 'Terms are needed to allow teachers and pupils to discuss many aspects of language. But it is important that the terms are introduced as they are needed . . .' (5:16). There is no attempt to prescribe what terms should be taught, because individual contexts will vary. The report does, however, indicate the kinds of terminology that may be needed, under separate headings.

- *'Language forms'* (eg sounds of English, spelling words, sentence, grammar, text structure) (5:28-30).
- *'Language functions'* to discuss aspects of written and spoken language (eg describe, report, explain, argue) (5:31-32).
- *'Communication and comprehension'* to discuss the way meanings are expressed (5:33-34).
- *'Language acquisition'* to describe and discuss how language is learned (5:35).
- *'Language varieties'* to discuss how language differs and changes (5:36-38) (eg differences between spoken and written English, dialects, slang).
- *'Literary texts'* the language to discuss literary texts (eg genre, written effects) (5:39-40).

Not all of these categories will be drawn upon in primary schools, though some will be used from the very early years (eg alphabet, story, poem, word, letter) and others will be introduced throughout Key Stage 2 (eg sentence, paragraph, adjective, noun, consonant, vowel, accent, dialect).

Meeting the teacher's needs

If teachers are to be able to use terminology about language appropriately, they will need to have a secure grasp of such terms for themselves. Katharine Perera (1987) identified the needs of teachers thus: 'It is obviously helpful if primary teachers . . . have sufficient command of the technical terms to be able to read books written for teachers about children's language. Furthermore, it is almost certainly easier for teachers to identify their pupils' linguistic strengths and weaknesses if they have the vocabulary for describing them.'

The Non-Statutory Guidance (Part 2, June 1990) has this to say: 'Teachers' knowledge about language will be used in three major ways, all of which should be provided through a systematic, methodical approach to knowledge about language, including grammatical structure:
- in *creating contexts* in which pupils' competence and implicit knowledge are developed;
- in *intervening* in pupils' language use in order to raise issues, to invite reflection, to suggest possibilities for further development;
- in *providing content* and *lines of enquiry* for pupils' learning about language' (D7 2:6).
- 'Knowledge of linguistic terminology will help teachers to discuss pupils'

language development' (D7 2:7).

Many teachers who have not received much teaching about language, in either their own schooling or their training, may well feel rather overwhelmed by the range and variety of knowledge they will be expected to have. In-service courses are available nationally, supported by regional co-ordinators and advisory teachers, to address some of these anxieties. The Language in the National Curriculum Projects (LINC) use the materials they have developed to support teachers, thus allowing them to make *explicit* their existing *implicit* knowledge about language, and thereby developing confidence in creating contexts, knowing when and how to intervene and providing content for pupils' development.

It is vital, though, that concern over 'naming the parts' does not obscure all the 'vitality and richness that can be found in language work in the classroom' (Perera, *op cit*). Knowledge About Language is a small part of English in the National Curriculum and it is for this reason that it should be integrated throughout all children's language work. *English for ages 5-16* (The Cox Report, 6:2) says: 'We believe that knowledge about language should be an integral part of work in English, not a separate body of knowledge to be added on to the traditional English curriculum . . . To treat it separately would be to risk giving rise to the misconception that it should be separately timetabled, taught and assessed, rather than integrated in the speaking, listening, reading and writing activities of any English lesson' – and any primary classroom.

Appendix

Bookmaking
Gillian Lathey

Why make books?

Children love to make books. Young children at home and school gain enormous pleasure from folding, sticking and stapling pieces of paper together to make books of all shapes and sizes and for a variety of purposes. Teachers can capitalise on this by providing materials and ready-made books in a writing or bookmaking area, and by extending children's bookmaking skills so that their work can be 'published'.

Publication gives status and permanence to children's writing. Once children become published authors and their books are placed in the class book corner or school library, or taken home to be shared with parents and friends, their work is certain to reach a wide audience. In this way children are encouraged to undertake further writing, and a clear link is established between reading and writing. Children also become more skilled at evaluating their own work, since not every piece will be suitable for publication. Some pieces of writing are personal and private, others may not develop quite as the author intended. A child working towards publication needs to talk with the teacher and other children about the organisation of the piece, the needs of the audience and the format of the finished book. It may be appropriate to encourage a child to write in his first language, or to provide a translation in order to reach a wider audience at home as well as in school.

In some schools parents have become involved in bookmaking. Some have worked in the classroom with children or joined workshops to write, illustrate and publish accounts of incidents in their own lives. These books, too, have been made available in more than one language where appropriate and have strengthened links between home and school, added to the school's range of reading material and given status to children's home languages.

To engage in the whole process of creating a book – from the first hurried jottings through various drafts to bookmaking and publication – helps children to understand that books are made by fallible human beings, and to develop a greater critical awareness of printed material. The development of such a critical awareness and the importance of providing opportunities to make a range of books are stressed in the National Curriculum Programmes of Study for Reading and Writing and the Non-Statutory Guidance (for Key Stage 1).

Bookmaking is, in itself, a satisfying activity and a learning experience, involving a consideration of design, colour-matching and other aesthetic qualities as well as mathematical activities such as measuring and estimating. If the time spent needs further justification, the whole bookmaking process could easily be matched to the four Attainment Targets for Design and Technology in the National Curriculum, from 'identifying the needs' of the audience through 'generating a design' for the book, 'planning and making' it and 'appraising its effects'.

Clearly, a wide range of materials is essential, so that appropriate choices in design can be made. A classroom writing area can be stocked with paper in a wide range of colours and sizes, plus staplers, a hole punch and tags for quick bookmaking, as well as ready-made stapled booklets. All off-cuts of paper can be kept for this purpose, including leftover gift wrapping paper for small book covers. In addition, a bookmaking area could be set up in an accessible part of the school for storage of equipment needed to make hardback books, and might include a display of books at various stages of the bookmaking process.

Different types of book have different uses across the primary age-range.

1 In a nursery class a hardback book, made by an adult with children watching and helping, can contain photos and captions as a permanent record of a visit or outing.

2 Children just learning to read need 'big' versions of favourite stories or poems for shared reading sessions (scrapbooks can be used for this purpose).

3 Older children can make their own hardback books and work through the publication process, but they too need access to materials to make 'instant' books: comics, 'flicker' books, mini stapled books etc.

Children's ideas for books are limitless, ranging from their own versions of favourite picture books to painstakingly illustrated stories based on TV characters and superheroes. Techniques used by children and teachers can extend to pop-up books, books with flaps to lift up, big books, tiny books – in fact books of all shapes and sizes. Bookmaking can soon become an established and well-loved part of children's classroom lives.

The following examples are intended to cover a range of bookmaking techniques. A list of suppliers of bookmaking materials is added after the examples.

Single-section sewn book (hardback)

A well produced hard cover book is attractive and durable. Children may decide to publish longer pieces of writing in this form, or collections of poetry and stories or a record of a term's project work. Many of the basic bookmaking techniques involved can be adapted once they are understood. Cover papers can be decorated in a way that is appropriate to content, using printing techniques, marbling, drawing and painting or even embroidery and appliqué. When making these books with a class of children, it is best to organise a rolling programme so that groups of children are at different stages of the process and can help each other.

What you need

2 pieces of A4 strawboard or thick card; 6 pieces of A3 sugar paper for pages; 1 piece of sugar paper, 10cm wide × height of the A4 board; 1 piece of scrim, mull or tarlatan, 10cm wide × height of the A4 board; 1 piece of linson, or buckram grain book cloth, 10cm wide × height of the A4 board plus 8cm; 2 pieces of cover paper the width of the A4 board × the height of the A4 board plus 8cm; folding bone (for making sharp folds); 2 bulldog clips; bookbinder's waxed linen thread; awl (for making sewing holes); needle; PVA adhesive diluted by one part to five parts of water; ruler and straight edge; Stanley knife; pencil; scissors; paste and spreader; newspaper; cloth; bookpress or heavy weight; kitchen paper.

What to do

1 Take the six sheets of sugar paper, fold them in half one at a time using the bone folder and interleave them.

2 Take the 10cm wide piece of sugar paper and the 10cm wide piece of scrim, fold them in half lengthways and trim the corners as in Figure 1. Place them round the spine of the pages with the scrim on the outside and hold them in place with small bulldog clips, top and bottom.

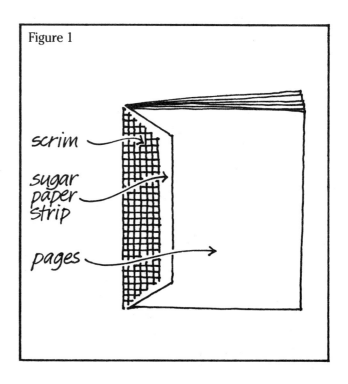

Figure 1

scrim

sugar paper strip

pages

3 Make a sewing guide for five hole sewing by taking a strip of paper cut lengthways from a piece of A4 and first folding it in half, then in thirds. Mark five sewing holes in the centre of the book on the inside using the folds of the sewing guide. Make holes using an awl, then sew the book together as in Figure 2, starting from inside the book. Trim the edges of the pages using a straight edge and Stanley knife.

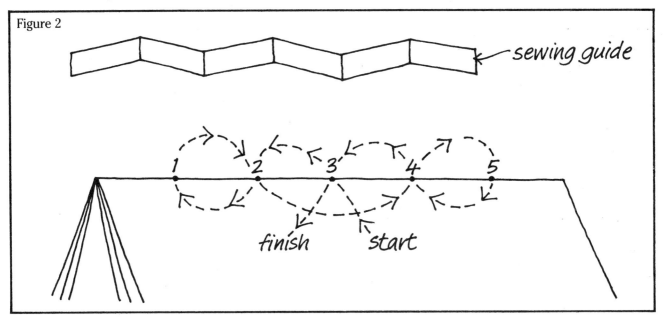

Figure 2

sewing guide

1 2 3 4 5

finish start

4 Take the 10cm wide piece of linson. Measure 4cm from each edge and draw a long narrow rectangle in the centre. Leaving this rectangle free, cover the rest of the linson with the diluted PVA and stick on the board as in Figure 3. Fold the linson over, top and bottom.

5 Take the pieces of cover paper, paste them and stick them to the boards, butting them carefully against the edge of the linson and smoothing out any air bubbles with a cloth. Trim and mitre the corners by cutting off the corners as in Figure 4, folding one edge of cover paper at a time, then pressing the edges with the bone folder. Place the corners of the book together and crease the spine.

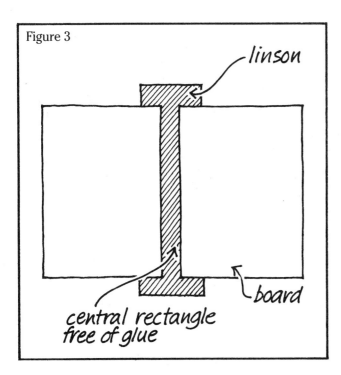

Figure 3

linson

central rectangle free of glue

board

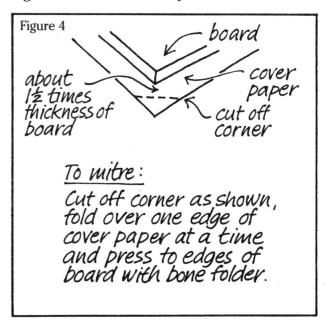

Figure 4

board

about 1½ times thickness of board

cover paper

cut off corner

To mitre:
Cut off corner as shown, fold over one edge of cover paper at a time and press to edges of board with bone folder.

6 Place the spine of your pages on this crease, and cover the scrim and sugar paper at the front of the book with the diluted PVA, protecting the pages with newspaper. Stick the scrim and sugar paper on to the boards, making sure that the spine of the pages stays in line with the crease in the linson as in Figure 5. Now do the same at the back of the book. Next paste down the endpapers.

7 Place kitchen paper inside the front and back covers of the book and wrap it around the outside. (Avoid newspaper for this purpose as the print may spoil your book.) Place in a book press or under a heavy weight. Change the kitchen paper after half an hour as some of the paste will have oozed out, then leave the book to press for at least two days.

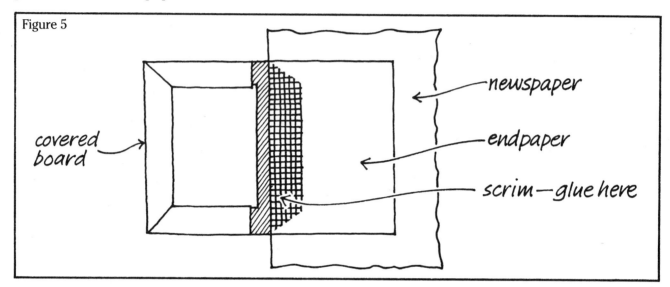

Figure 5

covered board

newspaper

endpaper

scrim—glue here

Adhesive tape book (hardback)

This is a smaller and simplified version of the single-section sewn book, using adhesive tape as the binding.

What you need
12 sheets A4 paper; 2 sheets A4 coloured endpaper; 2 pieces of A5 strawboard or chipboard; 24cm length of adhesive carpet tape (about 5cm wide); 2 pieces of cover paper, 25cm × 15cm; bone folder; paste and spreader; ruler; pencil; scissors; needle; thread.

What to do
1 Fold the 12 sheets of paper using the bone folder. Fold the two sheets of coloured paper (endpapers) in the same way and place them round the pages of the book.
2 Secure the pages top and bottom with bulldog clips and complete the five hole sewing process according to the

instructions for a single-section book. Trim the edges of the pages using a straight edge and Stanley knife.
3 Draw two lines, 1cm either side of the spine. Place a piece of newspaper between the endpaper and the pages of the book and paste the outer endpaper, leaving the margin free to allow for flexibility. Stick the board to the endpaper, smoothing out any air bubbles with a cloth. Now stick the board on to the back of the book in the same way.
4 Draw lines on the boards 2.25cm (or just under half the width of your adhesive tape) either side of the spine. Place the edge of the tape along the line on one of the boards, stick it carefully to the board and ease it over the spine to the other side of the book. Stick the tape to this board – it should reach the lines you have drawn so that it runs over the top and bottom of the book, over the boards and outer endpapers and down inside the spine.
5 Paste one piece of cover paper and stick it to the board, making sure that it overlaps

the tape by about 0.5cm. Smooth out any air bubbles. Mitre the corners, following the instructions for the single-section book. Turn the book over and stick down the other cover paper in the same way.

6 Paste down the endpapers, protecting the pages with newspaper. Wrap the book in kitchen paper and press it as described in the instructions for a single-section book.

Simple sewn book

It is possible to introduce very young children to the basic techniques of three hole sewing – needles and thread are not even necessary!

What you need
Paper cut to size; wool, narrow ribbon, or embroidery thread; scissors.

What to do
Show the children how to fold the pieces of paper one at a time by putting the corners together and folding. Once the pages are interleaved, make three equally spaced triangular cuts in the spine as in Figure 6, allowing the children to help wherever possible. Working from the inside of the book, the children can then simply push thread through the holes in the correct sequence and tie the ends. Alternatively, if the binding process is started from the outside and ribbon is used, the ends can be tied in a bow to provide an attractive finish to the book.

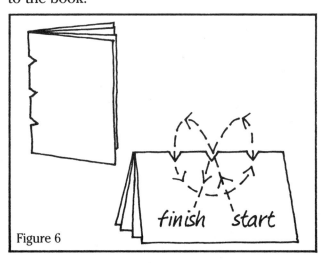

Figure 6

Zig-zag book

Zig-zag books containing children's work or photographs provide an eye-catching addition to any classroom display. It would appear to be a straightforward matter to make a zig-zag book – until you have had the experience of watching one slowly curl and 'flop'! A zig-zag book which is designed to stand as part of a display needs to be reinforced. Small zig-zag books about 5cm high will stand unaided because of their size, and make ideal mini alphabet books.

What you need
Sugar paper (for mini zig-zag books); strawboard/chipboard; manilla card; paste and spreader; cover paper; adhesive tape; Stanley knife.

What to do
1 Take two pieces of strawboard of a size appropriate to your needs. Cut two pieces of cover paper so that they are 4cm larger than the board all the way round. Paste one piece of paper and stick the board to the paper, mitring the corners as shown in the instructions on page 185.

2 Measure the width of the covered board and decide how many 'pages' you would like the book to have. Cut a strip of manilla card so that it is the same height as the board and in multiples of its width. If it is necessary to cut more than one strip of manilla card and make a join, ensure that the joins coincide with the folds and overlap by about 2cm as in Figure 7. This will reinforce the joins.

3 Using the width of the covered board as a measure, mark the folding points on the manilla card. Score the folds lightly with a Stanley knife and fold the card. Stick the first and last 'pages' to the covered boards.

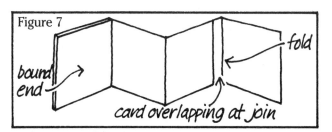

Figure 7

Photocopied books

It can be necessary to have several copies of a book, for example a child's story suitable for group reading, a book in children's first languages or a piece of work on the local environment which could be distributed (or sold!) in the wider community. Desk-top publishing programmes are one way to do this, but such a facility is not always available.

Photocopied booklets can be made from folded A4 paper. The first step is to make an original copy using white paper for both the inside pages and the cover. Use a black pen or typewriter for the text and black line drawings as illustrations. Once the original is complete, each A4 sheet can be photocopied, and the cover can be photocopied on to coloured A4 paper or, if your copier will take it, thin coloured card.

Bookbinding equipment

There is a range of bookbinding equipment available at stationers or through suppliers. The following have been of use in schools.

Comb binder
Comb binders are expensive, but worth the investment if a lot of bookmaking is going on in school. Local teachers' centres will usually comb bind books for a few pence.

Slide binder
Slide binders are readily available and a useful stop-gap to hold pages together while waiting for a more permanent binding. The pages will slide out if the book is not carefully handled.

Rings or tags
To bind a book using metal rings or tags involves punching holes in the pages. It is therefore necessary to leave a margin at the left of each page.

Display wallets and photograph albums
Display wallets can be used to display a collection of work which was perhaps not originally intended to form a book. An alternative is to use photograph albums with board pages and 'clinging' clear film which can be bought very cheaply in street markets.

Suppliers of bookmaking materials

Dryad Craft Centre
178 Kensington High Street
London W8

Falkiner Fine Papers Ltd
76 Southampton Row
London WC1

References and resources

Bibliography

Allen, D. (1988) *English, Whose English?*, NAAE/NATE.

Barrs, M. et al (1990) *Patterns of Learning*, CLPE.

Barrs, M. et al (1988) *The Primary Record Handbook*, CLPE.

Barrs, M. (1988) 'Drawing a Story: transitions between drawing and writing' in *The Word for Teaching is Learning*, Heinemann.

Bennett, J. (1985) *Learning to Read with Picture Books*, Thimble.

Bissex, G. (1985) *GNYS AT WRK: A Child Learns to Read and Write*, Harvard University Press.

Calkins, L. M. (1984) *Lessons from a Child*, Heinemann.

Clarke, M. (1976) *Young Fluent Readers*, Heinemann.

Clay, M. (1975) *What Did I Write?*, Heinemann.

DES (1975) *A Language for Life (Bullock Report)*, HMSO.

DES (1988) *Report of the Committee of Enquiry into the teaching of English (Kingman Report)*, HMSO.

DES (1988) *Report of the Task Group on Assessment and Testing (TGAT Report)*, HMSO.

DES (1988) *English for ages 5 to 11 (Cox Report 1)*, HMSO.

DES (1989) *English for ages 5 to 16 (Cox Report 2)*, HMSO.

DES (1989) *English for the National Curriculum 1*, HMSO.

DES (1989) *National Curriculum: Policy to Practice*, HMSO.

DES (1990) *English in the National Curriculum 2*, HMSO.

Ferriero, E. and Teberosky, A. (1983) *Literacy Before Schooling*, Heinemann.

Fry, D. (1985) *Children Talk about Books: Seeing Themselves as Readers*, Open University Press.

Goelman, H., Oberg, A. & Smith, F. (eds) *Awakening to Literacy*, Heinemann.

Graves, D. (1983) *Writing: Teachers and Children at Work*, Heinemann.

Hall, N. (1987) *The Emergence of Literacy*, Hodder & Stoughton.

Halliday, M. A. K. (1975) *Learning How to Mean*, Edward Arnold.

Harste, J., Woodward, V. and Burke, C. (1984) *Language Stories and Literacy Lessons*, Heinemann.

Hester, H. (1984) 'Peer Interaction in Learning English as a Second Language' in *Theory in Practice*, Vol 23, No 3.

HMI (1985) *Better Schools*, HMSO.

HMI (1990) *The Teaching and Learning of Language and Literacy: An Inspection Review*, HMSO.

Holdaway, D. (1979) *The Foundations of Literacy*, Scholastic.

Holdaway, D. (1980) *Independence in Reading*, Scholastic.

Hughes, M. (1986) *Children and Number*, Blackwell.

Kress, G. (1982) *Learning to Write*, Routledge.

Mackay, D., Thompson, B. and Schaub, P. (1979) *Breakthrough to Literacy Teachers' Manual*, Longman.

Meek, M. (1985) *Learning to Read*, Bodley Head.

Meek, M. (1987) *How Texts Teach What Readers Learn*, Thimble.

Meek, M., Warlow, A. and Barton, G. (1978) *The Cool Web*, Bodley Head.

NCC (1989) *English in the National Curriculum: Non-Statutory Guidance, KS 1*, HMSO.

NCC (1990) *English in the National Curriculum: Non-Statutory Guidance, KS 2, 3, 4, HMSO.*

National Writing Project (1989/1990) *Writing and Learning; Becoming a Writer; Audiences for Writing; A Rich Resource: Writing and Language Diversity; Writing and Micros; Writing Partnerships 1*, Nelson.

Newman, J. (1985) *The Craft of Children's Writing*, Scholastic.

Opie, I and P. (1987) *The Lore and Language of Schoolchildren*, OUP.

Payton, S. (1984) *Developing Awareness of Print: A Young Child's First Steps Towards Literacy*, University of Birmingham Education Review.

Perera, K. (1987) *Understanding Language*, NAAE/NATE.

Peters, M. (1985) *Spelling, Caught or Taught? A New Look*, Routledge & Kegan Paul.

Read, C. (1986) *Children's Creative Spelling*, Routledge & Kegan Paul.

Rosen, M. (1989) *Did I Hear You Write?*, Andre Deutsch.

Sassoon, R. (1983) *A Practical Guide to Children's Handwriting*, Thames & Hudson.

Smith, F. (1983) *Essays into Literacy*, Heinemann.

Temple, C., Nathan, R., Burris, N. and Temple, F. (1988, 2nd edition) *The Beginnings of Writing*, Allyn & Bacon.

Tough, J. (1976) *Listening to Children Talking*, Ward Lock.

Tizzard, B. et al (1988) *Young Children at School in the Inner City*, LEA Publications.

Vygotsky, L. (1978) *Mind in Society*, Harvard University Press.

Warlow, A. (1979) *Extending Reading in the Junior School*, ILEA.

Waterland, L. (1985) *Read With Me: An Apprenticeship Approach to Reading*, Thimble.

Weir, R. (1962) *Language in the Crib*, Mouton.

Wells, G. (1987) *The Meaning Makers*, Hodder & Stoughton.

Whistler, Theresa and children from Brixworth Primary School, Northampton (1988) *Rushaven Time*, Brixworth Primary School.

Widlake, B. and Macleod, F. (?) *Raising Standards: Progress in Coventry EPA Schools, during a two year period of parental collaboration in reading*, Coventry Community Education Centre.

Wray, D. et al (1983) *Developing Children's Writing*, Scholastic Bright Ideas Teacher Handbooks.

Children's Books

Ahlberg, Allan (1985) *Please, Mrs. Butler*, Viking/Kestrel.

Ahlberg, Janet and Allan (1982) *Funny Bones*, Picture Lions.

Ahlberg, Janet and Allan (1980) *Each, Peach, Pear, Plum*, Picture Lions.

Ahlberg, Janet and Allan (1983) *Peepo*, Picture Puffin.

Ahlberg, Janet and Allan (1986) *The Jolly Postman and Other People's Letters*. Heinemann.

Andersen, Hans Christian (many editions) *The Little Match Girl*.

Anno, Mitsumasa (1974) *Anno's Alphabet*, Bodley Head.

Anno, Mitsumasa (1985) *Anno's Counting Book*, Bodley Head.

Asch, Frank (1984) *Just Like Daddy*, Corgi.

Blake, Quentin (1981) *Mr. Magnolia*, Picture Lions.

Briggs, Raymond (1980) *The Snowman*, Picture Puffin.

Brown, Anthony (1986) *A Walk in the Park*, Picturemac.

Burningham, John (1983) *Come Away from the Water, Shirley*, Picture Lions.

Burningham, John (1984) *Would You Rather?*, Picture Lions.

Cameron, Ann (1984) *The Julian Stories*, Lions.

Campbell, Rod (1985) *Dear Zoo*, Picture Puffin.

Carle, Eric (1974) *The Very Hungry Caterpillar*, Picture Puffin.

Castor, Harriet (1985) *Fat Puss and Friends*, Puffin.

Dahl, Roald (1987) *Fantastic Mr. Fox*, Puffin.

Dalgleish, Alice (O/P) *The Bears on Hemlock Mountain*, Puffin.

Dodd, Lynley (1985) *Hairy McLary from Donaldson's Dairy*, Puffin.

Grillone, Lisa and Gennaro, Joseph (1980) *Small Worlds Close Up*, Julia Macrae.

Hayes, Sarah (1987) *Happy Christmas, Gemma*, Walker.

Hoban, Russell (1974) *How Tom Beat Captain Najork and His Hired Sportsmen*, Cape.

Hutchins, Pat (1971) *Changes, Changes*, Picture Puffin.

Hutchins, Pat (1970) *Rosie's Walk*, Picture Puffin.

Isadora, Rachel (?) *Ben's Trumpet*, Angus & Robertson.

Keeping, Charles (?) *Joseph's Yard*, OUP.

Keeping, Charles (?) *Charley, Charlotte and the Golden Canary*, OUP.

Lavelle, Sheila (1988) *Holiday with the Fiend*, Young Lions.

Lurie, Alison (1980) *Clever Gretchen and other Forgotten Folktales*, Heinemann.

Macauley, David (1988) *Castle*, Collins.

Macauley, David (1988) *Cathedral*, Collins.

McKee, David (1980) *Not Now, Bernard*, Anderson Press.

Munsch, Robert (1982) *The Paper Bag Princess*, Hippo.

Murphy, Jill (1984) *On the Way Home*, Picturemac.

Murphy, Jill (1980) *Peace at Last*, Macmillan.

Pearce, Philippa (1986) *The Lion at School and Other Stories*, Young Puffin.

Photo Talk Books, ILEA Learning Resources, Harcourt, Brace, Jovanovitch

Potts, R. (1982) *Tod's Owl*, Knight Books.

Prater, John (1984) *On Friday Something Frunny Happened*, Picture Puffin.

Riordan, James (1989) *The Woman in the Moon and Other Tales of Forgotten Heroines*, Hutchinson.

Roennfeldt, Robert (1981) *Tiddalick: The Frog Who Caused a Flood*, Picture Puffin.

Rosen, Michael (1981) *You Can't Catch Me*, Andre Deutsch.

Ross, Tony (1983) *Three Pigs*, Anderson Press.

Smith, Jim (1977) *The Frog Band and Durrington Dormouse*, World's Work.

Spier, Peter (1978) *The Great Flood*, World's Work.

Sterne, Simon (?) *The Hobyahs*, Methuen.

Stinson, Kathy (1985) *Red is Best*, OUP.

Sutton, Eve (1978) *My Cat Likes to Hide in Boxes*, Picture Puffin.

Viorst, Judith (1973) *Alexander and the Terrible, Horrible, No Good, Very Bad Day*, Angus & Robertson.

Vipont, Elfrida and Briggs, Raymond (1971) *The Elephant and the Bad Baby*, Picture Puffin.

Williams, Jay (1983) *The Practical Princess and Other Liberating Fairy Tales*, Hippo.

Wilson, Barbara (1978) *The Willow Pattern Story*, Angus & Robertson.

Zemach, Margot (1985) *The Little Red Hen*, Hutchinson.

Poetry

Balaam, J. and Merrick, B. (1987) *Exploring Poetry 5-8*, NATE.

Brownjohn, S. (1980) *Does it Have to Rhyme?*, Hodder & Stoughton.

Brownjohn, S. (1982) *What Rhymes with Secret?*, Hodder & Stoughton.

Calthrop, K. and Ede, J. (1984) *Not 'Daffodils' Again*, Schools Council/ Longman.

Kock, K. (1974) *Rose, Where did you get that Red?*, Vintage House (USA) N.Y.

Styles, M. (ed) (1986) *Start-Write: Helping Children Begin Writing Poetry*, EARD Cambridge.

Styles, M. and Triggs, P. (1988) *Poetry 0-16 Books for Keeps Guide*.

Computer Software: Publishing/Word Processing/Spelling

'Write' – ILECC/ILEA

'All write' – ILECC/ILEA

Front Page Extra – MAPE, Tape III

Pagemaker – (Stop Press) Advanced Memory Systems Ltd

Fleet Street Editor – Mirrorsoft Ltd

Typesetter – Sherston Software

Spellbank – Questlar

Spellmaster – Computer Concepts

Edspell – Learning and Training Systems Ltd

See also *Teacher Handbooks: Developing Children's Writing* (1988) Scholastic Publications.

Resources

'Books for Keeps' – Journal of School Bookshop Association. Published six times a year. Subscriptions: 6 Brightfield Road, Lee, London SE12 8QF.

Children's Book Foundation – Information on authors/illustrators/children's books of the year; all aspects of children's literature. BOOK FAX provides schools with regularly up-dated information, newsletters, children's book week details, author/illustrator lists, posters, etc. Details from: Book House, 45 East Hill, Wandsworth, London SW18 2Q2.

Language Matters – Journal of the Centre for Language in Primary Education (CLPE) – formerly the ILEA Centre, now in the Borough of Southwark.
Three issues a year. Subscription includes CLPE library membership.
Details from: Centre for Language in Primary Education, Webber Row, London SE1 8QW.
Some recent issues, still available, include:
'Learning to Write'
'Story and Storytelling'
'Texts that Teach'
'Developing a Language Policy'
'The PLR in Action'
'National Curriculum 1'
'National Curriculum 2'

'Free Stuff For Kids' – Regularly up-dated information on firms offering 'free' or 'nearly free' booklets, project material etc. The prospect of receiving material connected with their interests has children writing *real* letters with great enthusiasm! Details from: Exley Publications Ltd, 16 Chalk Hill, Watford, Herts WD1 4BM.